"Lyrically written, meticulously observed, and exhaustively researched, BEAVERLAND is going to break your heart—and then heal it with compassion, beauty, and wonder. As Leila Philip shows, America owes much of our wealth, our landscape, and our cultural history to the beaver. Like the exploitation of Native Americans and enslaved people, our relationship with the creature Roger Tory Peterson rightly called 'nature's foremost conservationist' is complex, bloody, disturbing, and cruel. It is marvelous that the beavers themselves, and the dedicated people working to protect them, may be the ones to restore our broken land, and heal our wounded relationship with nature."

—Sy Montgomery, *New York Times* bestselling author of
The Soul of an Octopus

"We can't have enough books about this wonderful creature—and this one is particularly strong on the remarkable history of the animal in our continent's history and imagination. A loud slap of the tail in approval!"

—Bill McKibben, bestselling author of *The End of Nature*

"BEAVERLAND is wonderful, captivating, and illuminating. I learned so much—about natural history, business history, the world of today's fur trappers, and the role of a large, strange rodent in America's ecological future. Leila Philip is a skilled and engaging guide through this beaver-influenced terrain."

—James Fallows, bestselling co-author of
Our Towns: A 100,000-Mile Journey into the Heart of America

"Before the Anthropocene we had the Casterocene: a North American environment profoundly shaped by millions of beavers. In BEAVERLAND, Leila Philip takes us on a fascinating tour of the beaver's effect on human history, and how, after its near extinction, we need to bring this rodent back for the sake of our ecosystems."

—Frans de Waal, author of
Different: Gender Through the Eyes of a Primatologist

"An astonishing, intrepid compendium about the world according to the beaver, including social, cultural, and ethnographic history, juxtaposed with personal narrative. Philip brilliantly paves the way for us to enter this unlikely shaper of our nation as she follows naturalists, researchers, trappers, and local historians, as well as visits her own backyard pond. She dives into many avenues of research, including the enslavement of Native Americans, the cunning greed of John Jacob Astor, the obsession of Dorothy Richards (who lived with fourteen beavers in her Adirondack house), and the lifeways of Indigenous peoples. Every inch of the way we know we are in good hands. BEAVERLAND is poignant, impeccably researched, and as artfully put together as any of this 'weird rodent's' houses, with an eye toward the beaver's role in the anthropogenic disaster of our changing climate and damaged ecosystems."

—Gretel Ehrlich, author of *Unsolaced: Along the Way to All That Is*

"BEAVERLAND may be the best-realized book about an American animal in years. A work of open-hearted and sometimes horrified discovery, it tracks the author's passion for her local New England beavers as it becomes a literary and journalistic quest to understand a classic continental story: how a world so extensively shaped by a singular animal collapsed when an economy destroyed them for money. Can returning beavers and their works save our future? However you answer that, this fine book is going to rearrange the furniture in your head."

—Dan Flores, *New York Times* bestselling author of *Coyote America*

"Leila Philip's BEAVERLAND is an engaging story centered on a nerdy anti-hero, the beaver. While she states that beavers are weird, she makes a strong case that people in the beaver world are even weirder. This book weaves humor and storytelling with profound thoughts about nature. Don't miss the beavers parachuting into the Idaho wilderness."

—Mark Kurlansky, *New York Times* bestselling author of *Cod* and *Salt*

"BEAVERLAND is a model for 21st-century environmental writing—a beautifully told story with lodes of well-researched history and ecology, and a lyrical ode to natural wonders that steers clear of romanticism and questions cherished environmental ideas. This book will surprise the hell out of you on nearly every page."

—Jenny Price, author of
Stop Saving the Planet!: An Environmentalist Manifesto

"Ranging across a continent and five centuries, BEAVERLAND explores our strange relationship with an odd creature capable of inexplicable engineering. In lyrical words and with deep insights, Leila Philip reveals how beavers shaped our environment—and how humans have unraveled their creation."

—Alan Taylor, Pulitzer Prize–winning author of *American Republics: A Continental History of the United States, 1783–1850*

"Are beavers smart? asks Leila Philip in this captivating personal journey through history and streams that brings secretive creatures to life: beavers and those who trap them. The other animals that engineer their world—beavers—create complex, biodiverse landscapes while we do the opposite. This engaging tale of how beavers shaped America's rivers and streams for millennia, and how their comeback is now helping restore waterways, invites us to wonder who, really, is the smart one."

—David R. Montgomery, MacArthur Fellow, author of *Dirt: The Erosion of Civilizations*

"In this engaging and informative book, Leila Philip tells the tale of North American beavers as seen through human eyes. Philip uses diverse vignettes, from Native American creation stories to visits with contemporary trappers, beaver believers, and scientists, to gradually build a story of beavers and humans through time. Plenty of basic information about beavers is presented in digestible bites along the way as Philip deftly evokes place, mood, people, and beavers."

—Dr Ellen Wohl, author of *Saving the Dammed*

"Leila Philip brings intelligence, enthusiasm, and an open mind to her inquiry into the lives and histories of beavers, offering her reader a many-angled vision of her subject as she investigates the overlapping and often competing interests of the trapper, the developer, the naturalist, and the merchant. In doing so, she tracks the beaver's essential place in our history and our lives. But BEAVERLAND is also a plea—beyond our history, our markets, and our desires—for the pure appreciation of this mammal and its capacity to remake the world. Perhaps this is the greatest achievement of Philip's clear-eyed and beautifully written book."

—Jane Brox, author of *Silence: A Social History of One of the Least Understood Elements of Our Lives*

Beaverland

How One Weird Rodent
Made America

Leila Philip

12

TWELVE

NEW YORK BOSTON

Twelve
Hachette Book Group
1290 Avenue of the Americas, New York, NY 10104
twelvebooks.com
twitter.com/twelvebooks

First published in hardcover and ebook in December 2022
First Trade Paperback Edition: January 2024

Twelve is an imprint of Grand Central Publishing. The Twelve name and logo are
trademarks of Hachette Book Group, Inc.

The publisher is not responsible for websites (or their content) that are not owned by
the publisher.

The Hachette Speakers Bureau provides a wide range of authors for speaking
events. To find out more, go to hachettespeakersbureau.com or email
HachetteSpeakers@hbgusa.com.

Chapter-opening beaver silhouettes by Libby Corliss, based on photographs taken by
Cheryl Reynolds of the beavers of Martinez.

The Library of Congress has cataloged the hardcover as follows:
Names: Philip, Leila, author.
Title: Beaverland : how one weird rodent made america / Leila Philip.
Description: First Edition. | New York : Twelve, 2022. | Includes bibliographical
references and index.
Identifiers: LCCN 2022031713 | ISBN 9781538755198 (hardcover) |
ISBN 9781538755211 (ebook)
Subjects: LCSH: Fur trade—United States—History. | Beavers—United States—History.
Classification: LCC HD9944.U48 B43 2022 | DDC 338.3/7297—dc23/eng/20220805
LC record available at https://lccn.loc.gov/2022031713

ISBNs: 978-1-5387-5520-4 (trade paperback), 978-1-5387-5521-1 (ebook)

Printed in the United States of America

LSC-C

Printing 1, 2023

For Garth and Rhys,
my true north

Contents

Author's Note

On Indigenous Stories

When I recount the story of Great Beaver here, I do so with thanks to the many Indigenous people who for centuries, despite everything, managed to preserve this story in all its many versions and carry it down. Traditional stories always reflect the collective history and culture of a people and cannot be easily attributed to one author. Many Indigenous writers have noted how they were raised to think of traditional stories as living things that grow, develop, remember, and locate, and in doing so shape who people have come to believe they are, and how they exist as part of the land. Robin Wall Kimmerer (Potowatomi) considers the stories of her people a collective treasure. Historian Lisa Brooks (Abnaki) believes that the resurgence of Great Beaver stories along the Eastern seaboard during the eighteenth and nineteenth centuries reflects the Indigenous awareness of the cultural and environmental devastation of the fur trade. Numerous Algonquian stories reflect the disastrous effects of hoarding resources. The Canadian writer and activist Leanne Betasamosake Simpson (Anishanabe) considers Great Beaver stories to be resistance narratives that reflect deeply held Nishnaabeg values of reciprocity, diplomacy, and negotiation. Anthropologist Marge Bruchac (Abnaki) and other scholars point out the ways in which Great Beaver stories convey knowledge of natural history and, quite possibly, paleo-memories of the megafauna *Castoroides*, the real great beaver who was large enough to reach above the knees of the great mastodons of the Pleistocene.

The version of the Great Beaver story that opens this book was inspired by the many beaver stories that I searched out and read. These are listed in the Sources and further clarified in the notes for each chapter located in the Epilogue. In most Indigenous communities, only shamans or pre-scribed storytellers have the ability and authority to convey the deepest stories of a people's origin. The Story of Great Beaver, while it does not fall into this category, is still very much alive in the oral traditions of many Algonquian people. I am particularly indebted to the contemporary telling of this story delivered by Marge Bruchac in 2020 for the Pocumtuck Valley Memorial Association Museum in Deerfield. And to Linda Coombs of the Wampanoag Tribe of Gay Head/Aquinnah in Massachusetts for reading sections of the book from the vantage point of a Native writer and scholar.

On the Name America

The earliest recorded use of the name *America* for this continent occurred in 1507 on a two-dimensional globe created by the German cartographer Martin Waldseemüller.

This is usually considered America's birth certificate and the naming of the Americas, or "America," traces back to the Italian explorer Amerigo Vespucci, who explored the continent in the years following Christopher Columbus's first voyage in 1492.

And yet, we now know that Columbus did not discover this continent.

Amerrique in the Mayan language means "land of the wind." It is also the name of a mountain range in Nicaragua that was rich in gold and visited by both Columbus and Vespucci.

Ommerike is an old word in the Norse language meaning "farthest out-land," which is what the Norsemen who arrived here at the beginning of the eleventh century called this continent.

Em-erika could be an Algonquian word.

Prologue

Ktsi Amiskw, the Story of Great Beaver

This is a story, part true, often embellished, but nonetheless rich with wisdom about the forming of the Connecticut River valley. About how at the end of the last great ice age, the glaciers melted into vast, rocky slurries of ice, then moved across the land, scouring out valleys and ravines, canyons and lakes and river bottoms. Of how the land became littered with that ancient mud that had turned to rock, the boulders and stones and slabs that would one day be used to construct the stone walls of New England. And about how, long before that, a vast lake formed when the glaciers melted; a lake, teeming with billions of sea creatures that lived and died and drifted to the bottom, collecting over the eons until the lakebed was thick with fertile mud. And about how, after the great fight in the center of this story, the lake waters were released, revealing the rich alluvial riverbanks of the Connecticut valley, one of the largest in the world.

This is an old story, a sacred story: the Algonquian deep time story of *Ktsi Amiskw*, Great Beaver, told and retold through centuries and across the continent, from the Atlantic seaboard to the Great Lakes.

This is how it happened. Long ago, back in the time when men were as animals and the animals as men, one of the *awaasak*—the animal people— happened by. He had been swimming along that long, long river, the Quinneticook. Then he came to a place where the land opened out into a valley so wide and lush, it made him stop and look, and when he looked he saw the fast-moving water and how plentiful the tree people were on either side. He could feel the pull of the water, even this far from the ocean, and the strength of the tides, and usually he would not try to dam up such a strong

river, but this place had caught his eye. And so he began cutting down the
tree people, laying their huge bodies across the river in a lattice pattern.
Before long the water began to swell on either side. He kept working until
he had built a strong dam that stretched all the way across the river. When
the river spread out, rising up the banks, he built his dam higher. Soon the
entire valley was flooded. Great Beaver heard the cries of the humans who
had begun to plead and run along the banks, but he ignored them. The
women who tended the fields were the first to see the flood. They tried to
get *Ktsi Amiskw*'s attention: Ktsi Amiskw, *please stop, please move your dam, our
fields are beginning to flood, soon we will have no crops. We will starve.*

But *Ktsi Amiskw* ignored them, slapped his huge tail, and told them to
quit whining and go away. The women grabbed their hoes and baskets
and rushed back to the village where they appealed to the village elders,
entreating them to speak to Great Beaver. The village elders put down their
pipes and walked out to find the beaver. They admired *Ktsi Amiskw*'s growing pond for some time. Such a handsome dam, might he not remove a few
tree people and let some water out, lower the lake enough for the women's
fields to remain dry? They flattered him and attempted to negotiate. But
Great Beaver only rose up on two legs and leaned back on his great tail to
see them more clearly. Then he leapt up, dove into the water, and again
slammed his tail. Who did they think they were telling him he must move
his dam? They could go someplace else to grow their crops of beans and
corn and squash.

In despair, the humans appealed to Obbamakwa, the shaper. If he didn't
stop Great Beaver from flooding the valley, they would surely perish. Obbamakwa wasn't keen to interfere with the world once he had formed it. But
he could see that if he didn't do something, the humans would starve. He
went to Great Beaver and told him to take apart his dam and let some of the
water out. But Great Beaver would not listen. Instead he grew belligerent.
Tell the humans to move, he said, *why should I care about them?* Obbamakwa saw
he had no choice and grabbed one of the tree people to use as a great club.
But *Ktsi Amiskw* dashed away. The great fight began. Great Beaver dove
down into the water and Obbamakwa dove after him, swinging at his head.
Wherever Obbamakwa's great club came down, huge boulders split to form
cliffs; his blows created ravines and waterfalls; they cleaved passages in

the rock that became river rapids; they shaped the eastern seaboard and the shorelines of the Great Lakes. In some versions of the story, like the one told in southern New England, Great Beaver is killed. In Northampton, Massachusetts, there is a mountain in the shape of a prone beaver called "Beaver Tail Hill" (later renamed Sugarloaf by English colonists). But in the telling of the Micmac and the Passamaquoddy, the northern Algonquian people of maritime Canada, and the Algonquian people of the Great Lakes, Great Beaver is too clever. He escapes, swimming fast through the waves of the lakes.

The story of Great Beaver has been told for millennia; in the words of Abnaki poet Cheryl Savageau, it is one of those timeless stories that "wakes up" when it is needed. The story praises its hero's power and ingenuity, his persistence, but it also comprehends his flaws, which we know have little to do with the nature of a beaver and everything to do with ourselves. You cannot ignore your relations with others and expect to survive. For thousands of years the people who lived across North America understood that if you destroy the earth, you destroy yourself.

But what does it tell you that this story, one of the oldest on our continent, a parable of the creation and destruction of an American paradise, has for its protagonist a fat furry rodent with four orange teeth?

Beaverland

The author's local beaver ponds, Woodstock, Connecticut

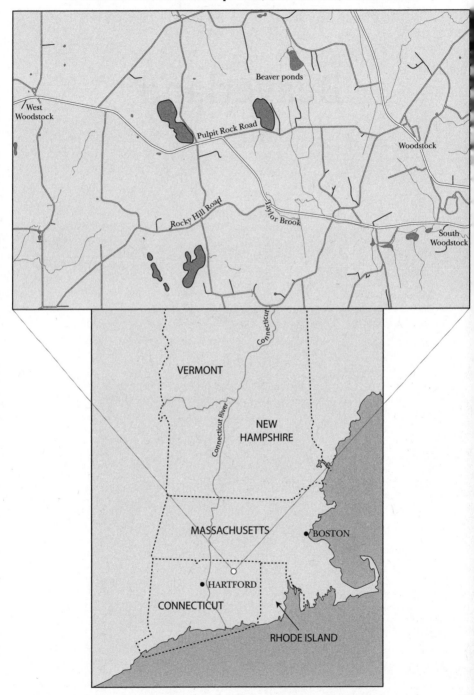

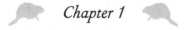

Chapter 1

At the Beaver Pond

I think there is an element of the sacred in the beaver, if only in its deep weirdness. One million years ago, beavers the size of bears roamed North America. They pose an evolutionary puzzle, like the platypus, or birds, which share some DNA with dinosaurs. When they dive, they seem more like marine mammals than terrestrial species, more seal than rodent. Their dexterous forepaws look startlingly human with their five nimble fingers and naked palms. They groom their lustrous fur with catlike fastidiousness. Their mammalian beauty ends abruptly in the gooselike hind feet, each as wide as the beaver's head. The feet are followed by a reptilian tail, which, it has been observed, looks like the result of some terrible accident, run over by a tractor tire, the treads leaving a pattern of indentations that resemble scales. Part bear, part bird, part monkey, part lizard, humanoid hands, an aquatic tail. Is it any surprise that beavers have fired the human imagination in every continent that they are found?

Pulpit Rock Road, named for a large boulder that sits on the roadside half covered in fern a mile from the beaver dam, is an old dirt road in my hometown of Woodstock, Connecticut, founded 1686, population 7,862. We have six dairy and beef farms in Woodstock, a bison herd, a commercial fruit orchard, and a multitude of backyard vegetable gardens. Forty percent of the woodland is wetland, which keeps the developers at bay. It's the quiet corner of Connecticut, the last corridor of dark night sky between Washington and Boston.

Pulpit Rock Road is the oldest road in town, one of the oldest in the state. Long before it was used by the first Europeans, it was one of the main paths of the Indigenous people who lived here, the Nipmuc, the Pequot, and the Mashantucket. The twelve Native tribes who lived in modern-day Rhode Island, western Massachusetts, and Connecticut sometimes met in the meadow just up from the beaver pond. The meadow is a glacial escarpment, with a rocky high spot safe from ambush, and the stream below brought game to hunt. Pulpit Rock Road is one of the last dirt roads in Woodstock. The highway department wishes to pave it over. The residents resist. We love it the way it is.

The road connects to the path that brought the colonists here from Boston sixty-eight years after the Pilgrims landed at Plymouth Rock. Thirty English families with names like Child, Taylor, and Eliot walked sixty-seven miles here from what was then Roxbury, just outside Boston. They first called the settlement New Roxbury, then renamed it Woodstock. John Eliot, the pastor of the First Church of Roxbury, Massachusetts, had heard that there were Native American Christians living in this area, early converts who might be thus amenable to having Europeans as neighbors. Soon after he arrived, Eliot walked down the then much narrower road a mile from the bridge, stood on the large glacial erratic along the pathway, and preached Christian values to the Native people who gathered, his new converts. What happened next is the old tragic history of death, displacement, and erasure. Within a few years, the land was divided into twenty-acre lots, and the new inhabitants went to work eradicating the forests. Today the woods have mostly grown back, and many of those first farming families have moved on, but the old stone walls of the early farms still stand. Walk twenty feet into the woods anywhere near where I live and you will run into poetic ruins of stone, usually studded with ferns and colored with fantastic spreads of lichen. Animals know the walls by heart; they are the Mass Pike of the woods, providing runways in all directions, or places for hiding and nesting.

The beaver dam by Pulpit Rock incorporates three large flat boulders laid out centuries ago to enable people to cross the small stream that had been named Taylor Brook. The stones were set apart so that the brook could pass through. When the beavers started damming up the brook, they made use of the crude stone crossing, a keystone from which they extended walls of mud, rock, and stick. The beavers moved in, their dam would flood the woods, and a pond would grow. Then a few years later they would move out and flood another area, letting the first one subside. The beavers I had begun watching as they moved into the woods by my house were the most recent colony to live here, in a location that their ancestors might well have lived in for hundreds of years, if not far longer.

Across the continent, Native Americans hunted beavers with spears, destroying their lodges, killing them as they tried to flee, eating their flesh, and using their fur. But Native American cultures as a rule upheld strong taboos against not hunting more *amiskw* than could be used (and that use was never enough to drive the beavers toward extinction). Beavers belonged to an animal nation and had to be honored after death. Most of the Indigenous peoples of North America ended up participating extensively in the fur trade, aiding European traders by bringing furs to swap for axes, iron kettles, blankets, trinkets, alcohol, and guns. This trade, and the ways it brought new technologies to Indigenous communities, is emphasized in much early American settlement history to justify the American fur trade. But it wasn't long before many Native Americans began to understand the ways in which overhunting could extinguish their own culture. Early French Jesuits in Michigan recount the Native practice of gouging out the eyes of a trapped beaver—an attempt to keep the animal from witnessing the desecration of its own death, and perhaps to protect the hunter from the wrath of the Great Spirit for his role in breaking a sacred taboo.

In the Bodleian Library at Oxford, a medieval bestiary dating from the early thirteenth century displays two beavers, meticulously drawn with long wolflike bodies, canine faces, and coats of silvery blue. Medieval depictions of beavers in Europe render them with serpentine necks, long canine legs, leonine paws, bushy tails, and removable testicles, flung at hunters to distract them. The Roman Catholic Church decreed that they could be eaten like fish as penance on holy days. For wealthy Catholics, the flesh did double duty—it was both delicious and a coveted aphrodisiac. Beavers appeared on heraldry in Great Britain from the Middle Ages onward; on the coat of arms of the city of Oxford, a robust beaver with a flashy blue-and-white-checked tail leans opposite an elephant. In one of the earliest Dutch maps of the New Netherlands, a beaver is a symbol of industry, holding a stick in its paws like a rabbit. By 1715, the most famous of London cartographers, Herman Moll, rendered beavers on his map of the new British colonies by drawing them as a column of dispirited factory workers trudging toward a dam near Niagara Falls. Each walks upright on its hind legs, carrying its allotted beam of wood across its shoulder, single file. As if capturing the mercantile fantasies of Europe, maps and pamphlets soon began appearing in which New World beavers are drawn living in condominiums—dozens of future pelts crowded into separate apartments within one lodge. The beaver is the most prominent feature of the first seal of New York City, the seventeenth-century seal for New Amsterdam. When the British took over, the seal was revised to include a Pilgrim and an Indigenous man, but the beaver remained, right smack in the middle between the two. Canada's first postage stamp featured a beaver, and the state of Oregon, founded in 1859, took the beaver for its state animal. The Massachusetts Institute of Technology, established in 1861, made a beaver its mascot. So did at least one sports team in every state of the Union. More roads, cutoffs, boat launchings, towns, and developments are named after beavers than any other North American animal.

Some of the oldest animal effigies to have been found are of beavers, and the Shigir Idol, the earliest wooden carving in the world, was sculpted using a beaver's lower jawbone. Throughout the ancient Middle East, beaver castor was used for medicinal purposes. In Iran, where beavers were called "water dogs" and considered sacred, they were protected by a system of fines; harming a beaver in ancient Persia could cost you 60,000 darics, although you could get out of it by killing one thousand snakes.

Yet the beaver's ubiquity is matched only by its weirdness. Indeed, beavers are considered "behaviorally weird," which means no one really knows when they started building dams. No one really understands how much intelligence, as opposed to instinct, is involved in that unique activity. Animal intelligence is measured by comparing the size of the animal's brain to the animal's overall body weight, something called the encephalization quotient, or EQ. Based on that simple ratio, beavers appear less cunning than rats or squirrels (though far better off than the bony-eared assfish, which has the smallest brain-to-body ratio of any vertebrate on the planet). But they have evolved in an intelligent way. Their eyes, ears, and nose are aligned, so that they swim like alligators, head barely visible, body submerged; yet unlike alligators, they do so not to hunt but to avoid becoming prey. Beavers can't see well. Their primary sense is smell. A beaver uses its nose to locate the cinnamon smell of birch and the licorice tang of aspen. They communicate through scent, depositing the castor oil that they produce in two internal glands to mark territory and introduce themselves to potential mates. While the visual area of a beaver's brain is small, a large area of their neocortex is dedicated to processing somatic sensory and auditory stimuli.

But are beavers intelligent creatures? It's a mystery. Throughout history, humans have studied their lodges and dams and canals, their skills at felling and transporting trees, their expertise at engineering. When three or four work together, they can roll a hundred-pound boulder and set it in their dam. Perhaps, like ants and bees, they have a kind of intelligence that we as humans simply cannot fathom.

A quiver on the surface, twitch of grass, and she is frozen. She turns one great webbed foot and grabs the pond's water, slowly turning as if she were a wooden top. Her small brown head with its bearlike ears lifts ever so slightly, the short blunt nose level with the water's surface, black eyes peering. The pond shimmers with insects; green wafts of algae thrum, each cell an engine of chemical reactions; photosynthesis turning sunlight to sugar, energy into biomass. She waits, floating in the sun-warmed water, senses flaring. Her nostrils widen, taking in the sweet stink of waterlogged weed and wood. Then a new smell: acrid, metallic. Her brain flashes danger, muscles pulse. She flings her head forward, thrusting her back out of the water, and dives. On the way down, her tail slams the surface, a paddle crack, a warning. Her head cleaves the water, clear nictitating membranes shielding her eyes like swimming goggles. She sees through the murk. She is not the predator, here she is prey. She dives and dives, her life a question answered by the speed of her flight.

Down she goes, hell-bent for the bottom of the pond. Her body swoops, all muscle now, propelling her through the pond as if following a groove. Her webbed toes spread like sails, grab the water, push. She dodges hazy shapes—sticks and branches, boulders and stones, water lily stalks and thick pond grass. The pond's surface now just memory, a distant lid.

She seems more fish than mammal now, her tail a rudder, her ears and windpipe sealed from the water. Though the dive slows her heart rate, electric currents of fear zing through her body. Her short front paws scramble, the surprising fingers ripping through the thick strands of water lilies. On the surface, the lilies bloom in elegant profusions of yellow and white. Down here they are a dark maze through which she must maneuver.

She swims deeper, into layers of welcoming silt, her inner lips closed behind her teeth, keeping water from her lungs. The mud-filled water ruffles her mouth while along her back the dark slurry curries her fur. She feels its weight and pushes harder still; she knows she is almost there. Then that sudden coolness like absolution and she parts the dark curtain. She slows, turns, glides along the canal. Only there, moving along the intricate highway she and others have clawed through the mud on the bottom of the pond, can she rest, swimming slowly through the underwater pathways. Ahead she senses a rising darkness. She dives once more, then swims up through a tunnel and breaks the surface. She fills her lungs and climbs quickly out into the dome of the lodge, safely home.

I stand on the bridge and wait. Eventually I know the beaver will surface and swim back here to the dam. I wonder if I spooked her with my shadow or my scent. Beavers can stay underwater for as long as fifteen minutes before their lungs need air, and in that time can swim over two hundred yards without needing to come back up. I scan the pond's surface. She could pop back up anywhere.

Coda sits by my side, leashed, her retriever head cocked toward the pond, pensive, her upper lip slightly curled in concentration. Her long-distance eyesight isn't great, but it's better than a beaver's. Her sense of smell is two hundred times greater than mine. I have learned to follow when she suddenly leaps off the trail, because chances are she has discovered something. Once a ten-point buck, shot and left in the woods. Once a headless coyote, legs bent as if still running in the tall meadow grass. Once the body of a wood duck, the jeweled head ripped off by an owl, a scattering of red drops of blood and the brilliant-colored feathers on white snow. As I look over the pond, I run my fingers through the soft fur of Coda's head. She sighs, leaning into my leg. We wait, the sun just a flare. Birds are settling down into whistles and chirps and that one achingly beautiful flute sound that seems to echo through the trees. Time passes. The surface of the water turns orange, then hot pink, almost crimson. Now Coda is restless and jostles my leg, pointing her head very decidedly away from the water toward the road. The pond is just a three-minute walk from our front door, but it feels like a world apart. Okay, I say, scanning the pond one last time. The beaver won't return until night. Beavers are crepuscular, most active once the sun begins to sink. I let Coda lead me back up the road toward home.

A small tug of water, a pulse down deep and she can feel it, movement where there should be stillness. She lifts her head from the water, bringing up a green frond of water lily draped over her head like a towel. She flicks an ear, turning it toward the new sound. She lifts her nose, taking in the dusky sweet pond scents, now twirled with something new. What? Coolness, silt, and she begins to sense it now, the outer layer of cells on the thick skin of her tail registering a change in water pressure. The sound is moving water, a subtle current flowing.

Something is wrong at the dam. The beaver whips around and dives. Once again she is swimming hard through the channels at the bottom of the pond, those dark lifelines, but this time headed away from the lodge to the dam. She rises up and breaks the surface, moving fast now along the top. At the dam she quickly finds the source of that tug and pulse, a hole through which water is flowing. She dives again and comes back up with handfuls of mud, which she presses quickly into the sides of the dam. Again she dives, now with a stick in her mouth. The next dive brings up a rock carried between her front paws and her chin. Mud, sticks, rocks are jammed into the hole. The beaver will not stop until the hole is plugged, the wretched sound of trickling water gone. This quick repair was done in the dangerous light of morning. Later, when darkness covers the pond, reducing the risk of predators, she will be back with others, bringing more sticks and freshly cut saplings to reinforce the dam. Beavers can fell a five-inch willow in six minutes; whittling down a trunk like an enormous sharpened pencil, a full-grown beaver can fell and then tow a hundred-pound sapling, swimming against the current.

And now I see that telltale ripple in the pond that always makes my heart leap. As it comes closer, I make out the dark head, the blunt beaver nose that curiously is draped in pondweed. The beaver is swimming so hard; she's a silver crease, heading right toward me. When she reaches about ten feet from the dam by the bridge, the beaver flings herself into a sharp dive and her tail slams the surface. I almost jump at the crack of sound. She rises back up, no longer draped with green pondweed, and again she dives. How I admire her ferocity. She is tracking me now, swimming back and forth along the length of the dam, one dark eye locked on my standing figure, glaring. She flicks her tail again. The first tail slam was to warn the others; the rest were for me. Beavers know the difference between individual tail slaps. They will routinely ignore those of juveniles, understanding their teenage love of drama, but will respond instantly to an alert sent by a mature beaver like the one swimming before me. This beaver wants me to leave her dam—now.

Do beavers have emotions? We can only guess. The one person to study beavers in close quarters, Dorothy Richards, the "beaver lady" who bought a farm in upstate New York in the 1930s, had as many as fourteen beavers living in her farmhouse at any given time. Richards thought beavers had a sense of humor. The ones she lived with would routinely steal her oriental rugs, making as if to drag them to their beaver pond. When she caught them, putting her foot on the rug to stop their progress, they would drop the rug, stand up on their hind legs to look up at her, and wriggle excitedly, making chuckling noises. Richards heard it as happiness. So did Enos Abijah Mills, who described in his 1913 classic, *In Beaver World*, how his pet beaver Diver would play tricks on him, then wriggle and squeak excitedly once caught.

Okay, Coda, I finally say, let's go. All I want from this beaver is to know that she is there, doing her work. She is my connection to something wild and uncertain, not just out there but in myself; the sight of her is all I need.

I don't need to stay, causing her more aggravation. Coda looks back toward the swimming beaver quickly and then turns up the road toward home.

Beavers are a keystone species, an organism so critical to the survival of a biological community that they function like the keystone in a medieval archway, that one shaped block that forms the apex of the arch and upon which the entire span of bricks depends. Remove the keystone and the arch collapses. For better or worse, beavers, like humans, have an inordinate impact on their environment. Many animals use tools and are important to biodiversity, but only beavers and humans dramatically alter the landscape to create the environment they need (or want).

Beavers need water, so they cut down trees and flood forests to create ponds. In doing so, they kill trees but create new habitat for hundreds of animal species that rely on those new waterways. Once they abandon a dam, having determined that life there is no longer manageable due to lack of food, it begins to drain and the pond grows back as meadow, then underbrush, then eventually forest, the soil enriched by years of accumulated pond rot and muck. They are forest Shiva, destroying illusion to create insight, putting into motion cycles of growth and regrowth, creation through destruction. And today, beavers are back in many North American landscapes. In fact, here in the East, they are everywhere, but considered so ordinary and unremarkable that they tend to be overlooked.

I am not the first self-trained American naturalist, who after catching sight of a beaver dam began looking for the animal that had created such a thing, only to become obsessed with learning about them. The study of beavers in America has long been the terrain of American eccentrics. America's first anthropologist, Lewis Henry Morgan, would spend twelve years tracking the forests of the Upper Peninsula of Michigan to study beavers. His 1868 book *The American Beaver and His Works* became the first authoritative account of beavers in the New World and has remained a classic. Forty-five years later, the first spokesman for the national forests under Theodore Roosevelt, Enos A. Mills, who wrote *In Beaver World*, would fall so in love with beavers that it would end his career in government service. In his 1913 book, Mills recounts observing fourteen different beaver ponds in the

Rockies over a period of twenty-seven years. He had a pet beaver he named Diver that loved to accompany him, riding in his mule's packsaddle. While Morgan was an industrialist who admired beavers, Mills was our first advocate for beaver preservation. Not surprisingly, Mills fell out with Roosevelt.

The next major North American beaver advocate would appear in Canada about twenty years later. By 1935, a wilderness guide and fur trapper turned beaver advocate named Grey Owl had enthralled audiences throughout North America and Great Britain. But Grey Owl was a conman. His real name was Archibald Stansfeld Belaney, born and raised in Hastings, England. When he was sixteen, partly to escape the expectations and disciplined ways of the two maiden aunts who had raised him, he ran away to Canada. Not only was his biography as a half Apache, half Scotsman a sham, but he was a habitual bigamist who abandoned multiple wives and children.

Archibald's writings nevertheless inspired other wildlife preservation advocates, including a shy but determined woman who had grown up in Little Falls, New York, and had recently bought an old farmhouse at the confluence of two streams. She determined to save the beavers on her property and went on to dedicate her life to their study, working tirelessly on education and outreach. In her tiny farmhouse, with special permission from the state, since beavers are wild animals, Richards took care of a pair of beavers and their progeny. Her slim memoir, *Beaversprite: My Years Building an Animal Sanctuary*, details her years with these successive generations of beavers and all that she learned about them. On one page she smiles broadly as she sits in her chair, an elderly woman by then, a huge beaver filling her lap. The beaver is sitting up, staring at her devotedly as it calmly holds an apple with both hands, eating. In another photograph she is seated at a table, "having lunch" across from her favorite beaver, a female she named Eager. The beaver sits in a chair at the table, upright on her hind legs in order to reach a plate of carrots.

But my own beavers were gone. Days passed, then weeks, without sight of that brown head surfacing. Evenings I stood on the bridge and waited, Coda by my side, but the beavers did not appear. A hole appeared in the dam and water began to trickle through. I could not believe how bereft I felt. Without my noticing it, my daily walks down to the beaver pond had begun to anchor my days. As I had watched the beavers move in and the water had risen, so had my sense of hope. On sunny days, the pond shone through the woods like a lost locket. When it was overcast, the water gleamed the color of beaten tin, an open eye. Even in winter, covered in snow, the pond caught the light and held it. Climate disaster was looming and we were as yet tragically unable to take appropriate action, but down at the pond it was possible to believe in nature's resilience. And in my own.

Each time I visited my mother now, she was shrinking before my eyes. There in the steaming bathroom, heater on high, helping her bathe, I'd watch the water travel down her body, following the wrinkled map of her skin, and felt floodwaters of grief but also a strange sense of calm. While I was there, the roles of child and parent almost completely reversed, me half-soaked from trying to help her in and out of the shower, my mother equal parts delighted then irritated, time came loose from its ruthless circle, becoming a spiraled thing, curving away then bending back in, holding us together. But it was clear she didn't have much time.

My mother, who had run our family farm in the Hudson valley right up until she was ninety, suddenly began needing help to get through her day. I was driving the two hours from my house to Claverack to help care for her as much as I could, but I lived in a constant state of wrench; I also had a family of my own and was a busy college professor, and then there were the beavers. When I was with my mother, I was taken out of my life, and there was nowhere else I wanted to be. But I also could not stay with her all of the time.

I felt almost uneasy about my obsession with the beavers, as if I had fallen into what was now a well-known trope in American nature writing—a woman of a certain age journeying into the natural world to discover solace. But my beavers were so completely determined, how could I not fall for them? I loved how chunky and awkward beavers appeared, so unlike the slim icons of female beauty most of us baby boomers had absorbed despite our best efforts. When I wasn't at my desk, I was swimming laps at the local Y, or walking the woods with Coda, or working in the garden, and my legs and arms had thickened with muscle. Beavers had become more than just a connection to the wild, they had become my animal guide. Annie Dillard had locked eyes with a weasel and saw in that weasel a wildness she envied. I loved how the beavers were unconcerned about the consequences of going all out for what they wanted.

I didn't want to sit at a table and have lunch with my beaver like Dorothy Richards, yet how I wished I could see them once again swimming in their pond, that token of the wild just down the road from my house. But my beavers were gone. I knew what I had to do.

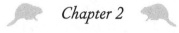

Chapter 2

On the Trap Line

Want to see a beaver lodge up close?"

Herb Sobanski is grinning like a Boy Scout, knee deep in the freezing swamp water. "Sure," I say and move toward him eagerly, too eagerly in fact, and I almost lose my balance. Each step in my rubber hip waders feels like I am walking on balloons. The cold water surrounds my legs, then my thighs. I walk forward slowly, pressing down to find solid ground, leaning on the broken sapling Herb had pulled from the brush and handed to me to use as a walking stick. He steps forward, testing the water with his trapper's pole, a wooden staff with a small metal plate on the end that resembles a short-bladed hoe. He'll use the pole to pull traps out of deep water and snag waterlogged branches to help hide traps in places where he thinks an animal will pass through, making what fur trappers call "sets." Strapped to his back is a large barrel-shaped wicker pack basket. He moves methodically, careful not to lean over too far in any direction so that the pack does not tip as he tests the depth of the water before taking each step. Herb stands in front of me, then slips between two large buttonwood bushes and is gone.

"Going to get thorny," he says when I push through and meet him on the other side. He waits for me, holding back the branches of a pricker bush with one end of his pole. I pass carefully through and Herb follows. The branch snaps back. We aren't far from the edge of the beaver pond where Herb has his trap line, but visibility is limited to the space between clumps of brush. Marsh grass rises up from the water in a series of brown humps. In the distance, I can see the tree line ringed by a line of white spires, trees that died when water flooded their roots. They stand solemn as columns in an ancient ruin. We are only thirty miles from Hartford, but here in the swamp it feels so remote it could be Maine or Vermont. Stands of conifers ring the pond, and huge glacial boulders punctuate the shoreline. The air feels tight as a bow, the sky stretched out in a brilliant swath of blue, even though the forecast is for snow. Time becomes the steady slosh and suck of our trudge through the water, the almost silence of the winter swamp.

"Hey, would you look at that!" Herb's excited voice breaks the stillness and he reaches over to bend down a branch to show me a delicate bird's nest in which lies a cluster of bright red berries. "This is why I love this," he says. "I always see something new." He forges ahead, a bit faster now, and I struggle to keep up. Then I see it. Just behind the next stand of bushes, a huge mound of sticks and mud juts up from the surface of the water in that iconic pyramid, a beaver lodge. We walk up until the water grows too deep to wade farther. We are about five feet from the lodge, which from this close up looks like a huge pile of pickup sticks. Saplings stripped of bark are criss-crossed and interwoven with branches, wider at the base and tapered at the top so that the lodge takes on an almost perfect teepee shape and rises up a good eight feet from the surface of the water. The lodge is too wide to see around, but Herb points to the top left side with his pole. "See that? Fresh mud there on top, so you know it's active." He studies the lodge for a few minutes in silence, then abruptly looks over the pond, which we can now see clearly; the water must spread over a good thirty acres, a silver sheen. "There's the feed pile," Herb says, and points again, this time to an area of water to the right of the lodge where the tips of a few branches poke up from the water between patches of snow and ice. Herb nods appreciatively. "They'll eat that all winter. Swim over and take a branch back to the lodge. Open up a beaver's stomach, nothing inside but sawdust."

I scan the feed pile, wondering how deep the pond is there. Beavers build their feed piles by first anchoring a latticework of sticks on the bottom of the pond. Then they add saplings and branches to build an underwater brush pile. Now that I can no longer see the beavers at the pond by my house, I've been reading about them. Beavers are herbivores; they eat twigs, branches, sticks, grasses, ferns, water lilies, and other pondweeds. Beavers don't possess cellulase, the enzymes necessary to digest cellulose. Despite this they manage to digest about 30 percent of the cellulose they eat. Micro-organisms in their stomach, caecal microbes, turn cellulose into nutrients.

Another beaver weirdness: It consumes plants, then expels a blackish sub-stance called coecotrophe, which it holds with its paws as it eats. Only after digesting its food twice does the beaver expel waste, which by then is a ball of sawdust, lightweight and odorless.

Herb walks on and begins to poke the water at the edge of the pond with his pole, looking for beaver poop, then he suddenly stops, gesturing to the top of a far tree. I look to where he is pointing and make out a large sprawling nest. "Osprey!" he blurts out. "I knew they were out here. Isn't this beautiful? Man, I love this." Herb plunges ahead without waiting for my response, heading for the far bank, but I wait. I stand there for a few minutes, the near-freezing water beginning to deep-chill my toes, in awe of the lodge's size and complexity. I have never been so close to a beaver lodge before, and to see it snug in its pond, a hidden gem of the wild, is thrilling.

But where I see the mystery of raw nature, Herb sees mostly a prob-lem that the state called him in to resolve. The beavers living here have flooded this area so extensively that their ponds are getting too close to a local water reserve. Beaver carry *Giardia lamblia*, a microscopic parasite that causes infection in humans, historically called "beaver fever," and the state is worried about potential contamination. On our way in, we had passed a well-kept white clapboard house with sloping lawns leading down to a newly built and landscaped pond. The people who built the house have also filed a complaint, as beavers from the state forest soon found their newly planted and expensive landscaping. Beavers love white and red birch and willow almost as much as poplar; the bark of each of these trees is loaded with sugar, a tasty carbo load. Based on the damage to their trees, the state issued them a permit to remove the beavers. The state then called Herb and told him they wanted all the beavers removed from the adjoining state land.

That was last summer. Herb convinced the landowners to wait. On prin-ciple, Herb will not trap out of season, considering it cruel and wasteful. Beavers trapped in spring or summer have kits in the lodge that will starve without their parents. The meat can't be used due to fear of parasites, and since their fur is only thick enough to have value in the winter, the pelt is useless. Herb has been trapping this site for about two weeks and already removed ten beavers. Today he plans to check the six traps he set the day before and figure out if he still needs to keep trapping or if his work here is done. Checking traps the next morning is an ethic for him; animals tend to move around at night and he wants to get them as soon as he can after they are caught in case they are in the trap and still alive. He also doesn't want to lose beaver to coyote, mink, or bear that might come along and feed on them before he gets there. Now that he has located signs of recent activity, he knows he has more beavers to catch.

By the time I reach the far bank, Herb has put down his pack basket and is taking out a few tools. The pack, which belonged to his father, is his favorite. Herb could use a more modern pack of any type, but he likes the nostalgia of a wicker pack that is the same style as those in nineteenth-century paintings and engravings of American fur trappers. Tied to the outside is a small sack of the kind that mountain men carried; called a "possible sack," this pouch kept dry their most valued items. A nineteenth-century fur trapper made his possible sack from buckskin and used it to hold flint, tobacco, bullet molds, and powder. Herb's possible sack is tan canvas and holds matches, a flint, his trapper license, spare tags printed with his trapper license number, permission letters from landowners, and some bullets, although today he has left his gun in the truck.

In almost forty years of trapping, Herb has only met a conservation officer once in the field, but he is required by law to be able to prove he is a licensed trapper. Back at the truck by the heavy metal gate that marked the beginning of state land, I watched Herb methodically assemble his gear on the bank, then chuck it into the bottom of the pack: hatchet, a coil of wire, wire cutters, a pair of metal pliers with exceptionally long arms called a trap opener, thick elbow-length yellow rubber gloves, four wooden stakes, then a handful of steel traps and cables, each length of cable wire fitted with extra swivels required by state trapping regulations, and a bottle of lure he made from beaver castor. I had watched him carefully lock his truck, then stash his keys in a pocket. Herb never packs water or food.

By the time he heads out, the wide wicker pack extending from the back of his neck down to just above his hips, he has morphed into part modern woodsman, part mountain man. He wears rubber and neoprene waders and a camo-pattern jacket, but his back has disappeared beneath his pack and his face takes on a look of grit and determination. Monday through

Friday, Herb is usually at home, working remotely to input data for the insurance company he's worked for since he was twenty-seven. Thirty years at the same company has earned him some flexibility. He can shift his work hours during trapping season to accommodate running his lines. Or he can use vacation days, as he has done today. With his pack filled, he's eager to get going. After checking this trap line, he will head over to two sites where he has been called in to remove nuisance beaver.

While Herb put together his equipment, I had nervously assembled and reassembled my own gear. Did I really want to witness beaver trapping? When the beavers on our pond disappeared, I resolved to try to find out what had happened to them. I reached out to neighbors along the road, some of whose families traced back to Woodstock's founding. This left me wondering about the environmental impacts of colonization on the beaver pond, because I learned that in town memory, beavers had always been here. Neighbors also mentioned that Woodstock had a town trapper, and suggested I check to see if he had trapped them. I was shocked to learn we even had a town fur trapper, but gave him a call. He assured me that he hadn't trapped the beavers, but from him I learned that fur trapping was alive and well here. I went to a gathering of fur trappers, thinking I might find out more about the disappearance of our beavers. No one knew, or if they did, weren't going to tell me. But I met Herb Sobanski, who could talk about beavers endlessly and cared more about them than anyone else I had met. When he offered to take me out on his trap line, I knew I should go.

We have been traversing for a good while now, walking the narrow dams beavers have built through the woods and flooded to create a swamp. All along we see trees half gnawed, or gnawed down completely. When beavers take down trees they leave a telltale stump sharpened to a pencil point. Usually the top of the tree has been dragged away, but sometimes in larger trees the beavers only chew off the branches, leaving the log where it fell, shorn clean of limbs. Beavers don't eat the wood of trees, only the bark. When taking down a tree, they'll bite out a chip of wood, quickly spit it out, then bite again, a furry chain saw.

The beaver demolition and construction here extends far beyond the pond. As we move into the woods I see that the swamp now spreads out from the far side of the beaver pond and down through the woods in a series of smaller bodies of water that resemble woodland rice paddies, each following the slope of the land. What once was lowland forest is now completely flooded—acres and acres of water spreading out through the trees. I stop for a moment to take in the sight. I'm in Beaverland.

Prehistoric beavers the size of grizzly bears had roamed Asia, Europe, and North America during the last great ice age, their gigantic incisors gnawing woody vegetation even before the first mammoths. They lived alongside saber-toothed tigers, giant sloths, and armadillos as big as Honda sedans; they were part of the group of super-sized animals called megafauna that populated the late Pleistocene. When the glaciers of the last ice age melted and the vast flooding finally ceased, the modern ancestors of today's beavers went at it, felling trees and building dams throughout Asia, Europe, and the Americas. In North America, beaver dams, ponds, and waterworks established hydraulic systems that created much of the rich biodiversity of the continent. That was the primordial Beaverland—North America before European colonization, when as many as four hundred million beavers filled the continent.

The great boreal forests that sprang up, threaded with beaver-made waterways, would have looked something like what I see now—half waterworld—streams spreading out through the forest as great fans of water, overspilling banks, then receding in rhythm with the seasons. Unlike the streams and rivers we know today, mostly degraded so that their currents carve channels through the earth, picking up speed and causing more erosion as they cut deeper into the ground, these messy, slower-moving streams and rivers from the time of Beaverland contracted and expanded like tides; they were arteries and veins of water pulsing life into the land.

Water was surely going to be the story of our century; it already was. Too much water from extreme storms in one place was causing loss of life and billions in economic damage, while too little water in another was causing drought that was equally deadly if not more so. Meanwhile, rising seas were erasing coastlines. We could use beavers again to help our water problems, especially here in the East, if we were smart enough—if we were open and humble enough. That Indigenous communities across North America understood the role beavers play in keeping water in the land is clear from the many variations of Great Beaver stories throughout the continent, and the rituals that surrounded the handling of a beaver's body. The first Euro-peans thought these superstitions were ridiculous, but they served to limit overkilling. If you hunted beaver you must care for the carcass by throwing the bones back into the water from which the animal had come, by hang-ing the skull from a tree, and always, at all costs, by preventing dogs from gnawing the bones, otherwise you might suffer a bad hunt, disease, even death. Such was the power of the keepers of the game, the animal bosses that ruled the nations of animals. It was foolish to anger the boss beaver.

"There you go," says Herb, startling me out of my reverie. He points to a large pine tree gnawed through at a point about two feet from the ground. The tree, a white pine at least eighty feet high, has a trunk so thick I can just circle it with my arms; it looks as if some huge creature has bitten a chunk right out of the side. "Fresh sign since I was here," says Herb. "That's inter-esting; they usually don't like pine—too sticky. Careful here, it gets deep."

Before I know it, Herb walks into the pond and is up to his chest in murky water, checking his first set, half submerged in an island of swamp grasses. "I think a muskrat might have set off my trap," he explains as he examines the water and pokes at a deep spot with his trapper pole. I don't see any signs of a trap at first, then I notice the two slim sticks placed with a small branch laid across the water to connect them. Herb had planted the guide poles to mark the spot. One has the trap connected to it by a chain and is pounded in deep enough to hold fast if the animal somehow survives the snap of the jaws and tries to make a run for it. Trapping on state land in Connecticut is first come, first served, with trappers competing for lines. There is an etiquette about leaving sets alone and not putting your sets too close to the existing sets of fellow trappers, but Herb has had traps pulled out by other trappers and thrown in the bushes so that they can take over that location. He has had traps stolen. He has had traps ripped out, demol-ished, left twisted and broken along with notes telling him that fur trap-ping is evil. When he recounts the sabotage, he shrugs it off.

Herb now stands on the bank, staring down at the set. His chiseled face with its short grey beard looks cold, but he plunges his bare hands into the slurry of half-frozen water, checking that the traps are still connected.

He resets the one stick that was tilted and makes sure that the other is secure. He is fastidious about securing his sets. "The last thing I want is for a beaver to swim off with my trap," he explains as he fiddles with the sticks one last time. "I'll lose my trap and the beaver will have lost its life for no purpose."

Herb has been running lines for muskrat and beaver with his own traps since he was nine years old. He has pictures of himself out trapping with his father when he was three, a sweet-faced towhead, seated atop the pile of muskrat his father and grandfather had trapped in the swamps near where they lived in New Britain. Herb's grandfather emigrated from Poland. They were workers, Herb was careful to explain, when I asked what brought his family to Connecticut, not farmers. His mother's family came down from Canada as lumberjacks and worked in the mills. Herb went along with his father and grandfather, but as he put it one day, his father was a lousy teacher and Herb learned by watching them and reading trapping magazines. Herb's father had old copies of *Tips for Trappers*, published by Sears, Roebuck and Company. This was the same magazine that Martha Stewart consulted, back when she was still Martha Kostyra and trapping muskrat with her two brothers. Herb loves the irony of the fact that Martha Stewart, today an icon of American suburban perfection, grew up trapping fur.

Herb and his three sisters and brother lived in a two-room apartment in what he calls "the projects" of New Britain. His father was a machinist at Pratt and Whitney and his mother stayed home. Herb remembers many dinners of elbow macaroni and tomato sauce and that home was not a happy place. He and his father went out into the woods every chance they got. Herb skinned his first muskrats when he was eight, and he still remembers the thrill of selling them to the local buyer. They'd sell what furs they had in early December to have money for Christmas. Herb, however, didn't use his money to buy presents. Instead, he bought more traps.

Herb and his father trapped together in the early 1970s. By then, beaver had not just returned to the Connecticut landscape, they were becoming a problem. Today an estimated two million beavers live in North America, thriving in every state except Hawaii. Even Alaska now has beavers. That trappers like Herb are regularly called in to remove them reflects one of the greatest conservation success stories of the twentieth century, a program called the North American Model of Wildlife Conservation. This model dates back to the turn of the century when the impassioned writings of John Muir called on Americans to preserve their remaining wilderness. In 1872, the U.S. government founded Yellowstone, its first national park. President Theodore Roosevelt would rally wealthy sportsmen to the cause of wildlife, and in 1907 states began receiving federal support for laws protecting game and wildlife, partially as a result of the Lacey Act, which had been passed several years earlier. In short order, Roosevelt founded the National Wildlife Refuge System and the U.S. Forest Service.

America was ready for a conservation movement. With the recent closing of the western frontier, the country was abruptly and keenly aware that it was losing the wilderness that had once defined the nation. As president, Roosevelt championed wilderness preservation and especially the rigors and tests of hunting, which he believed were critical for preserving the American national character, those defining ideals of self-reliance and of resolve, and freedom. Hunting could keep Americans from going soft.

In 1903, nature writer John Burroughs would take on writers like Ernest Thompson Seton who delighted American readers with his anthropomorphic tales of wild animals like Lobo the wolf, calling them "sham naturalists." Roosevelt would take up this refrain a few years later when he wrote his famous essay for *The Atlantic* criticizing writers who he felt were "nature fakers." For Roosevelt, a true relationship to nature had to do with acknowledging our proper ancient roles in this world as either predator or prey. Seen in this light, our primary relationship with animals is to respect them as prey and hunt them responsibly as predators. Of course, for Roosevelt, that included big game hunting. It is because of his love of the hunt that we have the diorama displays of animals in the Natural History Museum in New York City—even *Castor canadensis*, the North American beaver. Roosevelt's concerns now seem both highly relevant and wildly insufficient.

In his time, Roosevelt garnered great support for wilderness preservation and conservation by pointing out the simple fact that you can't hunt if there is no wildlife, and there is no wildlife if there are no wild places. An idea was hatched to give all the wildlife to all the citizens of the country, who already owned the public lands, with the theory that they would then have a vested interest in preserving it. This was the origin of the North

American Model of Wildlife Conservation, and it initiated the integral relationship between hunters and wildlife conservation that continues today.
The idea was simple: You had to pay to play. Hunters, anglers, and trappers would help restore and maintain wildlife through purchasing yearly
licenses. Today, upwards of 70 percent of state budgets for wildlife management, research, and the purchase of habitat come from these funds,
which in 2019 funneled $20 billion into wildlife management and conser-
vation programs along with hunter education and the infrastructure of
state parks. Since 1937, an 11 percent excise tax on the sales of guns and
ammunition has funneled over $56 billion into conservation agencies. The
entire scheme is weirdly American—and deeply counterintuitive to those
who don't hunt, who can't see the logic in conserving wildlife so that hunters can have wildlife to kill, and recoil at the idea that the sale of weaponry
helps preserve the lives of animals. But the program has also been fantastically successful. In the eastern United States not only beaver, but moose,
wild turkey, fisher cat, bobcat, Canada geese, whitetail deer, coyote, fox,
and bear are thriving.

The idea that some things in the natural world should not be bought or
sold or owned dates back to the ancient Romans and Greeks. But in Europe,
and particularly in England, all wildlife in the king's lands belonged to the
king. In medieval times, tracts of woodland were divided into an estimated
sixty-nine royal forests and permission to hunt them was granted only to
nobility. Herb and other fur trappers like him would have been jailed for
poaching and either whipped or hanged. Here in America, memory of the
king's forest was in part what fueled several states to make sure that the right
to hunt was written into their state constitutions.

By the late 1700s beavers were largely gone from Connecticut and the
rest of the East, and they were declared officially extirpated in the state
in 1842. Efforts to bring them back to Connecticut began in 1914, as part
of the larger national effort to restore wildlife to the American landscape.
That year, two beavers, shipped in from Oregon, were released in Union,
just a short drive from where Herb ran his trap lines. New York had already
led the way, restoring five beavers shipped down from Canada to the
Adirondack Park in 1905. By the 1930s beaver populations had grown large
enough for New York to allow a season for beaver trapping. Connecticut's

beavers settled in well, and by 1950 the population had grown to the point where the state opened its own beaver trapping season. The most famous beaver reintroduction program was led by the Idaho Fish and Game Department. In 1948, Idaho officials instituted a program in which seventy-six beavers were flown into remote areas in boxes, then thrown out of the plane to descend by parachute. The first beaver that parachuted down was named "Geronimo." Upon impact the boxes broke open and the beavers, unharmed, at least in theory, ambled off to find water. After World War II, throughout the country restoration programs brought wildlife back and controlled their size by setting hunting quotas; trapping and hunting was guaranteed to any citizen who could afford a license.

In the United States, all wildlife and all federal lands belong to all American citizens, and along with other natural resources, are protected, at least in theory, by the Department of the Interior via the Fish and Wildlife Service. Within federal guidelines, each state can mandate different rules for hunting and fishing. Fur trapping, once an arena of lawless exploitation, is more highly regulated than hunting or fishing. Every spring Herb pays $34 ($240 for nonresidents) to obtain a trapping license from the state of Connecticut. With this license, he can trap on state land. Each of his traps must be marked with his identification number, he must check them every twenty-four hours, and he must not trap on land or within fifteen feet of the entrance to the lodge. On private lands he must get the permission of the landowner. A state wildlife control officer must tag all furs before they can be sold, and trappers are bound by each state's trapping regulations.

Herb is one of fifty-two trappers listed by the state as on call to do volunteer trapping. He also donates his time as a trap educator, running classes for the state that are free to residents. Herb is evangelical when it comes to trapping. He believes in the importance of keeping it alive as a cultural legacy. He also knows that if he volunteers for the state education programs, the state fur biologist and the officer responsible for beaver nuisance calls are more likely to call him instead of a professional nuisance wildlife operator (trapper) when they need beavers removed. Herb gets many calls every year, not just about beaver but also for skunk, raccoon, fox, opossum, and coyote. His services are free. A professional trapper usually charges $200 for setting up, then $50 to $100 per beaver caught.

Today more of us who live in the eastern United States are in closer proximity to more wildlife than at any time in the past hundred years. Along with a surge in wildlife, however, has come a surge in human-wildlife encounters and problems, particularly with beaver. Fur trappers like Herb and fur biologists and wildlife managers who work for the U.S. Fish and Wildlife Service talk about managing populations of wild animals like beaver, fox, raccoon, and deer so that the carrying capacity of a given area can be maintained. By that they mean the point at which the population reaches the limit of food and other resources that its habitat can sustain. Overpopulation leads to starvation and disease, which trappers like Herb will point out is nature's way of curtailing a given population. But the state wildlife biologists who routinely calculate populations of wild animals in order to predict carrying capacities often ignore recent studies which show that while beaver populations surged in the 1980s, their numbers have tended to stabilize since then. They also readily acknowledge that today what really matters is the *social carrying capacity* of a given area. By that they mean the subjective point at which, in the public's mind, the problems created by animals like beavers outweigh the benefits. Collisions between deer and other wildlife and motor vehicles, for example, cost by one estimate as much as $12 billion annually. Wolves in Yellowstone and in Voyageurs National Park in Minnesota now hunt beyond park boundaries, preying on cattle and sheep. In 2019, beaver caused an estimated $500,000 of damage in Massachusetts by flooding roads, train tracks, septic systems, and agricultural land, as well as felling trees in, from a human perspective, all the wrong places. The state of Connecticut does not keep track.

Before long Herb turns right and heads toward the woods. Once again we walk between tall grey spires of dead trees. "Widow makers," Herb comments just ahead of me. "They can fall without a sound, kill you flat. I'm always nervous when I'm out here alone and there's a wind." But today there is no wind; we slip through the ghost forest.

"Beavers need pretty deep water to get around," Herb explains, sloshing forward, "so they build these dams and increase the size of the pond. They can't travel well on land, needing water to get to food."

Surrounded by the woods now, we follow lines of beaver dams, each a narrow unsteady walkway of mud and sticks. My front foot suddenly sinks into mud down to my ankle and I almost slide off the narrow trail. "Careful," says Herb. "It's deeper than you think." I stare into the cold water, so crystal clear I can see patterns of fallen leaves on the bottom. Soon we are off the dam and once again shadowing where the animals have traveled. I begin concentrating on smaller and smaller details: a chewed stick, a dab of fresh mud, some trampled grass, all clues to what the beaver has done, is doing, may yet do. Soon my senses are so alert the air feels raw; I can feel the woods coming to life in a new way and it is as if I am meeting some outer limit of myself. I keep following Herb through the swamp. The water is freezing cold and we are miles from where we began.

Scientists call beavers "ecosystem engineers," meaning they create new habitats, new ecosystems when they build their ponds. The dead trees that now ring the marshy edge of the swamp bring nuthatches, woodpeckers, and other species of birds that feed on the insects in the rotten wood. Great blue herons stalk the shallows and red-winged blackbirds herald in the trees. In the highest points, osprey nest. Meanwhile, the life forms in the water itself increase exponentially. Wetlands are a soup of life, each teaspoonful containing millions of organisms. Water from beaver-altered streams and wetlands has been measured to contain fifteen times more plankton and other microbial life than wetlands without beavers. Zooplankton in particular love the nutrients provided by beaver poop.

What Herb knows is that beaver ponds are visited by all kinds of animals. When he wants to trap raccoon or skunk, fisher cat or coyote, he'll make sets for those animals nearby. For the past two years, he has been participating in a statewide study of bobcats, and he'll set out cage traps for them later in the season. The wildcats are being tagged and released in an effort to map their movements, feeding patterns, and population.

Herb stops and looks down, then points to show me his second beaver set, placed just off the rim of the mud-packed dam, which holds the next terrace of water, slightly above the lower pond where we stand. Water leaks from the low wall or trickles over the rim in so many places that the dam is as mesmerizing as a fountain. At first I can't find it; the rusted metal of the trap's base or pad is almost perfectly camouflaged in its nest of waterlogged leaves. Then I see the three-inch plate. The sight makes me shiver. The jaws of the trap have been pulled apart as wide as they can go and are hidden under a thin layer of leaves, but all it will take is enough pressure on the pad for the trigger to release and the trap to spring.

"Beaver will cross over here," Herb says, "and if not beaver, a mink or an otter might." He explains how he has set the pressure in the foot pan so that it will trigger with the weight of a beaver or otter but not for smaller animals like mink. He always uses the largest trap allowed for beaver because he doesn't want to risk them getting partially caught. His foothold trap is meant to catch the foot of an animal and hold it fast until the trapper arrives. Herb doesn't like to use foothold traps on beaver unless the water is too shallow for traps designed for the beaver to swim through. In his pack are a variety of trap sizes and styles, because as he emphasizes in his trapper education course, every situation is different. By law, beaver traps must be set underwater, and this trap has a wire attached with a catch on it so that once the beaver feels his foot caught and dives down, the wire prevents the beaver from swimming back up.

"The beaver's instinct is to swim to deep water when in danger," Herb explains, "so when he feels his foot caught, he'll swim out, then soon go unconscious from lack of oxygen, then he'll die." I nod. The thought of a beaver running out of air to breathe while still alert, struggling to surface, is terrible.

Blind set, curiosity set, runway set, false den set. Scent mound set, dam set, bottom edge set, channel set. Herb has a name for each: This one he calls a channel set. He prefers trapping beaver with a Conibear trap, invented by Frank Ralph Conibear in 1958. A trapper in Canada for over thirty years, Conibear wasn't happy with the existing foothold traps, which he considered inhumane and inefficient. He kept tinkering until he had designed a trap that would kill instantly, snapping like a mousetrap. Conibear's design, called a body-grip trap, looks like a large metal square. In 1961, the Humane Society awarded Conibear its first certificate of merit, but not everyone believes that his design is humane. Within months I'd watch a public hearing for a proposed bill to ban their use turn into an all-out culture war.

In 1992, Herb contributed to a collaborative study of trappers, wildlife biologists, and veterinarians organized by the Fish and Wildlife Service to develop a set of best practices for fur trapping. They published their "Best Management Practices" in 1996. The gruesome foothold traps with serrated teeth were banned. Foothold traps today clamp shut with jaws padded with rubber and offset to reduce the impact. I'd seen trappers snap them on their hands to demonstrate that the pressure could not break the animal's paw or leg, but that isn't good enough for most people. Anti-trapper sentiment runs deep. This is a sore point for Herb and just about every trapper I have ever met.

"I don't like the killing part," Herb said. "What I like about trapping is figuring out how to catch the animal, but the killing has to be done. Still, you have to have compassion for the animals. That means I do what I can to make it quick."

After I first asked Herb if he would take me trapping, he wondered if I was an undercover "anti"—trapper slang for animal rights activist. "People won't protest a Walmart taking out a hundred acres of wildlife habitat, or a developer doing the same thing," he'd said, "but the same people who lobby so that I can't trap don't protest the treatment of animals at factory farms. Jesus, have you ever seen a chicken farm? What a nightmare. But they'll go after a small-time trapper like me because, let's face it, just one guy…that's an easy target." Herb has one word to characterize people who eat factory-farmed meat but protest fur trapping: hypocrites.

In the next grove, Herb shows me a second lodge, smaller than the first.

"It's abandoned," he says. "See how there is no fresh mud on the top? Otter will move in and use it, so will muskrat. But I have another beaver set here, can you see it?" I look through the brush and again see nothing at first, but now I know to look for the two short guide poles and quickly see them in the brown grasses.

"I see it," I answer.

Herb grins. "We'll make a trapper of you yet." I smile back, but inside I am not so sure. The glint of the foothold trap under the water is a sober reminder that we are tracking different things here. Herb is on the hunt for beavers, and I am on the hunt to try to understand why. We walk on, quiet. "Going to get a bit deep, but I think you'll be all right," Herb says. I watch him walk through the water, sinking up past his knees. He stands six foot three, a good twelve inches taller than me; I follow carefully, easing my way forward. The water is now up to my hips. Then, in front of us, is an embankment and what looks like a deer path down to the edge, trampled grass right up to the water.

"There you go," says Herb, "that's what we're looking for, a beaver highway. See how fresh the mud is there? They've been through recently." He points across the pond where another lodge rises from the water, this one looking like a sleeping camel with two humps. "A double-decker," exclaims Herb, his voice raised in excitement. "Probably why I caught so many beavers here already." He shakes his head. "I'm always learning something new out here. It's humbling. Trapping gets me up close to the animals and I can study them. Beavers are magnificent, really beautiful."

Herb caught five the first day he set his traps last week and five the day after. Normally he would have stopped there, as he always tries to leave a few beaver so that the colony can survive. But the state has given him strict orders to remove all the beaver from this area. Herb believes that by trapping beavers he is helping the state, individual landowners, and the beavers themselves by preventing overpopulation and potential starvation among the lodges.

Before long we are walking along a flooded roadbed, heading directly back into the state forest. On either side the swamp stretches out between black lines of beaver dams that extend deep into the trees. We continue in companionable silence. We still have three more sets to check. The sky starts to cloud over and the air grows damp; snow is definitely on the way. Soon our waders hit more solid ground and we pick up our pace. Herb points out the many places where water has brimmed up and over the sides of the beaver dams. As long as the pond stays full, the beaver won't try to fix every spill point. Some dams look like fountains, water spilling out in regular patterns that the beaver let be. To Herb, each of those points is interesting, because while beaver will leave them alone, other animals like muskrat, mink, and otter will use them as handy points to cross over the dam. "This is really minky out here," says Herb, "just the kind of place they like to hunt. They'll swim all around this kind of an area. I can envision mink and otter traveling through here. They really travel. I'll come back here later for mink, and otter."

We stare at acres of water spreading out on either side of the road. A lone bird trills. Water trickles. It is so beautiful it is like an ache.

When we reach the far bank, Herb points out another lodge, this one extending from the bank. Near the entrance, the beavers have dug a large channel through the bank in order to connect this pond to a smaller one nearby. "They really are excellent engineers," says Herb. We admire the deep channel cut at a perfect ninety-degree angle.

Beavers make channels like this one to connect ponds and create pathways they use to travel into the woods. They are also shipping lanes, used to float fallen trees and branches back to their lodge or toward the dam. Researchers have recorded beavers working together to tow and push large saplings along canals. It was this engineering skill that enthralled Lewis Henry Morgan, whose classic work *The American Beaver and His Works*, published in 1868, wrestled with questions of beaver intelligence. Morgan concluded that beavers must have the ability to solve problems because they don't adapt to their new habitat; they shape the land until it adapts to them. Morgan saw them construct a twenty-five-foot-long dam within a few hours. Some of the dams he recorded extended a quarter of a mile into the forest. The largest known beaver dam stretches through the southern edge of Wood Buffalo National Park in Alberta. Discovered by satellite imagery in 2007, it spans the forest for 2,790 feet—half a mile long, and twice the length of the Hoover Dam. This beaver dam is the largest animal construction on earth.

Herb checks his final beaver set, a trap set near a huge tree that has fallen back away from the pond, exposing a matrix of roots. Washed clear of dirt, this root ball looks like an enormous Celtic knot. I notice another beaver trail leading from the bank to the water, a good twenty inches wide where the grass has been flattened and then at the edge of the water becomes a muddy slide. I ask Herb why he hasn't made his set here.

"Feel beneath," he says, pointing to a spot about three feet from the trail on the bank. He moves over so I can walk out to the spot where he has been standing. "Now feel the bottom, can you feel that? It's their channel." I move my foot through the soft layer of pond mud and then my boot abruptly drops, following an indentation, which is clear of mud. My boot crunches on gravel. A beaver channel! In part because they have poor eyesight, beavers claw channels throughout the mud at the bottom of the pond to form roadways they can travel along by feel. This system of underwater highways enables them to swim with speed and accuracy, maximizing flight. More than once I'd watched beavers on the pond near my house dive down to this invisible highway and surface a good fifteen minutes later way across at the end of the pond.

When I finish checking out the channel, Herb points to a nearby tree where a glimmer of white in the grey bark indicates where a beaver has begun to chew.

"They are starting to eat here," says Herb. "This is a new path. Not far from here is where I caught a huge beaver last week. Fifty-eight pounds, a real beaverzilla. I could hardly fit him in my pack, then I had to pack him all the way back out."

It's time to make our way back. We've been walking for two hours, have checked four sets, and so far, to my relief, each has been empty. Any live beavers are hiding in their lodges. On our left, beaver dams eel their way in and out of the tree line, a thin dark line against which the water brims. The sky has grown overcast now, the air even heavier with coming snow. For the first time I am aware of growing tired, each footstep leaden with mud and water. Herb looks at the vista of pond stretching out into the distance. It is clear that he doesn't want to take any more beaver and has a dilemma of sorts. He has other sites to trap.

Then we find the beaver. "Unless my eyes aren't good," Herb says, pointing ahead to where I can just make out the guide poles of his next set, "I think there's something in there." He wades over to check the set. He studies the poles, then sticks his bare hands into the icy mush and with a rush of water pulls out the trap and along with it a dead beaver. I am immediately alert, pulled from my reverie of walking in the woods, preparing myself for what is to come.

"A yearling," Herb says quietly, his tone serious now as he pulls up the metal trap and works to free the mass of dripping fur. "Pelt won't be worth much, but it's good eating. This would be a good one for you to try." He throws the beaver onto the bank, where it lands with a thump, the tail flapping, then resets the trap, submerging it with his hands. By the time he has the trap positioned, his fingers are beet red. He shakes them quickly. "We got a guy who is going to make us beaver sausage." Herb swears beaver tastes good, especially as beaver chili.

I'm not listening. I'm looking at the beaver, which lies on the bank looking as if it were just resting, as if it might still swim away. I stare at the front paws, the tiny fingers each tipped with a narrow black claw, the naked palms. Beavers use their front claws to dig through the mud, to pat mud and sticks into the growing walls of their dam. They use two hands to hold food. One naturalist observed a colony of beavers eating lily pads by first rolling the edges up with their hands, then eating them with great deliberation the way a human might relish a hot dog. I had watched beavers from a distance for months, and now that I am close enough to one to touch its glistening hide, I have a sudden urge to pick the beaver up and run.

To me a beaver is a symbol of the wild, like those animal tracks I have found by the creek. A wildness I want to think is still out there. I still feel this way. But being with Herb has blurred the lines. One can make the case that Herb, like other trappers who utilize every part of the animal they catch, are the ultimate locavores. Herb plans to "harvest" the beavers he traps; they are, as he and the other trappers like to say, a "sustainable resource." I want to understand what this means, but something in me still balks. For Herb this beaver on the ground before us is both food and commodity. He will use the fur, the castor, even the tail. All of that is admirable, so why do I feel such resistance? I've drawn a line in the muck and on one line are animals we eat—cows, pigs, chickens, and sheep—and on the other side are wild animals meant to live in the woods and be their wild selves. I don't want to think about beavers having to be controlled, or "harvested." Although to be honest, being out here has complicated my sense of what I even mean when I say wildness. Once we drive out of this woodland, we'll be just ten minutes from a strip mall. Everywhere I look is in fact a landscape that has been human-altered for centuries. Maybe that was it—the beavers were something we could not control, a part of the natural world we had not altered. Perhaps it was the fact that just thirty minutes from Hartford, I could be out with a fur trapper and imagining myself close to something wild at all.

"Can you grab that for me?" Herb says casually. I nod, relieved to be out of my head, and lean down to grab the beaver's front leg. The fur glistens like the coat of a Labrador retriever. The beaver is surprisingly heavy. "There you go," says Herb approvingly. I lug it back to the stand of pine where Herb had left his wicker trapper's pack when he stopped to release the trap. As carefully as I can, place it in, headfirst. The large rubbery tail, that fantastic paddle, pokes up over the edge. I finger the tip where the tail has a slight notch, a tear or a bite healed over. I am implicated now. No longer an observer.

Back at the truck the question pops out before I have time to think it out. "Why do you trap? You could just go out and look at animals, be in the swamp that way." He answers simply, "If you don't kill the meat you eat you are just putting that killing on someone else." Herb looks at me then. He is revealing something new about himself, our conversation reaching a different level. Behind his glasses I see his eyes narrow, as if he is wondering if he can continue. I nod, although in a way I think he is still dodging my question, because he wasn't living off the beaver or muskrat or otter or mink, all of which he was trapping out there.

"Not everyone can kill," Herb continues. "It's not for everyone. But I respect the animal. If we didn't manage the populations, there would be so much disease and starvation, people don't realize. Why do I trap? Not for the money. I have lots of other ways to lose money!" He laughs, a hearty chortle, and turns to put the key in the ignition. But before he can start the engine, we both stare. A hawk sweeps down, talons extended, and grabs something from the meadow, then in a great flap of wings swoops back up. I can just make out a small animal dangling from its talons. The moment is like a chimera, like something half-dreamed, a moment of pure unequivocal ferocity, violence, and death, wild.

"You see that!" Herb's face lights up, his voice emphatic. "That's what I mean about being out here. You ask me why I trap. Even if fur prices are down I'll still go out. Out here, it's spiritual—I gave up on religion a long time ago." He swings his arm out to gesture toward the swamp. "This is my church."

Herb begins to tell me about his father, what a lousy dad he was, how much he drank to get away from the tedium and relentless shifts of factory work. How miserable his mother was. But through it all was trapping, something they shared in the swamp out behind the New Britain projects where the train ran through. "I buried my dad with a trap," Herb continues, "and a beaver skin. He was a veteran and was entitled to a salute, but the guys who showed up, they just played a tape, it was pathetic." A pained look crosses his face. "I think about my dad every time I go out trapping. My grandfather, too."

We've packed up the beaver and gear. The truck bumps over the dirt road, and at the entrance to the state land, I jump out and pull open the heavy metal gate. Once through, Herb stops the truck and double-checks that I have locked it securely.

It is 11:30 and we've been out for three hours, but Herb still has two more locations to check. After driving for a good twenty minutes, we pull into a neighborhood of sad houses: They need paint, the front steps have broken rails, and weeds push up around shrubs. "This used to be a nice neighborhood," says Herb. "Now it's full of drugs." He pulls in front of a small white house and Herb unpacks his gear. We walk down a sloping lawn toward the stream that runs through at the bottom of the yard. "He's been getting water flooding halfway up his lawn," explains Herb, "over his septic." There is trash along the sides of the stream, and tires and bits of metal have been thrown into the weeds. It is such a contrast to the woodland beauty of where we have just been that I am astonished that Herb even wants to trap here, but he slogs through the water and starts pulling out the sticks that beavers have stuffed into the culvert. In short order he has found the underwater route the beavers have been using here and sets two traps. Herb doesn't look back when we load the truck and head toward the last stop, a car dealership that has had problems with flooding in several of its lots.

At the car dealership, Herb drives to the back lots, which have been built right up to the edge of a low-lying wetland, and are now flooding when it rains. Even before beavers had begun to dam the area, the ground dips down so low that it must have flooded. The parking lots may well have been built before Connecticut's laws were introduced to protect fragile inland wetlands like these, or perhaps in violation of them. The beavers didn't cause the problem, but they are making it worse.

"This seems more like a human problem than a beaver problem," I say.

"Oh, sure," answers Herb, "you can count on people being dumb. The beavers are just being beavers, but they are there now, and the people, well, they aren't going to move." He shrugs and starts getting gear from the car.

Herb gets to work, and within an hour has put in two sets by the short dam beavers have built within a stone's throw of the parking lot. On the way back he smokes the cigarettes he can't smoke in the house. He's in a hurry now to get home because he's always there by 3 p.m. in order to meet his two children at the school bus stop. His daughter and son are ten and thirteen, and the bus stops in front of his house, but it is important to Herb to be there waiting. By the time we reach his fur shack, snow has started swirling down. I thank him for the day, pull off my waders, grab my gear, and head east toward home.

I drive back, past old mill brick buildings and empty tobacco barns. I think I am beginning to understand from Herb's ability to read the land for signs the intimacy between the trapper and the animals he traps. Herb has shown me something else as well. To love a place is to know it in its brokenness, wrote Wendell Berry. Herb was showing me how to know the brokenness of place, accept what was and learn to find beauty in it; at the car dealership he saw only the beavers. He wasn't focused on an idea of wilderness out there; he was finding the wild right here in Connecticut. Still, I wonder, where is his outrage at the polluted wetlands and the destruction of wildlife because people had foolishly built too close to streams and swamps?

Herb seemed to withdraw into himself and got on with the job; the beavers were still there and they were still wild. I was clearly on the side of the beavers. Herb was, and yet he wasn't. When I thought of beautiful landscapes my mind went to other places than northeastern Connecticut. I imagined the landscape of the Hudson valley where I had grown up, sunsets over a line of blue mountains. Or I thought of the rugged mountains and hills of southern Oregon where I had worked as a tree planter, then a ranch hand. I was, more often than not, focused on somewhere else.

Even before I met Herb, the beavers had been changing how I saw the place where I now lived. However fern-studded and beautiful, the lines of stone walls through the woods of New England troubled me. They seemed a constant reminder of all the ways we had ripped through the continent, extracting the hell out of everything from the natural world. In *Changes in the Land*, environmental historian William Cronon estimates that each colonist took down an acre of forest per household every year, and by the mid-1800s over 80 percent of the New England forests were gone. It would be some time before I would uncover the awful truth behind the building of many of the stone walls in my hometown. What I saw at first was how nature was consuming them, the roots of plants and trees slowly but surely dislodging the stones in those laboriously constructed walls, then winds toppling them. For wildlife, the stone walls had become an efficient trailway teeming with food.

Meanwhile, down at the beaver pond near my house, I had been witnessing nature's powers of regeneration. First the beavers arrived, then the assorted company of wildlife that followed, from muskrat and otter to wood ducks and heron and on: a beaver-generated ecosystem. But all of this I had seen from a distance. With Herb, a fur trapper, I was actually in the beaver's world, learning how to read the woodlands for beaver sign, that language of broken twigs and creased blades of grass, all of which I had missed until now.

Some days later, when sun pools across the table and I make pancakes for my mother and myself, I tell her about my day in the swamp and my interest in learning about fur trapping.

"Why?" my mother asks, direct as usual.

"They know things about animals," I parry, but the truth was, I wasn't sure yet who these fur trappers were, exactly.

"It's sadistic," my mother says bluntly, summing up what others thought but wouldn't say.

I could understand my mother's reaction. When most people heard that I was researching contemporary fur trappers they grimaced or gave me a sideways glance. In terms of human experience, not much is worse than the feeling of being trapped. Physical entrapment is scary, but just as terrible are the myriad ways we can come to feel trapped in emotions or psychologically by others or by ourselves. The minute we think of being trapped we feel panic. Fur trappers like Herb don't believe that animals experience the same emotions that we do; for them, trapping is humane if it is done well and the animal dies quickly. The fact is, we are only beginning to understand what animals actually experience in terms of what we call emotions.

I remind my mother that a man she respected was a fur trapper. Every spring that I could remember she had bought shad roe from Everett Nack, a commercial fisherman, part-time carpenter, hunter, and fur trapper. Nack had a pet raccoon and loved baby skunks, yet he sold raccoon and skunk pelts to make Daniel Boone–style hats. He was also an environmental vigilante. One weekend when I was in high school, he let me go out with him on the river tagging sturgeon. When dawn broke, we skimmed the Hudson's tides in his small boat, and when we reached the nets, pulled them up to find huge fish, with shark-like tails, dinosaur-like plates, and long pointed noses. Nack quickly tagged them, while I kept an eye out for guys from the Department of Environmental Conservation. Tagging sturgeons, which were an endangered species, was illegal, and that was exactly why Nack was out there. He would end up proving that an endangered species was in the river and thus environmental protections needed to be put in place to restrain the pollution being dumped downriver by large power companies. The power companies had managed to suppress any state environmental studies, which is why Nack took things into his own hands.

Everett Nack had been a legend in the Hudson valley, admired by Pete Seeger and others dedicated to the cleanup of the Hudson River, and I knew that my mother admired his vigilante ways. But when I remind her that he was both a fur trapper and an environmentalist, she says, well, yes, but he was different. In her mind fur trappers are still gnarly macho types who, like gunslinging cowboys, kill animals for sport. I could see I wasn't going to change her mind and so I let it go. She was dying by then. Each week when I visited, it was clear that we didn't have many more mornings to sit at the table together, enjoying pancakes and the morning sun, and I didn't want to argue with her.

I was still far from understanding Herb's insistence that trapping was spiritual. I turned to a book that Tom Decker, the head of the Fifth Division of the U.S. Fish and Wildlife Service, had recommended. Decker, an avid hunter and trapper, oversaw projects from up and down the Atlantic coast, and he'd shown me an anthology by James Swan titled *In Defense of Hunting.*

Swan argues that hunting is necessary for human survival because it links modern people to their Paleolithic past; although we no longer need to hunt to survive, denying innate human violence is dangerous. His references are dated—he cites Carl Jung's famous statement that a "part of the soul is a leopard," and also Eric Fromm's ideas that in the act of hunting a man becomes one with the animal—but still seem relevant. Swan puts modern hunters into three groups: meat hunters, those who hunt to put food on their table; recreational hunters, those who hunt for sport; and nature hunters, those for whom hunting is "a sacred act with as much as or more meaning than participation in organized religion." The first two types of hunters are the norm. Forty-five percent of hunters surveyed respond that they hunt to put meat on their table, while another 38.5 percent hunt as a sport and a hobby. This group includes a percentage of what Swan calls "slob hunters" who give the sport a bad name by relying on military-grade guns and scopes, and technologies of all kinds over skill; they also often mix hunting with drinking. What really interests Swan is the third category, "nature hunters," a much smaller percentage, only 17 percent of those surveyed, who are in the woods out of a deep, abiding love of nature and the natural world.

"The path of the nature hunter," writes Swan, "leads them not toward violence and mayhem, but towards respect, awe, humility, and even love for the animals hunted." And this sense of awe often leads them to describe hunting as a religious experience; a sacred act, which means they have reverential feelings for nature perhaps best described as love, yet they turn around and kill what they love. After being on the trap line, I thought I understood some of this better. Walking the trap line felt like being in the grip of an ancient, immediate, and emotional way of moving through the world. You were instinctively on guard because it began to feel as if the roles could quickly reverse; a predator could become prey.

Three of our most famous nature writers, Henry David Thoreau, Aldo Leopold, and Edward Abbey, considered hunting to have virtues. Up in Canada, Archie Belaney (a.k.a. Grey Owl) had given up his trap lines but stressed the value of that "wild life." While Thoreau never hunted, he thought every American boy should know how to handle a gun. Leopold felt that duck hunting connected him to the natural world. "The out-of-doors is our true ancestral estate," wrote Abbey. "How can we pluck that deep root of feeling from the racial consciousness? Impossible!" For him, hunting was central to survival.

The National Trappers Association has tallied about 250,000 licensed fur trappers throughout all fifty states. But no one really knows exactly how many trappers are out there, because most of them like living as far off the grid as they can. Much like the animals they hunt, fur trappers feel safer traveling along the edges of things. But being an outlier does not mean a lack of fraternity, or that there is no code of honor, or set of rules—the rules were just different and appeared paradoxical, the way a community of hermits seems like a contradiction in terms unless you belong to a monastery yourself.

The fur trappers I came to know were bonded by a common enemy, the antipathy they believed most people, and particularly environmentalists, had for them. And while the beaver population was on the rebound throughout North America, the population of fur trappers was not. They were becoming an endangered species. They felt trapped.

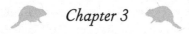

Chapter 3

Looking for Astor in Astoria

Somewhere in the churning waters of the Atlantic during the fierce winter of 1783, just off the coast of England or close to the Chesapeake Bay, we don't know exactly where, several first-class passengers on the American vessel the *Carolina* paced the deck. They were officers of a great and powerful trade organization, the Governor and Company of Adventurers of England Trading into Hudson's Bay. They had come above to speak in private about weighty matters, matters of great importance, concerning a particular trade item that had already made them fabulously wealthy.

Little did they know that a passenger, a young man who had paid five guineas for a bunk in steerage, had also ventured to the upper deck and was listening. The money to be made was so fantastic that at first the young man thought they must be talking about speculation in tulips, but even a butcher's boy knew the follies of tulip mania that had bankrupted seventeenth-century Amsterdam. No, the men were talking about something of great practical value that sold for such staggeringly high prices in London it made his head spin. They were talking about beaver.

The men discussed methods of baling and sorting and transporting furs, as well as strategies for obtaining the beaver pelts most prized by European hatters, the *castor gras d'hiver*, which were taken from beaver caught in their winter prime. What the young man overheard next made him tremble; beaver skins sold in London for twenty shillings a pound, and a prime beaver pelt weighing two pounds could be traded for trinkets and knick-knacks worth no more than three or four shillings from willing Native people. Fur could be traded for iron kettles and hatchets, English blankets, ammunition, guns, and rotgut rum, but also a handful of cheap jewelry, blue glass beads, ribbons, pins—even a packet of sugar buns.

Hunched down against the wind, the young man did the math. Four shillings for a pelt worth forty was a huge gain even with the cost of transportation. He had paid the equivalent of twenty-five U.S. dollars for his passage, and it had taken him four years of hard work as a laborer in London to save up enough money for this fare and to buy seven flutes, which he planned to sell when he reached Manhattan. He had so little money to spare, he had wrapped the flutes in his one suit and extra shirts and underwear in order to avoid paying the extra charge for freight. His plan was to open a music business in New York, but this talk of the fur trade, which seemingly required almost no capital to enter, was rapidly changing his mind. His goal in coming to the New World was to get rich. Forget selling music; he resolved to find out more about this lucrative fur trade. He made his way to New York City, found work peddling bread, and as soon as he could, sold the seven flutes and used that money, along with cunning, self-confidence, stamina, and ambition, to buy pelts of beaver, then other furs. In an almost unbelievably short time, he was rich.

Within fifteen years after landing in New York City, Johann Jacob Astor was America's first multimillionaire. His American Fur Company was America's first multinational corporation and a plunderer's dream. He would find a way to dupe the young nation's shrewd and passionate third president, Thomas Jefferson, in service of a scheme to create the first American trade monopoly. And his dream was borne on the back of the beaver.

When Astor left England in 1783, the Little Ice Age, which began in the 1400s, was still dramatically cooling the Northern Hemisphere, bringing winters of intense snow and cold. That December was particularly harsh, and the transatlantic passage from Bristol to Baltimore, which should have taken just over three weeks, ended up taking four months. The *Carolina* pitched and heaved through gales so fierce that at one point Astor put on his suit so that he would be properly dressed should the ship capsize and they all die at sea. But the experienced captain managed to sail them safely across the storm-tossed Atlantic. The Chesapeake Bay was frozen solid, and for weeks they waited aboard for the ice to break up. Astor's fare had included salt beef and biscuit for the duration of the voyage, so he remained on board. Finally, on March 23, he did what most of the other passengers had already done; he climbed down from the icebound vessel and set out on foot over the ice to the city of Baltimore.

The young German immigrant made his way to New York City to seek out his brother, who had emigrated years earlier and ran a butcher shop. But Astor had left his village in Germany to escape working in the family butcher shop alongside his father and did not want to fall into the same trap in a new setting. He found work at a bakery. His days spent peddling bread enabled him to quickly learn the city, which in 1784 was a settlement of twenty-three thousand people. Eighteenth-century Manhattan was filthy and poverty-stricken and bristling with opportunity.

As soon as he had found a way to purchase trinkets for trade, Astor headed down to the city's waterfront looking for river men, sailors, down-and-out Indigenous people, and wandering farm laborers who might have a pelt or two. Astor plowed every bit of money he could obtain into buying more trade items that he carted throughout the city, seeking to trade for fur. As he had on the ship, he kept his eyes and ears open, and within a few months he landed a job in the fur business, working for a Quaker named Robert Browne, cleaning, sorting, and beating furs. By the following December—within six months of arriving in New York—his own stock of beaver and other furs had grown to the point where he was able to return to London to sell his first lot of North American beaver.

By the spring of 1785, Astor was ready to take his trading to the next level. Dressed in woodsman's clothes, a knife in his belt and a clay pipe in his mouth, he set off by steamer up the Hudson River to trade directly with Native American tribes on behalf of Browne's company. From that point on, Astor's fortunes in the fur trade rose like hot mercury. He continued buying furs for Browne, but also on his own behalf, setting out at an almost frantic pace on long journeys through the Poconos, then up the Hudson River to meet and trade with the tribes of upstate New York. The Oneida, Seneca, Huron, and Iroquois had been trading among themselves for centuries before the arrival of Europeans and were shrewd bargainers. From them Astor learned enough of their languages and ways to become a skilled trader. As one resident of Schenectady wrote, "I have seen John Jacob with his coat off, unpacking in a vacant yard near my residence a lot of furs he had bought dog-cheap off the Indians." Albany had been the eastern fur trade headquarters for Iroquois country since Henry Hudson had turned his boat around there in 1609. The early Dutch Walloons made this strategic site on the river a permanent settlement in 1632. Named for the beaver that founded it, Beverwyck had played a critical role in the New Netherlands as a beaver trading post. Through his trips up and down the Hudson valley from New York City to Albany, Astor was introduced to figures of importance in early New York.

By the time Astor arrived in Manhattan, the city seal had already been designed, not once but twice with the image of a beaver featured prominently. The original seal of New Amsterdam displayed a beaver lying on top of the flag of the Netherlands. When the British took over in 1664 and renamed the city New York, they removed the Dutch flag from the seal, added a Pilgrim and an Indigenous man, but kept the beaver. One of Johann Jacob Astor's good decisions soon after his arrival seems to have been to marry the daughter of the woman who ran his boardinghouse, Sarah Todd, a woman who understood the beaver's importance to the city's history. Sarah was by all accounts a levelheaded woman with excellent business sense.

When eventually Astor did open a small music business in the room below their lodgings on Queen Street (now called Pearl Street), he left the running of it to Sarah, who minded the small enterprise while raising their children. Sarah was hardworking and practical, but her family was related to one of the oldest Dutch families, the Brevoorts, giving her social connections that Astor made use of. It was Sarah who encouraged Astor, then an awkward young immigrant with a thick German accent, to start visiting the Manhattan coffeehouses frequented by prominent fur traders and do everything in his power to befriend them. Sarah's family had watched the little settlement of Mannahatta creep steadily north. It may well have been her business savvy that later influenced Astor to take some of the fur profits that he was always keen to plow back into the fur business and begin purchasing real estate on the outskirts of the city. Astor would go on to purchase an area known today as Greenwich Village. He also bought a largely rural area, Eden Farm, which today we call midtown and Times Square.

An up-and-coming fur trader in eighteenth-century New York needed access to high-quality Canadian beaver and other furs. Astor had been making a tidy profit, and his buying trips were taking him not only up and down the Hudson valley but also west into the Poconos. But his next move was to continue up the Hudson past Albany, west along the Mohawk to the portage at Little Falls, and north to Montreal, the center of the Canadian beaver trade, where he arrived in the summer of 1788. On October 28, he ran an ad in the *New York Packet* advertising his new ability to buy and sell Canadian fur. "He gives cash for all kinds of Furs: and has for sale a quantity of Canada Furs, such as beaver...which he sells by large or small quantities."

Astor's ability to sell prestigious Canadian beaver put him on the map. Within two years he had formed an association with Thomas Backhouse and Company, an important London merchant. At twenty-seven, he had already managed to build a lucrative transatlantic fur business: His net worth in combined cash, merchandise, and real estate was between $30,000 and $40,000, about $850,000 today. He was only getting started.

During his now frequent trips to Montreal, Astor was wined and dined by the partners of the North West Company, which had been formed in 1783 by competitors of the Hudson's Bay Company, which had largely controlled the Canadian fur trade since its founding in 1670. These fiery Scottish traders introduced Astor to a means for buying furs on a much larger scale; instead of only obtaining pelts directly from Indians and trappers, a fur company or a fur trader like Astor could buy from other fur companies. The profit margin was lower, but traders could quickly amass stocks of fur. Most important, this enabled them to obtain the wonderfully valuable beaver from the northwest trading centers of Detroit and Michilimackinac. Those beaver pelts were so dark and lustrous they sent the London prices rocketing. Astor was beginning to understand that he could make a lot of money from the riches to be had in the interior of North America, and those riches were furs—magnificent beaver, along with lynx, mink, and fox, all of which fetched staggeringly high prices among Europe's status-conscious aristocrats.

Astor began thinking of the fur trade in a newly ambitious and highly illegal way. He did not mean to take for himself some of the wealth to be had from fur in the interior of North America—he meant to have it all. He simply needed to figure out how.

The British had controlled the North American fur trade since 1760, and despite the war of independence that freed the colonies, the continent west of the Mississippi was still unexplored and uncharted territory and French, with Canadians controlling the fur trade in the Northwest. Throughout 1793 and 1794, the Canadians stepped up their efforts to protect their market. They sent guns, money, ammunition, liquor, and wild promises to Native tribes, enlisting them in increasingly bloody encounters with American traders. At the same time the British imposed trade restrictions and illegally seized American ships on the high seas in an attempt to damage the international trade of the new nation.

War fever rose to such an extent that federal leaders were alarmed. With the hope of averting conflict, they urged President Washington to send a special envoy to London. Washington sent founding father John Jay, known for his skills as a diplomat. In 1794, under "Jay's Treaty," the British promised to withdraw troops and garrisons from all posts in the United States. Settlers and traders in the Northwest Territory might either remain or leave with their property intact, and both British and American subjects were given the right to cross the boundary between Canada and the United States at will. When Astor heard the terms of the agreement, he is said to have uttered one sentence: "*Now* I will make my fortune in the fur trade."

Astor flourished in a world of frontier lawlessness and cutthroat competition. But his great triumph was at hand when the size of the United States doubled with the Louisiana Purchase and a new era of westward expansion began. In 1803, Thomas Jefferson organized the famous Corps of Discovery expedition to explore these new lands west of the Mississippi and to map for the United States what British explorer Alexander Mackenzie had successfully accomplished for the North West Company in 1783: an overland route to the Pacific.

Thomas Jefferson put his expedition together carefully. Meriwether Lewis was a naturalist and astronomer and William Clark was a surveyor; together their skills enabled them to explore the new lands acquired in the Louisiana Purchase and chart a way to the Pacific. The expedition had two goals based on Jefferson's precepts. One was diplomatic, as they would be apprising the tribes whose lands they were traveling through of the new sovereignty of the United States under the Louisiana Purchase. This needed to be done carefully, for they hoped to shift trade toward American interests. The French were well established in St. Louis, then the westernmost fur trading post, and the English had control of Canada. The expedition packed many gifts to give to tribal leaders and sought to avoid conflict. Their second goal was ethnographic. Jefferson wanted them to observe and gather information from the Native people they met. In addition, Lewis and Clark were to survey, map, observe, and record observations of geography, flora and fauna, and the natural resources of this new western territory. In keeping with Jefferson's instructions, Lewis would dutifully record the animal species they observed and the names of the many tribes of Indigenous people they encountered. They found no remaining ice-age creatures, but plenty of elk, bear, wolf, coyote, bison, fox, lynx, too many squirrels to count, mischievous prairie dogs, myriad birds, and, most important of all, plentiful beaver of a size and quality Lewis noted he had never before seen.

No one knew for sure what lay in the far west beyond the Mississippi. Would they find the lost tribes of Israel, or the existence of surviving mastodons? In 1803, these speculations were bandied about and were not considered ridiculous. In 1739, mastodon bones had been unearthed near the Ohio River, and this record of the megafauna of the last great ice age revolutionized scientific thinking. Today we can't imagine knowing much about animals without an awareness of evolution and extinction, but in eighteenth-century animal science, both of those ideas were still years away. Charles Willson Peale, Thomas Jefferson's friend, managed to get hold of an almost complete mastodon skeleton unearthed in Newburgh, New York. He reconstructed the creature and in 1801 unveiled it to audiences who were by all accounts both spooked and titillated by the thought of giant creatures from a previous time. If there were massive hairy elephants, what else?

Lewis and Clark were on the trail for 537 days, a journey of 4,118 miles through uncharted territory. On May 14, 1804, they left Camp Dubois outside St. Louis and began following the Missouri River up against the current until it met the Yellowstone River, which they followed north and west until finally they came upon the mythic Columbia River, which they knew ran directly into the Pacific. Some days earlier, when they had first encountered the wide Columbia River estuary, Lewis had been so stunned by the river's expanse that at first he thought they had arrived at the Pacific. "Ocian in View!" he had exclaimed. "O! The joy." They soon realized that they were not yet at the mouth of the river where it spilled fast and furious into the equally rough surf of the Pacific; that majestic sight off Cape Disappointment would not come for days.

A few years after he returned, Lewis wrote bluntly of one of the goals of their expedition: "With hope of future gain from the fur trade." All along the way they had carefully noted the presence of wildlife but recorded with particular attention and enthusiasm the presence of beaver. On July 23, 1804, in Camp White Catfish, Iowa, Lewis recorded that they had killed two deer and caught two beaver for food. "Beaver appear plenty in this part of the country." On their journey they met a number of Native people, all of whom were actively trading beaver and other furs with white traders. They met a number of French beaver trappers en route, but in North Dakota on April 10, 1805, Lewis took the time to note that "the beaver these people have already taken is by far the best I have ever seen." Not long after that encounter, they came across an Indigenous burial site. A human body had been wrapped in buffalo cloaks and left under scaffolding upon which were two dogsleds and dog harnesses. The dogs were gone, but among the dead person's possessions was a small bag containing valuables. When they examined it, they found it contained scraping tools and red and blue dyes, but also the dried roots of plants, plaits of sweet grass and the long nails from the back feet of a beaver: a Native American medicine kit.

Beaver fed the Corps of Discovery throughout their journey west. The men also shot elk, deer, and later bison, but according to Lewis they were all keen for beaver. On May 2, 1805, Lewis noted that the "flesh of beaver is esteemed a delicacy among us." They particularly loved boiled beaver tail, which Lewis described as tasting like "fresh tongues and sounds of cod." In addition to surviving off of beaver meat and carefully noting the locations of potentially fine sources of beaver fur, Lewis also made one of the earliest observations of beaver adaptation. In Montana, not far from the Beaverhead River (which Lewis noted had been named that by the Native people there), he observed beavers out during the day and understood the significance. In his journal that day he wrote that the beaver he saw, "in consequence of not being hunted are extremely gentle and out during the day." Back east, where for decades by then the beaver had been voraciously hunted, they had become mostly nocturnal and crepuscular. In other words, beavers had quickly adapted to the presence of European hunters, and switched to emerging from the safety of their lodges only in twilight or at night. This makes sense; the beaver's other predators—coyote, bear, and wolf—are more active at night. In a landscape without the pressure of human hunting, working during the day would have been safer than venturing out after dark.

It would take Lewis and Clark two years to complete their historic journey to the Pacific and back, but as soon as he returned, Meriwether Lewis strongly urged President Jefferson to make haste and create a settlement and trading center on the Pacific. Jefferson was keen but lacked the funds.

Johann Jacob Astor knew his moment. He visited Jefferson and the two fueled each other's imaginations, talking for days as they developed visions for the limitless possibilities offered by West Coast settlement. Jefferson's thinking was geopolitical—he wanted to extend the reach of the young nation west and understood the national importance of opening trade with the Pacific. Astor's thinking was pure, unadulterated greed. He meant to create a trade empire. What Astor did next was remarkably bold, cunning, and corrupt—in order to convince Jefferson that his intentions were in support of spreading American democracy westward and not in the service of a trade monopoly, he created a fur company. On paper it appeared to be run by a board of twenty-five stockholders, but it was in fact owned only by one man, John Jacob Astor. That company was the American Fur Company, known as the AFC, which, along with its Pacific branch, the Pacific Fur Company, was a legal mirage. Astor had convinced friends and associates to lend their signatures, but they were a board in name only; they did not own a dime of the company, nor did they have any oversight or voting rights.

Resigned to the need to rely on private investment to open the country's westward expansion, President Jefferson granted Astor's company a government charter to head west following Lewis and Clark's route and found a trading post on the Columbia where it met the Pacific. Backed by the U.S. government, Astor was thus able to sway, barter with, and negotiate terms with the remaining settlers and Indigenous peoples. The trading posts founded along Lewis and Clark's route theoretically represented the combined interests of the U.S. government and the AFC, but in reality it was Astor's interests that prevailed. His company ran the posts, which meant it controlled the trade for all of the fur from the interior of the continent. The linchpin of Astor's plan was the establishment of a settlement on the westernmost edge of the continent, a trade gateway that could cross the Pacific.

In 1810, Astor financed two expeditions west, one overland following Lewis and Clark's journey up the Missouri River, and one by sea. The overland expedition would start in St. Louis, the most westward point of the fur trade, and establish trade posts at each of the places the Corps of Discovery had established camps. The sea voyage, led by Captain Jonathan Thorn, would set out from New York City and sail around Cape Horn to arrive at the mouth of the Columbia River. From this new colony, the first west of the Rockies, Astor's ships would be able to transport beaver and other furs to China, where they were in high demand, then head back to North America or to Europe filled with tea, spices, nankeen yellow cloth, and highly coveted Chinese porcelain. It was a ruthless, daring, and brilliant plan—and it almost worked.

In 1810, the *Tonquin*, commanded by the foolish Captain Thorn, sailed from New York Harbor and reached Cape Disappointment at the mouth of the Columbia River the following spring. Near-mutiny, a tragic loss of life, and a final explosion would end up destroying the ship, its cargo, and everyone aboard, but before this happened, enough men would find their way ashore and build a rough shelter. The spot was not ideal, but the despotic captain had ordered the men to build the fort so quickly that they did not have time to make proper measurements or locate the highest, most secure point. As soon as the rough structure was completed, the captain ordered them to raise the flag. The first American settlement west of the Rockies was founded. Of course it would bear Astor's name: Astoria.

On the wall of the Historical Society of Astoria, Oregon, is a map of Astor's westward expeditions. Next to the map there are two glass cases, one holding a gentleman's worn black top hat made of beaver felt, and the other an equally aged stuffed beaver, on a base. The beaver, whose fur has turned a light brown with age, nonetheless looks busy, in the act of gnawing on a stick. Peering down at these two objects from his portrait on the wall is Astor, who capitalized on the European hat industry's need for beaver felt. Despite the desultory air of neglect, the choice of objects is apt. The hat, the beaver, the map, and the man were like the four legs of the table on which stood the economic history of young America.

On the map, a dotted line from continent to continent shows the route of Astor's projected trade empire. In Astoria, his ships would load up with furs and cross the Pacific to unload in Canton. In China, they would load back up with valuable silk and tea, spices, and porcelain, then sail around Africa and straight to London. Once in London, the valuable Chinese trade goods would be unloaded and they would fill back up with British trade goods in hot demand in America. They would cross the Atlantic for New York Harbor, unload, then reload with goods from there and head west, sailing around the tip of South America. Before arriving in Astoria, the ship would make a brief stop in Hawaii for more exotic trade goods.

In the portrait, Astor is simply dressed in a black suit with a white cravat. He has a slightly disheveled look, as if he had finished a long day of work, and beneath his eyes dark circles tinge his face, giving it a worn, almost tired look. His rather portly belly indicates his success in the world, and the painter has taken care to depict his jacket as slightly pulled apart to accommodate his girth, revealing a triangle of white shirt. Astor looks out with an expression of satisfaction, the gaze, slightly weary but still intense; it is the look of someone who has achieved his life's goal. The mouth does not smile but the lips are pulled slightly apart as if we have come upon him in a moment of contemplation. By the time the portrait was completed, Astor had already made a bundle trading beaver pelts in the East, but he was planning to build a financial empire by extending that trade west. No doubt he was thinking about his fortune.

In contrast to Astor's calm, the beaver is a study in agitation and appetite. Positioned so that it stands upright on its two back legs, the beaver grasps a stick in its two front hands. Its head is angled and mouth open wide, so it is poised to bite down on the stick, which the beaver holds with great resolve. The taxidermist has gone to great lengths to separate each delicate finger so that it circles the stick in a tight grip. The small eyes blaze: *Do not even think of grabbing this stick.* The Roman natural philosopher Gaius Plinius Secundus (AD 23–74) popularly known as Pliny considered the beaver vicious. "The bite of the animal is terrible," he wrote. "If they seize a man by any part of his body, they will never loose their hold until his bones are broke and crackle under his teeth." Pliny had a rather overactive imagination: For the most part, beavers are vicious only in regard to trees. But the ferocity of this stuffed beaver seems a perfect projection of the fur trade's appetite for beaver fur.

A few steps beyond Astor's portrait, the top hat, and the stuffed beaver, someone had thought to include a color reproduction of a portrait of Henry VIII, looking stout and kingly in ermine-lined robes. The accompanying placard gives a brief history of the fur trade in Europe. Ancient Egyptians traded with Arabians and Phoenicians for furs, coloring them with vegetable dyes. Ancient Greeks imported furs from Libya and especially from the Scythians, who lived north of the Caspian Sea and trimmed their clothes with beaver and otter skins. The Romans imported pelts from Germany. Senators of the Roman Republic distinguished their rank by wearing furs in addition to regular cloth togas. In Latin, *pelle* means animal skin. In AD 410, when the Visigoths took control of Rome, the city tried to keep them from ransacking the streets by paying a ransom, which included three thousand fur coats.

In medieval Europe an astonishingly wide array of skins was traded from all four directions, establishing a fur trade commerce. Furs from Germany, Ireland, and Scotland flowed to London. Furs from Spain, North Africa, and Sicily went to Paris. Furs from Sweden, Portugal, and Bulgaria ended up in Bruges. Russia with its northern territories full of prime fur became a major trade center, sending furs west to Europe. At one point, the best winter weasel was to be found in Armenia, which led to white weasel being called *ermine.*

The living quarters of the rich, especially stone castles, were heated only by fireplaces, which meant they were drafty and cold, even in summer. Fur was needed to make blankets and quilts, robes and covers, hats for outdoors and caps for sleeping, dressing gowns, and gloves. There were fur-lined pajamas, and babies were baptized in special fur-trimmed christening gowns. The standard medieval garb of the wealthy consisted of two layers of clothing, an undergarment or tunic, called a *cote* in Middle English, over which an overgarment called a *supertunic, surcote,* or *houpelande* was worn. Both of these layers were often made with fur. When venturing outside, people donned a cloak called a *pilche* that was usually lined with fur. At times members of court might be wearing as many as three different layers of animal skins.

While Astor might have donned a fur coat for warmth, in medieval Europe furs were an important sign of class distinction. By the fourteenth century, sumptuary laws, which defined permissible expenditures and the general consumption of the nobility, began to describe in detail which particular furs groups could wear (or not). If you were a commoner you could forget about wearing anything but sheepskin, rabbit, and maybe deer. The first statute of 1337 stated clearly that only the royal family, prelates, earls, barons, knights, and certain clerks who had at least £100 a year could wear fur. Royalty could of course wear anything they liked, and in the fourteenth century they favored sable and ermine, civet cat, otter, fox, and red squirrel caught in winter when their bellies were pure white with a rim of grey—and of course, beaver. Nobility and clerics could choose from a range of imported furs, but only knights and ladies with an income of over £266 a year could wear squirrel. Everyone else of gentle birth had to be content with facings of ermine on their hoods or robes lined with better-quality lamb's wool called budge. Furs were so valued they were included in wills and passed down from one generation to the next. The sumptuary laws spurred the socially ambitious.

Images of men and women in costly furs dominate medieval art. Illuminators loved to portray scenes of splendor, men and women dressed in the riches of their furs. In St. Mark's Basilica in Venice, one of the most arresting mosaics is of the temptress Salome, dancing in her scarlet, fur-lined robe. In England, royalty, such as King Henry IV, displayed their power through particularly extravagant furs: One of his robes, a nine-part affair, was made from the skins of 12,000 squirrels and 80 ermine. King Henry VIII ordered one robe made from 100 sable and 560 squirrel skins. It cost roughly £200—about six thousand times the daily wage of one of the plasterers working for him at that time in his Eltham Palace.

I am in the middle of the display room at the Historical Society, trying to count the number of ermine sewn together to make the facing of King Henry VIII's cloak, when the archivist comes up next to me and hands me a paper with the phone number of a woman who is doing work on native plants. I had asked her if she knew of anyone trapping beavers or doing work with them here. She thinks the woman might know something about beavers, but she isn't sure. It will be some time before I fully understand the significance of this connection between beavers and habitat restoration. Eventually I will learn that on the other side of the Columbia River, in Washington State, an ambitious beaver relocation project has been in place for the past decade in the Methow Forest, returning beavers to the mixed conifer forest to help battle wildfires. And that a few hundred miles to the south and east, beavers are being reintroduced to central Oregon high desert areas as part of salmon recovery. But I don't know of those projects yet; I just take the phone number from her. Then, reluctantly, I give up on trying to count the number of tiny white weasels sewn together to make the lining of King Henry's fine *pilche*, thank her for the contact, and head out into the grey Oregon afternoon.

At my next destination, the Maritime Museum, I stop only briefly to see an exhibit titled *Explorers of the New World*. Underneath a list of well-known names—Columbus, Verrazano, Magellan, Coronado, Cabrillo—I discover a surprising display of gorgeous maps from the sixteenth and seventeenth centuries when Europe was obsessed with finding a passage to the East.

One particularly beautiful map, the *Atlantis Pars Altera*, published in 1595 by Rumold Mercator, describes the North Pole. This is the first map in the world dedicated to the North Pole, and the detail is breathtaking. It is also wonderfully inaccurate. The landmass of the pole is drawn as a low pyramid, divided neatly into four quadrants; rivers flow out from the center in all four directions—east, west, north, and south. In the center is a large rock, identified as "Polus Arcticus." The map confirms what explorers kept searching for but didn't exist, a route right through the North Pole to the source of spices, silk, and tea, the East. Of course, it would be those failed expeditions to find a way to Asia that resulted in the discovery of the New World; North America was the landmass they unexpectedly bumped into on the way.

Long before Astor, maps were important tools of empire. The kings and queens of England, France, the Netherlands, Italy, Spain, and Sweden sent their explorers to North America, and maps of the New World identifying its resources became increasingly vital to their empires. But the fur trade did not begin with these highly financed voyages; it began when high winds blew a fisherman off his course, and when the clouds lifted, he spied a strange new land. The coast of Newfoundland, or perhaps Labrador.

Throughout the 1500s, Bretons, Englishmen, Basques, and Portuguese had sailed regularly out across the rough North Sea toward Iceland and the great fishing grounds known to be off its coast. When the fisherman who had been blown off course made it back (who knows who or where or when?), he must have told others of his discovery. Or perhaps he kept it secret and ventured back alone. Before long fishermen from throughout Europe were heading out in search of this newly sighted land. They regularly braved great distances in tiny boats to search for fish, and word of a possible new fishing ground sent waves of them westward. Some ventured into the great Gulf of St. Lawrence. Some struck anchor off the coast of Maine. Others found their way south to a queer little hook of land later called Cape Cod.

They found plentiful fish, and, seeking fresh meat to supplement their fare of salt cod, ventured to shore. There they met Native people who brought out beaver skins as gifts and to trade. Not only did these people seem to have an endless supply of these valuable furs, but they treated them as if they were nothing, exchanging them eagerly for any small trinket. Once back in Europe, the fishermen sold the pelts for a fortune. Word got out and soon merchant ships were surging across the Atlantic and kings and queens sent explorers to chart and map possible beaver trade in the New World.

The French came first. The explorer Jacques Cartier landed in New Brunswick in 1534; then in 1603 the great navigator Samuel de Champlain began venturing through North America. In the next five years he would make over twenty trips across the Atlantic, and on July 3, 1608, he founded New France and Quebec. The Dutch East India Company sent Henry Hudson on his famed trip in 1609. The New Netherlands followed, with the Dutch establishing in quick order beaver trading posts in Mannahatta and up along the majestic Hudson River. In 1671, when the Dutch scholar Arnoldus Montanus published his volume *De Nieuwe en Onbekende Weereld* (The New and Unknown World), which included the first engravings of North American beavers published in Europe, he recorded that eighty thousand beaver pelts were being shipped annually from the New Netherlands. England was a bit late in the game, but made up for it in haste, in part because Samuel Champlain would end up so enraging the Iroquois that it would start a hundred years of war between the French and the Indigenous people. In 1670, King Charles II gave a charter to the Hudson's Bay Company, granting it fur trading rights over a vast expanse of what we know today as Canada. The HBC employed cartographers and explorers to extend fur trading networks throughout not just Canada but territories south, creating a virtual monopoly. They instituted the beaver pelt as the official trading standard, giving rise to the "beaver dollar." Herman Moll's 1715 map of North America, on which he had drawn the strangely human-like lines of beavers at Niagara Falls, came to be called the "beaver map" and was in great demand.

By the mid-eighteenth century, England controlled all of the North American fur trade from Florida in the south to the Hudson's Bay in the far north. And their reach extended from the Atlantic coast all the way west to the Mississippi River. By the time Astor set sail for New York, the North American fur trade was well established, but the big money, the beaver dollars yet to come, lay far away, across the continent, westward to the Pacific shore.

I leave the map exhibition at the Maritime Museum and drive to the overlook where in 1811, John Jacob Astor's ship the *Tonquin* arrived at the mouth of the Columbia River. I brace against the wind, and when I shut my eyes it feels as if the world is a kite loosed in its current. When I open them back up, the ocean stretches out in ridges of corduroy, row after row of whitecaps moving steadily toward the shore. Even on this cloudless spring day, the pounding of the waves is tremendous. The river's torrential current crashes into the surf in terrifying swirls. Yet it was here, in stormy weather in 1811, that the arrogant commander of the *Tonquin* ordered his best men into small boats to find a way across; the dangerous waters created huge sand-bars that they needed to sound in order to cross safely through. Even as the sailors stepped down into the pitching small boat they must have known they were lost. Still the despotic captain would not wait for calmer weather or even for the fog to lift, and when the first boat was swallowed by the waves, he sent another. Many men needlessly perished before the *Tonquin* made it to the other side. Three days later they planted the flag for Astoria.

Within a year of this accomplishment, Astor had a geopolitical problem to contend with, the War of 1812, which some historians now call the "bea-ver war" because it was a war motivated by control of the fur trade. The fur trade had brought constant conflict to North America. The Dutch had been first, but having never been interested in settlement, were soon pushed out. Sweden and Italy were dabblers. But England and France warred bitterly for control of the new land and its riches. Individual traders fought one another to secure furs, then the Indigenous people—their traditional cul-ture largely dismantled and along with it the intertribal balance of power—fought one another in a vain attempt to control the distribution of the new trade goods Europeans were bringing to their continent. Even after the American Revolution and the subsequent Jay's Treaty of 1794, which was supposed to secure lands west of the Mississippi for the new nation, Great Britain was unwilling to relinquish control of the fur trade in the Northwest. Within twenty years, under the leadership of George Simpson, the Hudson's Bay Company would begin their infamous scorched-earth approach of harvesting beaver along the Snake River. Their idea was to so overhunt beaver that they would create a "fur desert," a wasteland empty of commodities, thinking that this would discourage American settlers. Their plan would fail, but not before it wiped out most of the beavers.

When war broke out between Britain and America in 1812, it was osten-sibly over the issue of the Royal Navy's practice of preying on American ships. But in reality the two British fur trading companies, the Hudson's Bay Company and the North West Company, had become nervous about Astor's global trade scheme. In 1811 his sea route had established not only the fur trading post of Astoria, but just as significantly, an overland net-work. The infrastructure of his trade monopoly was in place.

In 1813, Captain William Black, commander of the British corvette the

Raccoon, received orders to seize the fort of Astoria. When he arrived, however, he was surprised to see a British flag already flying. Seventy-five men from the North West Company had taken matters into their own hands. Hearing of the British invasion, they had camped outside the fort and worked out a deal with Astor's men. Always practical, Astor agreed to sell the fort to the British for $58,000. Commander Black was not pleased. He insisted on storming toward the fort, and when he saw how small it was, he reportedly exclaimed in indignation, "What, is this the fort I have heard so much of? Great God, I could batter it down with a four-pounder in two hours."

Captain Black hung his own Union Jack flag and renamed the fort after the king. Fort George, as it was then to be known, came under British control. If John Jacob Astor cared, he did not show it. He knew the fur traders of the North West Company and they knew him. They had struck a deal, hadn't they? From his offices in New York, he still retained control of the entire fur trade route from St. Louis to Astoria. His ships circled the globe. He didn't care if the fort was under American or British control, so long as he continued to get rich.

In the end, his brilliant plan to control the fur trade and build a global trading empire would fail, but not because of his flaws as a businessman or his failure to understand the geopolitical forces of his time. He would fail for some of the same reasons we are facing environmental disasters today: He could not control the forces of nature. Astor could have a fatal impact on the beaver, but he could not dictate their rate of reproduction or their ability to regenerate. He could bend economies and politicians, laws and regulations, and hundreds of people to his will, but he could not control the animal he had so benefited from.

Once his fur company had a foothold in the West, particularly in the Rockies, it mobilized bands of company and free trappers, the famed mountain men, to procure furs. The period from 1820 to 1840 was the heyday of the mountain man, a time that Herb Sobanski and most of the fur trappers I had met romanticized. This system of sending European trappers into the wilderness was more efficient than trading for beaver pelts from the Native people. So efficient that in no time, barely twenty years, the seemingly endless resource of North American beaver fur that was to fuel

Astor's new trade engine was done. The beaver was gone. Astor didn't much care. When the United States finally regained formal possession of Astoria in 1818, Astor said he was too old to restore his outpost. By this time he had made so much money from the fur trade and had invested so much of it in real estate and other ventures that his fortune still multiplied.

I head out of Astoria, following the twisting road toward Portland, driving in the dark. In the car lights I see a glow of eyes. They are low to the ground and still. Coyote, I wonder? Then my heart leaps. It could be beaver. All along the way I had been following a river, then a wide wetland, a swamp. Beaver habitat. I slow the car down and peer into the darkness. There is a wild animal by the side of the road. On the postcard of the Columbia River I sent to my mother, I had written, "Looking for Astor in Astoria, no beavers yet." I knew she'd get the humor. I stop the car and wait. I listen. There's a rustle in the grass. But it's not the beaver I am hoping to see. Staring back at me are the wide, startled eyes of an elk.

The conversion of natural resources into power has always been the propelling force of empire. Africa had gold and ivory; Asia, spices, salt, and silk. The Atlantic Ocean rippled with cod. From the beginning of the seventeenth century onward, America had the beaver. Throughout the colonial period, beaver pelts instead of gold were the unit of trade. Demand for beaver fur enabled the New England colonies to pay off their huge debts. Then at the start of the nineteenth century, businessmen like Astor used beaver to rev up the engines of American capitalism. But natural resources like beavers are never infinite, and if you take too much and do not let those resources replenish, there is only one outcome; they run out.

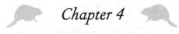

Chapter 4

Man's Land

February in rural New England is a cold, uncertain month. Our road freezes, then thaws, then freezes into ruts of mud and ice. The trees, spires of grey now, bend and wave like blades of grass, strangely supple in the fierce wind. When winter storms case their branches in ice, the sound of the wind moving through them is like the tinkling of myriad bells. Otherwise winter is a tyranny of silence. The woodpile shrinks. The cats fling themselves down by the woodstove, slovenly as drunks. The dog, Coda, sneaks up on the couch.

Down in their ponds, the beaver lie still in torpor, their metabolisms slowed so that they only need to leave the lodge for minimal amounts of food, to breathe, and to eliminate waste, pellets of chewed wood that sink to the shallows, then hover ghostlike among the leaves. Beavers cleverly reduce their need to breathe in winter by increasing stores of oxygen in their muscles. Colder weather signals their body to produce more red blood cells, which hold oxygen in the blood. And beavers have in their muscle tissue high levels of myoglobin, a protein that gives them a larger supply of oxygen from which to draw while under water. It is this protein that reddens meat. The meat of a beaver killed in winter is a deep purplish red.

Even with this remarkable winterized blood chemistry, beavers still need to breathe. For as long as they can, they will maintain breathing holes in the ice, swimming up through the slurry of freezing water. More than once, Herb Sobanski has been out on his trap line and heard the crack of a beaver slamming its head up from below, cracking the layers of new ice. When the pond freezes solid, the beavers will rely on the oxygen inside the domed cavity of the lodge and thin layers of air trapped below the ice when it freezes. In January, Herb had shown me how he locates icebound beaver by searching the ice for bubbles. When the beavers surface to breathe the air trapped under the ice, some of the air held in their dense wool is released into the water, forming bubbles, which quickly freeze into a faint trail.

Herb has a freezer full of beaver he has rough skinned but not finished, and now that the weather is bad for trapping, he'll spend most of the month in his fur shack preparing pelts. The beaver trapping season in Connecticut won't officially end until March 31, but in February, the traps freeze over or are hidden under snow. Herb usually spends the month skinning and preparing pelts from animals he has already caught, then heads back out in March. I've been out with Herb on his trap line several times by now, but we haven't been able to go over many of my questions, as he only liked to converse briefly or when we were coming and going in the truck. He suggests that I come to the fur shack so we can talk while he is skinning.

The text arrives at 5 a.m. one morning:

Herb: Meet you at Man's Land after work
Me: time?
Herb: 6
Me: Okay
Me: Sorry…Where is Man's Land?
Herb: Didn't tell you?
Me: No
Herb: my fur shack !

By the time I arrive, Herb has almost finished skinning a coyote. The door is open, although above the entrance a metal sign has been tacked to the siding that reads "No guns allowed, except the one I am aiming at you."

I walk in. After visiting fur trappers and fur trapper gatherings I am used to these nods to American gun culture. Herb has two kids in a public school here, less than an hour from Newtown, but the closest we have come to talking about gun control is to agree that no one needs a military-grade rapid repeat rifle to hunt deer. Herb encouraged his wife, Sherri, to get a pistol license. He thinks I should get one, too.

As soon as I step in, Herb calls out a cheery "Welcome to Man's Land." He stands next to a coyote skin that hangs limp as a towel from a hook and gambrel. From nose tip to bushy tail tip, the coyote must be over six feet. Herb wears a black oilcloth apron and thick yellow rubber gloves that reach up to his elbows. He has the coyote's ear in his hand. He sees me glance at the floor around the coyote, which is covered with bloodied newspaper. "I'm almost done here," he says, "just finishing the ears. The rest of it is out back in the woods if you want to see it. Gave it to the hawks. I'll get the skull later. I'm not into that kind of stuff, but a guy I know is; he cleans them and sells them, I guess."

Not far from where Herb works is a crude wooden trough hammered together from two-by-fours. A large beaver lies on the trough, facedown, and in the corner on a pallet I see three more beaver. My watch reads 6 p.m. Herb has already had dinner with Sherri and their two kids. The rest of the evening he plans to spend here in "Man's Land," skinning, fleshing, and stretching fur. Located about a hundred yards from his house, at the bottom of the short slope, the garage is spacious, with room for two cars and a second story, the wood siding stained forest green to match the house.

Herb and his family live in a modest-sized and well-kept contemporary house flanked by Herb's pride, a pool. All summer the Sobanski yard is a vision of the good life of the American suburb; the large deck has a table and chairs and a green-and-white-striped awning. By the grill, wide stairs lead down to an in-ground pool, surrounded on all sides with bright-colored hibiscus as well as elaborate, artful combinations of flowering plants assembled by Sherri. Piled in one corner is a jumble of colorful swim noodles and floats. The family dog, Mack, a sleepy beagle, regularly escapes the heat under the table. Both Herb and Sherri are songbird enthusiasts, and throughout the yard, bird feeders swing from branches and poles. Each spring the couple eagerly await the heroic return of migratory birds.

In contrast to the yard's suburban emphasis on leisure, the fur shack is a place of work. Tools and bits of equipment, lines of traps and chains, neatly assembled on nails, line the back wall. Everything seems organized, each tool on a separate hook: pliers and screwdrivers, hammers, wire cutters, and grips of various sizes along with links of chain and saws. On a shelf above the tools sit two chain saws and a large sign reading *National Trapper Association* with the association logo. On a nearby rack, several pairs of waders hang inverted not far from a shelf holding three old-fashioned wicker trapping baskets.

It takes me a minute to register what I see before me: Herb at work fleshing a coyote. This is an elemental scene, a human taking the fur of an animal. Trappers call this rendering the animal, or processing the fur. "Coyote are stinky," says Herb. "I wanted to get this out of the way before you got here." He first brushed the coat to remove burrs and leaves, then rinsed it with water. Some trappers go all out with their coyote, shampooing each pelt with baby shampoo and rubbing the coats with baby oil before taking them to auction. Coyote are sold fur side out, and fur buyers assess size of the pelt, the length and thickness of the fur, the range of color, and the overall quality of the fur finishing, then they offer a price. Herb explains quickly that a neighbor had shot the coyote that morning and dropped it off, asking if he would skin it. The neighbor wants to get the coyote pelt tanned, which is why Herb is taking extra time with the ears and the feet. I listen, still adjusting to the sight of a canine skinned and hanging from a hook and the silent beaver waiting in the trough, and to the smell, a combination of chain saw oil and rank flesh. It is not that the sight of an animal carcass is new to me: On my family's apple farm in the Hudson valley, I'd often seen a deer strung up in our barn in late fall. White-tailed deer with their gorgeous brown eyes routinely chewed so many buds off our young trees in winter that we sometimes lost whole sections of orchard. The man who helped with pruning had rights to hunt our land along with his buddies. In my immediate family, no one shot deer, but my father kept a .22 locked in the gun closet for woodchucks, which also created problems on the farm.

I tell myself skinning a coyote is no different than skinning a deer, even if it looks distressingly like my dog, then search for a clean surface on which to put down my bag. As usual, my writing is both a bridge and a barrier. I am here as a novice and my questions are a bridge; I seek to understand how a fur trapper thinks about trapping, killing, and taking the fur and meat from wild animals. What is it about fur trapping and finishing fur that Herb values so highly? I put my tape recorder on the table and hit record. Then I grab my notebook and pen, this habit reminding Herb that I am on the hunt here, too, a writer documenting what I observe.

"Urban coyote?" I ask, walking over to touch the coyote's rough fur.

"Isn't all wildlife urban by now?" Herb quips back.

Coyote are like beavers; as humans have moved into their habitat, they haven't gone anywhere, they've simply adapted to doing what they do in an altered landscape, often in ways humans find troublesome. The coyote has a particularly beautiful coat, the area along the back of the neck and over the shoulders thick with a wolflike mane of long black guard hairs. Eastern coyote are now popularly called "coy wolves" because of their large size, but the idea that they are a contemporary cross between a coyote and a wolf has been disproved. The wolf DNA in the eastern coyote is a holdover from an ancient time when coyote first branched off from wolves. But they do have larger jaws than western coyote, enabling them to take down larger prey. Herb has been participating in a wildlife study that tracks coyote DNA in order to understand their range and feeding habits. Whenever he traps a coyote he puts a few hairs in a small tube and sends it to researchers at Providence College.

"Okay, that's it," says Herb, taking the coyote hide down from the hook and placing it on a nearby surface. Even without a body to support it, the coyote hide still seems full of life, the thick fur glancing off the table, each hair a striation of brown and black that catches the light. In *Roughing It*, Mark Twain described coyote as a "living breathing allegory of want." Summing up over two hundred years of cultural hate for cayote, as they were then called, Twain writes that it was a "long, slim, sick and sorry-looking skeleton with a grey wolfskin stretched over it, a tolerably bushy tail that forever sags down with a despairing expression of forsakenness and misery, a furtive and evil eye, and a long, sharp face with slightly lifted lip and exposed teeth."

Even today, coyote are as much the focus of hunting, trapping, and general misinformation as beavers. Coyote are so adaptive, like beavers, that they disrupt our usual divisions of what is urban and what is rural. Wild animals are supposed to live in the woods, but as coyote and beavers and wolves keep demonstrating, in twenty-first-century North America, they regularly don't. Wolves ignore the boundaries of Yellowstone and Voyageurs National Park and sometimes prey on cattle and sheep. A pair of coyote den in Central Park. Coyote have been photographed riding mass transit in Portland,

Oregon, and walking onto Wrigley Field. In Chicago, Dr. Stan Gehrt, who heads up the longest urban coyote research project in the country, has identified a generation of coyote that now teach their young to wait at traffic lights and avoid eating rats, saving the coyote from getting hit by cars and from ingesting fatal doses of rat poison. Meanwhile, beaver have held up the subways in Toronto, and every year Herb is called to trap beavers living in the banks of the Connecticut River in Hartford.

"I can show you how to flesh and stretch it later if you want," says Herb, watching me admire the coyote's magnificent fur. "For coyote like this, I'll stretch the hide on a board. But first, let's get to what you came to see."

Herb's first step is to weigh the beaver. He hangs it quickly from a handheld scale. "A big one," he says. "Forty-five pounds. This'll make a nice pelt." He nods quickly to point out the other beaver on the pallet. "I've got to get all of these done for the sportsman's club—they like the meat for their game night." Herb lays the beaver down, face up, and pats the belly. By the fall of their second year, beavers are mature and average forty to sixty pounds. The largest beaver on record is still a 110-pounder caught in 1921 on the Iron River in Wisconsin.

"Energy," wrote William Blake, is "eternal delight," the source of life, but without breath to fill its lungs, the beaver lies inert, a strangely flaccid thing. The beaver's mouth shows glimpses of orange teeth—a stark reminder of the life that once filled it. Before I know it, Herb has removed the front paws and the feet. The sound of the cutting is horrible, but Herb picks up a foot and fingers the toes apart to show me how it is webbed like a goose's but with what looks like a dewclaw on the back of one leg. "They'll use this to groom themselves," he says. "Just amazing. They'll spread oil through their coat with this, waterproofing. Beavers are such incredible animals." Spread out on the board, the beaver's webbed hind foot is as wide and large as my hand. He throws it in a bucket. "I'll give those to the hawks along with the coyote. Nothing's wasted in nature." He doesn't show me the front paws with their slim fingers, for which I'm glad.

Herb now takes a small blade and cuts a decisive line from the tip of the beaver's chin down to the end where the tail begins. The dark fur parts, revealing a sudden redness of flesh. He works quickly, cutting the fur away from the base of the tail, then in one swift motion severs the tail completely.

"Mountain men just loved eating these," he says. "They said it tasted fatty, like butter or lard." He hands it to me and for a moment the sensation in my hand is as if I am holding a thick paperback. The tail is surprisingly heavy, but despite its scale pattern, the tough skin is buttery soft. I feel along the rounded edge to where it is indented with a jagged nick. "Probably got bitten along there," Herb explains. "Could have been a snapping turtle, plenty of them around."

The beaver's tail might just be its oddest feature, but it is also the most versatile: paddle, prop, rudder, water sensor, energy source, and air-conditioning system in one. On land, beavers use their tails to help them balance when they sit up on their two back legs to look around. In the water, they both steer and propel themselves by sculling their tail from left to right in a swift sideways motion. Cells on the surface of the tail are so sensitive that through them beavers can feel changes in water pressure, which is how they know to rush to their dam to repair breaches even when they are too far away to hear the sounds of trickling water. During winter, the extra fat beavers store in their tails enables them to survive for months with little food. In summer, the web of tightly meshed blood vessels that spread throughout the beaver's tail helps keep it from becoming overheated; body heat is released through the walls of individual cells via this network of blood vessels.

For some strange reason, the beaver's tail even influenced fashion. During the 1950s, a hairstyle called the beaver tail was as popular for women as the ducktail was for men; in both cases the hair was combed up and styled into what was considered to be an alluring bouffant resembling a duck's rear or a beaver's flat paddle. Herb's use for the beaver tail is more practical: He uses it to make bait. Coyote, it turns out, along with mink and fisher cat, can't resist rotted beaver tail. When I hand the tail back to him, Herb carefully tucks it into a plastic container and snaps down the lid. He's learned to keep beaver tail in strong containers because mice also love it.

Throughout history, humans have coveted the tail of the beaver. In medieval Europe, fried beaver tail was called "forest cod," and appeared regularly on banquet tables. In Germany, it was so highly regarded that it came to be reserved only for the emperor's table. Beaver was an especially desired delicacy because it was rich and fatty, and due to the fact that beavers spent so much time in the water, the Catholic Church considered the meat to be "cold" like the flesh of fish. The church forbade the eating of "hot" meats during times of abstinence and atonement because these foods were believed to excite libidinous passion and sex was forbidden on holy days. But through this loophole of its fishy qualities, the church ignored the fact that the beaver is a warm-blooded mammal and allowed the consumption of beaver tail. For the 166 holy days, including all Fridays, Catholics who could afford the delicacy enjoyed fried beaver tail without guilt.

This ruling by the Catholic Church was highly ironic. Since Roman and Greek times, beaver tail had been valued as an aphrodisiac, considered especially helpful for aiding in the "advancement of priapus" (Priapus being a minor Greek God whose most distinguishing feature was his large erection). How beaver tail came to be considered the Viagra of medieval Europe remains a mystery. But Native American regard for beaver tail was also tied to the belief that it aided male potency. In his 1637 abstract on New England, *New English Canaan*, British writer Thomas Morton reported that beaver tail was considered to be so helpful to "masculine virtue," that its consumption was reserved for the sachems or tribal chiefs. He suggested that the importation of beaver tail would so "delight the ladies of Europe" that it could become a tidy business.

There were other reasons that beaver tail was reserved for the tribal sachems which the early explorers completely missed; for the Indigenous people of North America, beavers were powerful "animal people" who must be honored after death by certain protocols lest their spirit return to make the hunter sick. Early French explorers, the *coureurs de bois*, were also generally oblivious to these protocols, but learned a taste for beaver tail from the Native people they met and passed this culinary secret of the woods along to American trappers. They also used it as a cure for frostbite. The mountain men of the Rockies, in particular, valued beaver tail as a much-needed source of fat in a diet of lean game meat. Trapper accounts and diaries ignore beaver tail as an aphrodisiac, but opine frequently on its creamy flavor when roasted over a spit.

Herb has never eaten beaver's tail and doesn't intend to try, although he has eaten beaver meat and loves a good beaver chili. He hasn't been able to convince his wife or their children to eat beaver in any form except in the shape of cute, beaver-face cupcakes that Sherri bakes for the annual fall rendezvous. Herb remembers his father and grandfather eating "marsh rabbits," the raccoons and muskrat that they caught in the swamps near Bridgeport. When Herb was ten, in his second year of running his own trap line, he convinced his younger brother to join him in roasting muskrat over an open fire. The experiment was not a success. Herb's little brother, who grew up to become a dentist, not only never ate wild game again, he never went out trapping or hunting again either. He and Herb go fishing on occasion. His brother's daughter, who attended Connecticut College, is now a devoted animal rights advocate and a member of an organization named after its mission, the People for the Ethical Treatment of Animals (PETA). She opposes fur trapping. When I asked Herb about his niece's position he answered philosophically. "She's doing her thing. It's okay. She has her views and I have mine. We're still family." His brother considers Herb a "fine woodsman" but says he'd have to be starving before he'd set a trap.

Herb is now ready to skin the beaver and takes up a knife with a rounded blade. One hand pulls the hide up away from the flesh as he follows the contours of the body with the blade in the other. His movements are precise, practiced, and quick. Soon a dark river of fur cascades from one end of the trough, revealing the surprising beauty of the beaver's body—muscle, tissue, bone. Herb turns it over and continues working, carefully cutting the pelt away from the forepaws and legs, and finally from the head. One final quick swipe of blade and the pelt comes free. Herb flips it up, then spreads it out between his hands, pulling the fur to its full length. "There," he says, "just beautiful, isn't it?" With the palm of one hand he presses the gleaming fur back to show me a layer of lighter grey underfur. We stand for a moment and admire the glistening pelt.

Beavers keep themselves warm with an outer layer of water-resistant guard hairs and an underlayer of shorter fur. The outer hairs are so thick that even a postage-stamp-sized bit of fur contains over 126,000 individual strands—more hair than most of us have on our entire head. The underlayer, called beaver wool, is made up of short hairs each serrated with a tiny barb so that they interlock, forming a layer of remarkably dense fur. Once sixteenth-century hat makers in Europe discovered that this uniquely barbed wool could be compressed to produce superlative felt, they went crazy for it. Eurasian beaver were soon so overtrapped that they were eradicated from even most of the remote wilderness areas of Russia. And when the beavers were gone, the mythology of their soft fur lived on. In "The Triumph," seventeenth-century poet Ben Johnson compares female beauty to the usual tropes of lilies, fresh snow, and pure white swan feathers, then suddenly swerves into a rhapsody on beaver down. This connection between beaver down and feminine beauty would carry through Western culture and cross the Atlantic. Here in the New World, by the twentieth century, beaver became a slang word for female genitalia.

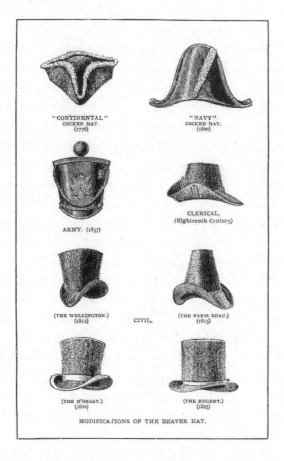

This illustration, from the 1907 annual report of the Forest, Fish and Game Commissioner of the State of New York, shows some of the many ways in which beaver fur was used to create men's headgear.

The fame of beaver wool has a simple answer. In the days before Polartec, Gore-Tex, or any form of spandex, beaver wool provided warmth in harsh conditions. Native Americans knew that the warmest, most comfortable coats were those made from used beaver pelts because through wear and tear the guard hairs were rubbed off, enabling the wearer to enjoy the luxurious softness of the underfur. From the sixteenth century on, the lust for beaver wool sent explorers flying across the rough seas in search of the New World.

"Beaver helped make this country," Herb says. He throws the fur over his shoulder where it hangs like a lounging cat. He turns his focus to the rest of the beaver, which now looks disarmingly similar to a large uncooked beef roast. Herb turns it over and makes a deep cut along the stomach. The innards tumble out in a gush of dark blood. He scoops them into a bucket to throw out for the hawks, alongside the coyote. Next he takes up a small knife, sharpens it, and begins cutting out the oil sacs that he'll use for bait, followed by the most valuable part of the beaver: the castor. A few practiced cuts between the pelvis and the tail and Herb holds the castor sacs up. Each is about the size of my clenched fist.

Castoreum, the granular yellow substance with a musky smell that beavers produce in their castor sacs, was used for medicinal purposes from the earliest days of European history. The Latin name *castor* is derived from the Greek name Kastor, one of the divine twins (Kastor and Pollux) worshipped by women in ancient times as a healer and preserver from disease. In his classic from AD 77, *Naturalis Historia*, the Roman naturalist Pliny listed castoreum's many medicinal uses, including as a cure for headaches, constipation, and epileptic fits. Considered fantastically valuable, these medicinal "beaver stones" traveled along trade routes from western Europe to Asia and Persia. Ingested as shavings or mixed with alcohol, then later injected into the body, castoreum became a medical wonder. The list of ailments it was thought to cure grew to include dysentery, the retention of urine, worms, fleas, pleurisy, gout, induration of the liver and spleen, rheumatism, insomnia, poor vision, hysteria, memory loss, and even insanity. When beavers are first mentioned in Western literature by Hippocrates, who wrote between 450 and 350 BC, it is the wonder of castoreum's medical properties that he brings to the attention of readers. In the sixteenth century, the Syrian Christian physician David of Antioch writes a description of beavers, joining other prominent physicians of the Middle East in lauding the medicinal values of castoreum.

Throughout the early history of Europe, the hunt for beaver castor led to some fantastic misunderstandings about beaver anatomy, most noticeably the belief that when pursued, beavers remove their testicles and cleverly throw them at hunters, so distracting their assailants that they get away. The early Greek writer Aesop may have rendered the best-known version of this castration fantasy in his iconic tale "The Beaver and His Testicles." In Aesop's story, written in 600 BC, a beaver, pursued by castor hunters, promptly gnaws off his testicles and throws them at the hunters and their dogs, which become so distracted by this prize that the beaver can flee. "As soon as the hunter lays his hands on that magical medicine," wrote Aesop, "he abandons the chase and calls off his dogs." This account is bizarre on several levels. First, it confuses the testicles with the castor sacs. Beaver testicles are internal, along with all of their other glands. The lack of visible testicles was clearly what distressed early hunters; the word *castor* also comes from the Latin *castrum*, meaning to castrate.

By the twelfth century, the beaver's imagined ability to bite off his own testicles had become an established religious allegory of the importance of chastity and obedience. In the *Aberdeen Bestiary*, a gorgeous thirteenth-century illuminated manuscript featuring a long blue beaver with a serpentine body and lionlike paws, the entry begins blandly enough: "Of the beaver there is an animal called the beaver, which is extremely gentle; his testicles are highly suitable for medicine." But soon the tale becomes an erotically charged religious parable, for the beaver not only bites off his testicles and throws them at one hunter, he is then canny enough to rear up and display his castrated state to a second hunter. Upon seeing that the beaver has no testicles, the second hunter leaves the beaver alone.

The takeaway? So may the chaste man learn from the beaver how to confuse the devil.

The text of the bestiary is without ambiguity: "Thus every man who heeds God's commandment and wishes to live chastely should cut off all his vices and shameless acts, and cast them from him into the face of the devil. Then the devil, seeing that that man has nothing belonging to him, retires in disorder." Today, the closest that beavers come to featuring in religious allegory might be the kindly beaver couple of C. S. Lewis's *The Chronicles of Narnia*. In his famous work of Christian allegory, the beaver couple resembles the beaver guides of Native American beaver stories—they lead the children from the human world into the fantastic otherworld beyond the wardrobe.

We no longer use beaver castoreum for medicine. Whatever medical benefits castoreum provided beyond a placebo would have come from the salicylic acid in the beaver's diet of willow bark. From the time of Hippocrates on, people throughout the world knew to brew willow bark into a tea that could help relieve a number of symptoms from reducing fevers and thinning the blood to muting pain. In the late nineteenth century, scientists discovered how to make aspirin from willow bark essence, and beaver stones became a thing of the past.

We still make use of beaver castor, but mostly we eat or drink it. If you like raspberry, strawberry, or vanilla ice cream and vanilla pudding, you have probably eaten beaver castor. If you like strawberry Twizzlers, raspberry soda, raspberry Jell-O, or any kind of raspberry- or strawberry-flavored candy, you definitely have. Labeled a "natural food additive," by the FDA, beaver castor is routinely used by the food industry because it works; castoreum gives off natural whiffs of vanilla, raspberry, and strawberry scent and enhances those flavors in food. If you like whiskey you can choose from several high-end castor-scented blends; it also is used in a range of expensive vodkas and bourbons, including Tamworth's elite 88 proof Eau de Musc; European liqueurs flavored with castoreum have names like Belvedere and Baversnaps.

If you wear perfume, you are also probably wearing castoreum, which has been used as a fixative in perfume since the nineteenth century. Castor's musky odors are blended into high-end perfumes like Chanel No. 5 and Shalimar. Valued for what the industry calls its "leathery notes," it helps create the musky scent of many expensive brands of men's cologne.

Beavers also find the smell of castoreum alluring, although strictly for purposes of communication. They excrete this musky scent by mixing it with urine, then spraying their unique *eau du castor* on small piles of mud. These castor mounds become that beaver's message, warning, classified ad, or call to arms, depending on the context. In *The Lives of Game Animals*, nature writer Ernest Thompson Seton called castor mounds "mud pie telephones."

When beavers emerge from the lodge in spring, their first task is the marking of their territory with castor mounds. Beavers are peaceful among their own family group but will not tolerate outsiders, and castor mounds function like the New England stone walls of colonial farmers—a barrier that both connected and separated good neighbors. Beavers are one of the few monogamous rodents and mate for life, but free males and females will paw mud into castor mounds in early spring to advertise that they seek a companion. In summer, when male beavers tend to roam the woods, searching out possible territory for new ponds, existing castor mounds will give them notice that beavers already inhabit a given territory. When Herb wanted to draw a beaver out, he would make a mound of mud and put a few drops of castor oil that he had extracted from trapped beavers. Especially in March, this served as an irresistible lure; beavers would swim up to investigate the new beaver scent and encounter his trap en route. Herb only needs a small amount of castor for lures; the rest he will sell at the spring fur auction. Last year Herb made as much on beaver castor as he did on beaver pelts.

With the castor pouches removed and carefully set aside, Herb is ready to carve the meat. He carefully cleans the knife again, then points to the rib cage. "See that strip of meat there? People like that. But first I have to get out the saliva gland—you'll get sick if you eat that. Same for the two glands under the arms." Herb feels along the carcass with his fingers until he has found the right spots, then cuts these glands out. Now he is ready to carve out the meat. After the thin strips from the rib cage are removed, he points again with his knife to two thick muscles above the legs. "Beaver hams," he says, "are considered the best part."

Once the meat is in its plastic bag, it looks like the dark meat of chicken. Herb puts it in a waiting cooler. "I've been donating meat for fifteen, twenty years and no one has gotten sick from it," he says proudly. Later, he'll rinse the meat then freeze it along with the rest he's harvested. In a week, he'll drive it to a local sportsman's club, which cooks it up for their annual wild game supper. Called "beast feasts," these wild game dinners are standard fund-raisers for the various local clubs, but they also bring together locavores like Jesse, a member of Herb's trapping organization whom I'd seen earlier in the fall at the trapper rendezvous demonstrating how to trap bear. Jesse is a young man who, along with his wife, feeds their family of two small children only with locally raised produce, dairy and chicken, or meat that they trap or hunt. Last summer, Jesse's wife shot a moose in Maine, and that was what they ate for the rest of the year, interspersed with wild turkey and beaver.

Not all of the Native tribes of North America ate beaver, but some did, roasting the entire beaver over a fire. Others cut beaver flesh into thin strips and cooked them over a low fire until they became dry and brittle, making beaver jerky. They pounded beaver meat with berries into a paste that was mixed with animal fat and molded into pemmican cakes that lasted for months. Many Native American teachings and stories venerated the sagacity of the beaver, and some tribes, like the Blackfeet of the northern plains, upheld prohibitions against even harming them. According to the Cherokee, the earth was created by the Great Spirit with help from the beavers. The Crow believed that in their next life they would come back as beavers, and the dead were buried in beaver blankets. In the Northwest, many Indigenous peoples, including the coastal Salish-speaking peoples of Western Washington and British Columbia, considered beavers to be a cursed race who, having fallen out of favor with the Great Spirit, had been punished by being turned into beavers. That was why beavers worked so hard, to atone for their misdeeds.

Trappers, explorers, and early historians give many accounts of Native American superstitions about the hunting and handling of beaver once they were taken. It was a widespread Native custom that a beaver's carcass must never be fed to dogs, as was the habit with most game. Often trappers found beaver skulls and whole skeletons hanging from trees.

Throughout North America, the beaver's scapula was used by many Indigenous people in religious ceremonies, and in the Northwest, even its teeth, decorated with lines and circles, or colors, were used like dice for games of chance. Here in Connecticut, beaver ribs and teeth were fashioned into digging and gouging tools. Before Herb discards the carcass, he'll cut off the beaver's head, but not for religious reasons; he will put it in his freezer to give to the same guy for whom he is saving the coyote skull. "I don't charge him anything for it," Herb explains. "I just like to see every bit of the animal used."

Fur, tail, castor, oil sacs, meat, skull. Herb has taken from the beaver all that he can and dumps what remains into a bin outside for the hawks. He has a wildlife camera pointed to the spot so he can capture images of the hawks and coyote that will descend to pick or gnaw off the remaining flesh. Mice will chew the bones; insects, worms, and microorganisms will consume the rest. Turning toward me, he removes his gloves and suggests we head upstairs to start on the pelt. He takes the stairs two at a time, the beaver's fur still swinging from his shoulder.

I hurry to grab my things and follow. Herb is clearly eager to get to his favorite part of the process: finishing the fur. But halfway up the stairs he stops and heads back down. "I forgot the castor," he says with a grin, then adds, "I suffer from CRS...can't remember shit. Go on up." While he retrieves the castor I walk up into the spacious second-floor room, filled with a long table and a bookshelf along one side. Hanging from the rafters are rows of drying beaver castor glands, while all around the room are furs in different stages of finishing. Leaning against the far wall are groupings of wooden boards, fur stretchers, each corresponding to the different sizes and shapes of animals. Part of the art of finishing furs like coyote and fox is choosing the right stretcher, one that pulls the hide out enough to show the fur and the full size, while not overstretching it. An overstretched hide will twist and warp in an uneven pattern once it is off the board. Pelts are graded on size, as well as the quality of the fur and the skill of the finishing most of all.

Along the far wall hang finished pelts of fox, coyote, and skunk. Herb considers himself a water trapper, and beaver is his main pursuit, but when he is asked to trap other animals as part of his service as a volunteer trapper, he usually says yes. For a nominal yearly fee, Herb could become licensed as a wildlife control operator, a professional who removes wildlife for payment, but he doesn't want to make trapping that kind of a business. As I have come to see, a big part of his ethic as a trapper is what he calls "helping people out."

As soon as he is back up the stairs, Herb slips the castor sacs onto a waiting nail pounded into the long beam where it joins a line of castor sacs already hanging there in various stages of drying. Not far from the beam, where the ceiling meets the wall, Herb has tacked up a line of round fabric patches with different logos and colors of fur trapping association meetings from different states. So far Herb has collected over twenty, including a patch from Georgia where he trapped muskrat and nutria one winter. Herb is active in trapper organizations, including the National Trappers Association, based in Illinois. The NTA hosts an annual conference each July which is a watering hole for trappers from around the country, but each state has its own licensing program. Connecticut has five hundred registered trappers and two different trapping groups—the one Herb founded and the one he used to belong to before he got into a dispute with them about trapping regulations.

I walk over and finger a light grey coyote pelt. Herb admires his handiwork. Skinning and fleshing, and preparing his furs, is a point of pride for him, as it is for most trappers I've met. A well-finished fur also brings a better price. "Last year my coyote was graded top lot up at NAFA," he brags, mentioning the largest fur auction in North America, the North American Fur Auction in Canada that he shipped fur to the year before. "I don't want to do it if I'm not going to do it well."

Herb lays the beaver skin out, fur side down, on his fleshing board, a tapered length of wood that sticks out from the wall at a slight angle. Taking up the sharp bow-shaped blading tool, he begins to scrape the hide, moving in quick strokes away from him. "Beavers are fatty. You have to scrape them really clean, while being careful not to cut through it." In a few weeks, I'd watch fur buyer Harlen Lien at the local fur auction looking through the piles of beaver. He'd examine the flesh side as carefully as the fur for signs of proper finishing.

Herb works quickly, and his expertise is evident—in just under ten minutes, he has scraped the entire skin. "If there's a mistake to be made," he says, picking up the pelt and studying it, "believe me, I've made it."

For the first time, Herb suggests a break. He lays the beaver skin down on the table, pulls off his apron and gloves, and reaches for the pack of Marlboro cigarettes tucked into the pocket of his T-shirt. He won't smoke in the house, but here in Man's Land, it is clearly one of his great pleasures.

It takes Herb a few minutes to search out an ashtray. I look at his bookshelf. The shelves are filled with stacks of his favorite trapping magazine, *Trapper & Predator Caller*, and books. There's a copy of Robert's Rules, which he uses for administering the trapper organization, a copy of *Iron John*, by Robert Bly, numerous books on American history and King Philip's War. There is a copy of *In the Spirit of Crazy Horse*, by Peter Matthiessen, and several books on mountain men, including one on southern trappers called *This Reckless Breed of Men*.

I take a seat at the long table for our break, and as soon as I turn on the tape recorder, Herb blurts out, "I'm a Republican, guess you figured that out." I nod, wondering why he wants to state this, but not surprised either. I'm a college professor who drives a Subaru. More than once while driving to a trap line Herb has asked me if I've seen the news and mentions a headline he saw about Hillary Clinton having broken the law or leading a cabal of baby-eaters. He states these speculations as if they are facts. A previous morning when we'd stopped at the usual Dunkin' Donuts near Herb's trap line to get coffee, he had suddenly turned to me in the middle of our talking and said, "Man, you think about things a lot!" It was both a compliment and a caution. But I had the sense that in the end, my tendency to ask questions and reflect on things was okay—I was a college professor and a journalist after all. It's literally my job. But soon after, he had asked me if I knew any libertarians. His eyes narrowed, the way he did on the trap line when he was pondering beaver signs or how to fix a problem. I told him I did. His eyes relaxed then. He nodded. Our conversations about politics often go like this, both of us aware of the other's political allegiances, respectful but cautious.

I'm curious about why he's brought up politics now and am about to ask him when he announces emphatically, "But I haven't even voted since Reagan!" When I ask why, he shakes his head. "When I want to catch an animal I learn all about it. If I want a beaver I'll read books, I'll study it…I can't believe how dumb the American public is. They'll believe anything. Hell, people even think pro wrestling is real!"

We both laugh, but Herb isn't done with this thought. "Is it just me or are there smart people on the fringe but most Americans are pretty stupid?"

"Well," I say, hedging. I am afraid of what opinion I might let slip if we really start talking about the 2016 election.

Herb is suddenly agitated. "Does it matter what we even think? It's all a game and they're just playing with us." He jumps up from his chair and reaches over the table to pick up a small wooden box. "When things get overwhelming, I come here and I think about how to get a weasel to go into this box." He hands me what looks like a bluebird box with a top that slides open. Inside I see a jumbo-sized mousetrap made by the Victor mousetrap company. "That's the biggest Victor trap you can buy," says Herb. "It's a snap trap. Putting snap traps outside is illegal in Connecticut," he continues, "but I'm on the citizens' advisory council to see if we can add trapping weasel to the list by using sets like this. They're worthless as a pelt, maybe get a dollar for them, but it's a thing some guys want to do."

I look at the proposed mink trap. When Herb was a kid during the heyday

of unregulated fur trapping during the early '60s, it would have been common practice to staple mousetraps to trees, then set them with a piece of
bait, a method that often caught owls and other birds of prey. Those cruel
forms of trapping have since been banned, along with steel traps with serrated teeth. State fur biologists set limits on the duration of the trapping
season and the number of animals each trapper can take per season. In the
fur trapping course that Herb teaches each fall for the state as a volunteer,
he shows a lengthy PowerPoint on trapping styles and practices designed to
maximize the four stated goals of "efficiency, selectivity, practicality, and
safety." Herb and other trappers argue that fur trapping is more regulated
than hunting or fishing. But animal rights activists question the level of oversight given that the state employs only a handful of conservation officers.

On the table sits a grey hat with "NRA" in big red letters stamped across
the brim. "One of the guys left it here," says Herb when he sees me looking
at it. "I used to be a member, but I could see the magazine was becoming all
about sport shooting and politics." He shakes his head and pushes the hat
aside along with the pile of trapping magazines spread out across the table.
"You have to know your shit when you're trapping," he says.

"What gets me," he continues, "is that landowners in Connecticut don't
have to follow the same rules as licensed fur trappers—they can trap in any
way they want. But who owns the wildlife? You can't just shoot any deer that
comes on your property. So why are landowners allowed to trap without following the regulations?"

Herb has lobbied to require landowners to follow the 1996 Best Management Practices for trapping as published by the U.S. Fish and Wildlife
Service, arguing that fur trappers are required to do so to protect the
wildlife and to "sustainably harvest" game, as they put it. But this created
problems with the oldest trapping organization in Connecticut, the CT Fur
Trappers Association, founded in 1957. Herb had been a member for years,
and served as president, but many members, those whom Herb calls "old-
school trappers," wouldn't support any limits on the rights of landowners
and farmers. In 2014, Herb left the CTFTA to form a new fur trapper organization that calls itself Connecticut Fur Harvesters. They emphasize education and spreading the gospel of fur trapping to younger guys and any
women willing to participate. To date, Herb's new organization has grown

to include eighty-seven members; they run a fall rendezvous and their own spring fur auction every year. The group meets monthly, here in Herb's fur shack. Mostly, according to Herb, they shoot the shit, but it's clear that this fraternity is important to him. They are a band, and often feel under siege.

When he isn't out trapping or in the woods, Herb is thinking about what he can do to protect fur trapping and conserve wildlife habitat. Last year, he became an elected member of Nutmeg, a statewide group of woodsmen, anglers, hunters, and fur trappers that lobby state legislature on wildlife conservation. On the table I see a pamphlet left over from the most recent meeting of his trapper organization. I had attended and listened to Herb talk to the group about a proposed bill to take 4 percent of all federal income from offshore mining and drilling and direct those funds toward wildlife conservation. Herb considers himself a pragmatist when it comes to the environment. I had asked him at one point why he wasn't protesting the Trump administration's opening of public lands in national parks and conservation areas to unprecedented levels of mining and drilling, since doing so would mean destroying huge tracts of wilderness habitat. But Herb shook the question off, replying that mining and drilling was going to happen, and since it was, the best thing was to make sure that 4 percent of that money went to support wildlife. Herb asked all of his members to write their senators to support this bill. Since the meeting, he has also sent an email to every trapper in the state letting them know that on March 1, a new bill banning the use of Conibear, or body-grip traps, will be presented to the state senate's conservation council in Hartford. Bills to ban fur trapping routinely surface in the state legislature, usually supported by the Connecticut chapter of the Humane Society and often by animal rights activists. Nothing gets Herb as riled up as the mention of the Humane Society or PETA. Every time I ask if he might work with them on wildlife protection in the state his answer is unequivocal. "They're haters. That's all, just haters. They've got no clue what goes into this work, none at all, or any idea who's really doing the damage. They've got some Bambi idea about what nature is."

On the fifteenth Herb plans to take the day off to sit in the long passage between the rotunda and senate offices in the state capitol, manning a table on behalf of his trapper organization. Three guys are lined up to help him, and a woman named Aili, who teaches bow hunting and plans to run in her district as a Democrat. Each of them plans to take time off from work. The table will be filled with pelts, along with literature about trapping and beavers; they hope to catch legislators as they pass by and talk to them about the services fur trappers in Connecticut provide.

Now that we are sitting as Herb smokes, I ask him the question I've asked before: "You clearly love wildlife and the outdoors. What is it about trapping?"

Herb pauses. I think he's going to respond with something about the role trappers play in managing wildlife, but instead he says simply, "I trap because I'd be lost without it…and I know what lost is."

"Lost," I begin, not knowing quite what to say. "You mean—?"

"Lost," he interrupts. "I mean lost, dark times. My dad worked for Pratt and Whitney as a toolmaker for thirty-eight years. My grandfather too. I tried it but I only lasted two years. I couldn't do the factory scene, the noise, the pollution, the alcoholism…I just couldn't take it."

Herb's face darkens and he glances down. When he looks back up, his expression is pained but resolved. He segues back to trapping. "Just when I think I know how to catch an animal…something happens you don't expect. Trapping is like that. I need that humility." He starts telling me about growing up in the projects of New Britain, once called the Hardware City, back when it was a manufacturing center. "I was an alcoholic from the age of fourteen to twenty-one," he says grimly. "My son saved my life. I thought, 'I can't keep drinking, what if I crash the car and kill him?'"

Herb takes a long draw on his cigarette and tells me about being raised Catholic despite the fact that his parents had stopped going to church years before. He was an honors student in high school and loved playing football. He went to college with the dream of becoming a game warden, but then he found himself distracted by other, more recreational pursuits, including alcohol and drugs. He had anger issues and ended up in the police station. When his father came to bail him out, Herb was told by his dad that he would only do this once—the next time Herb was arrested for anything, he was on his own. Herb says that hard line was what he needed to shape up. He managed to stay out of trouble after that; married and enrolled in a treatment program at the Institute of Living in Hartford soon after his son was born. He would become a dedicated member of Alcoholics Anonymous for the next twelve years. A divorce followed, but also years of therapy. Herb read the books of John Bradshaw, who coined the term "dysfunctional family," and then encountered the work of the poet Robert Bly, who had a following for his ideas on men's mental health. Herb continued to work toward sobriety and eventually remarried and had two more children.

"Did you have any heroes growing up?" I ask. Herb answers quickly. "My father and my grandfather." He pauses and adds, "I think my father would do anything to get outdoors. I'm a lot like him. If he wasn't out of the house trapping, he was out hunting or fishing. I admired the fact that he could do that for himself. I'm from the generation that had just three TV channels. TV is a Pandora's box; ever since it got opened there's been so much evil."

I ask Herb directly if he thinks he was medicating himself for depression when he was using drugs and alcohol, and his response is immediate. "Definitely. I take antidepressants now. But back then you didn't talk about these things. You didn't talk about anything. And if you did, it stayed in the family." Then Herb says it: "I was abused."

I am so stunned I have no idea how to respond. I nod, then Herb continues, as always, matter-of-fact. "I don't need to talk about it anymore. I did serious therapy." He gestures around the room, then, his arm moving in a wide arc, he says, "I use the past as a guidepost, not a whipping post. And I have this. It saves me."

Then he tells me a version of a Cherokee story. A young man tells his father that two wolves are battling inside of him. One tells the young man that he is selfish, and the other tells the young man that he is loving. The young man asks the father, which one will win? The father says, the one you feed will win. I look at the dark ink tattoos peeking out from where Herb has rolled up the arms of his shirt: a coyote howling under the moon, an eagle feather, and a dream catcher. "Resentment is the worst thing," Herb says. "All it does is eat at you."

With that, Herb stamps out his cigarette. "Let me show you how to tack up a beaver." He walks over to where a series of boards are leaning up against the wall. Each has a large round circle drawn on it that corresponds to the official sizes that fur graders will use when sorting beaver for auction: extra-large, large, medium, small. "You got skinny beaver and fat beaver," says Herb. "I need to line this one up to just the right circle…" He holds the pelt against the board, assessing its size. "No, see, that one isn't right, I think I need to move it down a notch." He picks up a hammer and dish of small finishing nails and begins nailing the edges of the beaver pelt to the board, pulling it as he goes so that it follows the drawn circle. Once dried, the fur, now called a beaver pelt, will resemble a large furry coin.

Herb is halfway through nailing the beaver pelt to the board when he starts talking about Jesus. He holds several small tacks in his mouth and reaches for them one at a time, then hammers them into the circumference of the pelt. "When I was in treatment," he begins, his words slightly muffled by his mouthful of tacks, "I read all the religions, I read the Koran, I read the Old Testament, the New Testament, front to back." He holds the hammer still for a moment, then blurts out, "What kind of a religion is it that celebrates nailing a man to a cross?" He hammers the next nail down too hard and it bends. He pulls it out and resumes pounding. "For me, the majority of critical things in my life were always initiated by something in nature. When my grandfather died, he lingered. I was called to go to his death, and on my way, I stopped at a light. I saw these crows and this huge red hawk sitting on an electric line. The crows are dive-bombing the hawk, just going at him, but he's not moving. I got goosebumps."

"You think it was your grandfather's spirit?"

"Exactly." Herb's voice is clear. "Things like that have happened in my life…" He pauses. "The killing part.…it takes a certain—" He cuts himself off, hammers a few more nails into the beaver pelt, then continues. "It's not for everyone. I get that. But I'm okay with that part of myself. I celebrate it."

What I learned in Herb's shack, watching him transform the beaver from wild animal to commodity, was the way in which fur trapping seemed to connect him to nature, not just through the ancient relationship of hunter and hunted, but through the physical work. To skin the beaver well, Herb had to know the secrets of its body, the twists and turns and idiosyncrasies of muscle and sinew, organ, tissue, and bone. The work itself of skinning involved a kind of knowing, a level of knowledge gained over time. Through this process an intimacy emerged. Herb was wrestling with that ancient question, *How shall we now live?* And for Herb, beavers were part of the answer.

By the time I head home, the air is crisp. Overhead the stars shine their cold indifferent light. January might be named for the two heads of Janus, one head facing toward winter's dark, the other toward spring, the coming light. But here in New England, February seems the month when each day hangs suspended, ready to veer back into darkness, but just as ready to bend toward the light of spring. When the ice finally breaks, the beavers will be released from torpor and, finding one another, mate underwater. One hundred days later, the kits will be born, unable to swim or dive until they grow big enough to learn from their parents.

Two weeks later, Herb texts me a picture. He is standing outside Man's Land with his take of fur for the season nailed to the side of his fur shack. Displaying the furs you have managed to catch, skin, and finish by spring is a fur trapping custom dating back to the era of the mountain man. In spring, the free trappers would emerge from the woods and head for the rendezvous, their horses laden with all the furs they had caught through the fall and winter. Standing next to the furs, Herb looks proud.

Then February tilted, sliding into fast motion. What we all knew could happen, finally did: My mother caught a cold from which she could not recover. She'd been so stoic and stubborn and patient and in so much discomfort from her compromised lungs for so long that at the end, I wanted only to give her comfort and help her let go. But when she took her last breath at dawn, just as a pink glow began to spread up from behind the Catskills, I felt stunned. And later, when I finally walked out of the hospital, it was into a world glazed with grief. My mother had lived a long life, and we had known the end was near, but it still seemed impossible that she was really gone. I knew I was lucky to have been with her at the end, but I also knew I was going to miss her for a long time.

Not long after he heard the news, Herb texted me: got something to show you.

When I arrived, he pulled a huge load of pussywillow branches out from the back of his truck. "For your mother," he said and walked them over to my car. I opened the door so he could put the branches in and tried not to weep. Out on the trap line one day when we'd passed some pussywillows, I had told him about how each spring my mother would round up all of us kids and the dogs and we would head out in a great hullabaloo through the orchards to the woods that soon became swamp. There we looked for signs of spring—tips of skunk cabbage, frog's eggs, and pussywillows, their silver tips the prize we took home. "Thanks," I said simply. I knew I didn't need to say anything more. Herb nodded and I headed home.

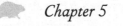

Chapter 5

Wild Fur

By the time the clock strikes eleven, every table in the Veterans of Foreign Wars event hall in Herkimer, New York, is heaped with wild animal skins, each pile rippling with color: brown and fawny red, greyish tan, black and white, grey with spots, striated brown and grey, copper red, chestnut brown, golden, blonde and cream, slate grey and black. There are coyote, piled like boards, glossy skins of mink and otter, round flat disks of "beaver dollars," the fur stretched into rounds. The room is packed with men wearing Carhartt and camo. Knives hang from belts, and boots echo across the floor. Above the muffled chatter comes the singsong drone of the auctioneer. This is the annual spring fur sale sponsored by the Fulton-Montgomery Fur Harvesters and Foothills Trapper's Association. You can buy opossum, fisher, skunk, and fox, a pelt of sumptuous bobcat, the tan belly patterned with spots of grey. You can buy, if you bid early and fast, some almost black beaver pelts from the Adirondacks. You can buy the most famous muskrat pelts in the country, "Montezuma rats," trapped in the marshes of western New York. And you can buy entire animals frozen for taxidermy. Today there are heaps of bushy raccoon from Pennsylvania, and slender marten from Wyoming. Someone has even entered a lot of blonde beaver from Montana. At the end of one table, several bobcats frozen whole seem to be prowling. And in the corner is the pile of winter mink that Henry VIII would have snatched if he were here, given his greed for fine ermine. A collective frisson fills the room; the air tastes electric. This is what remains of the historic North American fur trade.

Paul Johnson, a short, spry man with a chiseled Lincoln face, is the master of ceremonies. Right now he seems to be leaping across the room and

back, greeting trappers as they come in, making sure the three men working the tables to accept and register fur have everything they need. And the
fur trappers keep sauntering in. Wild fur fills their arms or they carry it in
like bundles of wood. Others have large bags slung over their shoulders.
Some men have used black plastic garbage bags; others have thick white
plastic bags stamped with black print. The black letters spell out *NAFA*,
North American Fur Auction, or the words *Fur Harvesters*. These two companies trace their roots back to the first fur trading enterprise in North
America, the legendary Hudson's Bay Company, and to its early competitors. When John Jacob Astor set up his fur trade and founded the American Fur Company, he was in brutal competition with these British firms for
control of beaver pelts, so valuable that they served as the first currency of
the transatlantic fur trade. The "made beaver" system of fiscal accounting
established by the Hudson's Bay Company (and thus used by others) made
beaver pelts the gold standard of the day. All other furs (and trade goods)
were priced in relation to that value.

Beaver accounting today is a great deal simpler, but Paul's wife, Shelley,
is already tucked into her chair in the small room to one side, doing the
books. Her door is closed and no one, I mean no one, is allowed to open
that door and break her concentration. It is Shelley's job to record the bids
as they come in and generate checks. By the time the sale ends, she will
have recorded the bids on almost $23,000 worth of wild fur, which seems
like a lot until you realize that once upon a time in North America, come
spring, fur trappers came staggering down out of the woods to the annual
rendezvous to meet fur buyers with loads of fur worth tens of thousands of
dollars. Beaver pelts, which averaged one to two pounds each, were sold by
weight; a hundred-pound pack held about eighty skins and was worth about
$12,000 in today's money. The lure of the trap line was considerable; in the
early 1800s a fur trapper made forty times the daily pay rate of the typical
farm worker back east.

In the room today are country fur buyers acquiring beaver pelts and
other furs direct from trappers the way John Jacob Astor did when he was
just starting out, first on the wharfs of Manhattan, then up the Hudson and
west along the Mohawk River to historic Native American trading sites like
the portage at Little Falls. The men I see, in work boots and Carhartts, or

jeans and hoodies, represent what remains of the legacy of the European
fur trapper, those renegades of American history who, like the cowboys of
the West, have come to represent an enduring and complex cultural trope
of American masculinity: the mountain man, a lone and self-reliant figure
who seeks freedom in the wild life. Today, the closest comparison to the
mountain man might be the long-distance trucker, whose job is grueling
but lucrative and done in the solitude of the open road.

I stand at the doorway and wait, adjusting to the odor. The furs have been
fleshed and finished but not tanned, so the hides are stiff and rank with the
smell of decaying flesh. The long hall decorated with flags and plaques has
only a few small windows, but today it is bright with the light from long fluo-
rescent tubes that span the ceiling. In the back is a counter that leads into
a small kitchen with coffee, donuts, and breakfast sandwiches out for sale.
Some trappers are standing there, coffee in hand. The auction has been
going for three hours, but furs keep coming in. Here comes a man carrying
in an entire bobcat, the large wildcat frozen whole for taxidermy, the face
still snarling.

There are some bags of green beaver, meaning unfleshed, which won't
sell for much, but most of the fur up for auction today has been finished,
meaning the animal was skinned, the hide fleshed, cleaned, and dried,
although each type of fur is finished in a slightly different way. Muskrat and
otter are finished flesh side out, to protect the fur. Beaver are stretched into
the round coin shapes I saw Herb display in Man's Land. Coyote and fox are
often finished with the feet intact and dangling. Once inside the door, trappers head first to the long receiving table on the right where furs entering
the sale are counted and the trapper is given a lot number. When the fur is
accepted into the sale it is moved to one of the long tables that fill the room,
in line now for the auction. Paul and the men working for the auction check
that each pelt has a tag. To be sold here, all furs must be tagged by the
department of wildlife for the state where the animal was killed; in this way
states attempt to monitor the populations of fur-bearing animals.

As soon as I step into the hall, Paul Johnson waves to me and smiles in
welcome. I interviewed Paul last fall at the annual fur trapper convention
held nearby at the Herkimer fairgrounds. Fur trappers are a community of
loners, but most belong to local trapper organizations that have annual fall

gatherings, still called rendezvous after the historic meetings of the *coureurs de bois*, the first French explorers who came to North America in search of fur. These smaller groups tend to belong to statewide organizations, and these statewide groups belong to the National Trappers Association. Here in New York State, every Labor Day the New York State Trappers Association hosts an annual convention, which is a three-day meet-and-greet for fur trappers, fur buyers, and companies that sell traps and other gear and supplies for finishing wild fur. On the outskirts, the convention is a huge flea market where you can buy everything related to the hunting and trapping life—antique magazines, cast iron camping skillets, mounted deer heads, and the traditional fur hats worn by mountain men. Trap collectors bring boxes of steel traps to trade and sell along with the coveted hand-forged iron traps from the beginning of the fur trade. You can find all types of gadgets and rural bric-a-brac, from waffle irons to lampshades made from deer hide. You can't buy guns, but you can buy axes and shovels and the odd box of bullets. And there are demonstrations on trapping techniques and lectures by famous trappers, and over meals everyone tries to catch up on the latest news of potential legislation that might prevent them from trapping fur.

Underneath the carnival tone runs collective angst about groups mainly located in cities and suburbs, of "antis" who seek to change fur trapping regulations, or stop trapping altogether. Fur trappers represent a sector of rural culture in America that believes itself to be under siege, so paranoia runs high. I always keep my notebook out in front of me, but initially when I came to the fur sale, I was regarded with suspicion. Harlen Lien, a fur trader I had gotten to know, was my passport, guide, and protector. The first time I went to the annual state trapper convention, a man at the entrance had grabbed his walkie-talkie as soon as he saw me. I heard him shout "Anti" into the receiver and I was immediately flanked by three men. Only when I said I was there to meet Harlen Lien did the situation deescalate. Later that day, Harlen introduced me to trappers and vendors, and after that, everyone I met was friendly and willing to talk.

I first met Harlen a few years ago when he came down from the Adirondacks to buy fur at the local spring fur sale. When the bidding was over, I introduced myself and explained that I was trying to learn about the fur trade for a book I was writing. He laughed and said, "It's a skin game." I could tell he was deflecting, maybe wondering if he should speak to me, this stranger taking notes. In general, I tended to observe at these kinds of gatherings; I kept my notebook and pen out but did not ask too many questions, letting people get used to the fact of me, because I was clearly not a fur trapper. But when I met Harlen again, some months later at another fur sale and asked if he would show me how he graded fur, he began to answer my questions. From that point on, he was incredibly generous with his knowledge and introduced me to a lot of people I probably would not have met otherwise.

I glance around the room. The long banquet tables, used for weddings and anniversaries, graduation parties and events, have been carefully covered in brown paper taped down at each end. They have been lined up parallel across the room. But instead of bringing side dishes, or presents for the newlyweds, everyone has brought animal fur. It takes me a moment to get over the fact that I am walking into a room filled with the hides of dead animals, hundreds of them. If they suddenly came to life, the hall would become a bedlam of claw and fang, tooth and nail. I push my way through the crowd toward the bidding table. Every coyote pelt reminds me of my own dog and for a few moments I struggle. Then I see a young woman in black stretch tights and black Polartec. It's Grace, the teenager I had met here a year ago. Last year was her first year putting up her own lot in the auction, a muskrat she had trapped at a pond. When Grace sees me, she waves eagerly.

"This year I have four muskrats," she tells me, proud of the achievement.

Grace is a striking fifteen-year-old with glossy dark brown shoulder-length hair and an easygoing smile. Glass studs sparkle in her ears and her dark eyes shine. Last year she talked about being part of the varsity volleyball team at school. She didn't have her own horse, but rode often and loved it. She lives outside Saratoga Springs, home of the Saratoga track and yearling Thoroughbred sale. She hopes to get into Skidmore when she graduates because through her dad, who works in the maintenance department there, she can get a scholarship. At last year's sale I had watched her walk up and down the aisles of pelts, stroking the gleaming fur. When the men running the auction needed a pen or more tags, or an extra hand to move furs along the table, she was ready to help. She is the only teenager I see here, one of only about twenty women, but as usual, she seems at ease.

Under her jacket Grace wears a T-shirt with the logo for her father's nuisance wildlife business, Final Step. The shirt spells out the company name above an American flag with a coyote seated, haunches down, nose up, howling.

"How was the trapping season?" I ask her.

"We did good," she answers, explaining that she and her father put their lots together with her uncle. "Thirty-two coyote!" she says proudly. She pulls out her phone to show me a picture of her father's fur shed. I see a small wooden hut, beautifully trimmed and stained a warm maple brown. Across the front are tacked coyote, then beneath them rounds of beaver, then some muskrat (hers), and skins of red and grey fox.

Grace and her father and uncle have been here since the doors opened, so she thinks their lots should be up soon. She pushes ahead eagerly and I follow. Soon we are near the bidding platform, which is a set of banquet tables pulled together to form a surface large enough for the buyers to circle. On top of the table is a small hard-backed chair on which sits the auctioneer, dressed in a red flannel shirt and jeans, with a short white beard and an angular face. His brown felt hat is tipped forward at a jaunty angle, and in the brim he's tucked a colorful splash of guinea hen feathers and red and yellow plumes. This is Bob Hughes, one of the last fur auctioneers in the country. A veteran trapper of almost seventy years, he has only a few minutes to assess the quality of the fur on the table and calculate a starting price. Now he is leaning forward, hands on his knees. It is his job to set the price, keep the bidding going, and manage the sale, which means keeping focused on the faces of the buyers, and knowing when to push and when to back off. More than once while I watch today I'll see him calm bad tempers.

The buyers surround the table. On the far side I see John Rockford, a trapper who runs a fur and fur supply business. Next to him is Harlen Lien, who is probably the last of the true country fur buyers. Harlen is inspecting the furs, which are grey fox. He lifts one of the slim pelts up by the nose, then lets it fall back down on the table and presses his other hand against the fur, making the hair stand up. He ruffs the fur a bit, almost as if he is roughly patting a dog, then he lifts the pelt and gives it a quick jerk so it snaps. There is a sharp crack. He turns it over and examines the flesh side carefully. Does he want these? He looks up as if he doesn't give a damn about those pelts, is maybe even insulted by having had to waste his time looking at them, and pushes them across the table toward the other buyers. The other buyers reach out and grab them, eager for their turn.

Harlen has been in the business since he first got hooked on buying fur back in his twenties. He had just finished a degree in wildlife management at the University of Idaho, and when he and his wife soon had two kids to support, he began trading fur to supplement his income. That was back in the '70s when the back-to-the-land movement was in full swing and living a simple life seemed part of the answer. Within a decade Harlen was making much more trading fur than in wildlife management jobs and became a fur buyer full-time. Until his kids reached school age, he and his young family drove all over the country, buying furs and mostly living out of their van. Harlen is a slim man of sixtysomething now with a square jaw, clean-cut good looks, and kind blue eyes. But when he is bidding, he is as swift as a mink, and his face goes blank with concentration. Now he and John, the buyer on his side of the table, lean slightly forward, knuckles down. They act like competitors, but as I will learn afterward from Harlen, this is a performance, because while John will win the bids on all the muskrat, he is actually going to sell them to Harlen later. There is nothing illegal in this. In fact, I'm pretty sure that most everyone here knows it, but hidden deals are part of the theater that everyone enjoys. And, for reasons that I'll never quite understand but have to do with the elaborate system of buyers and sellers and accounts that makes up the highly secretive fur trade, Harlen doesn't want people to think he is in the market for muskrat. Across the table, two buyers sit in chairs. I recognize them from the sale last year. One man, named Lee, has a round face and a quick temper. His brother is less volatile, and tends to let Lee place the bets. Harlen considers them rookie buyers.

I turn to see Tom Hart and two other fur trappers from Connecticut, Jim Koleman, who has begun to buy fur, and Al Jones, a retired lineman. Al is a short man with long straight grey hair and a long grey beard. He wears silver-framed glasses and sports a dark green ball cap. Harlen has stopped making the trip down from the Adirondacks to Connecticut for the spring sale because they don't have enough fur to make his trip worthwhile. Herb has gone ahead and trained to be a fur agent for the Canadian fur auction, Fur Harvesters, so that he can send furs taken by the trappers in his group north to the next sale in Winnipeg. Herb meant to come today to watch the auction but couldn't make it.

I walk over to stand next to Jim, a robust man in jeans and a blue sweatshirt.

"You buying fur today?" I ask.

"No," he answers, "just sightseeing. I'm here for the fun."

"You can sum the fur trade up in two words," Tom Hart interjects: "It's over." He enjoys the grim drama of his words, then grins. Tom is a large man with a blunt face, a jaunty walk, and a handlebar mustache. Something about the jut of his chin signals defiance, and while he is always pleasant to me, I wouldn't want to cross him. But when he talks about mink, his voice becomes animated. Tom considers himself a water trapper. He traps beaver, muskrat, and otter, but mink are his favorite. Every season he drives all the way to the Northeast Kingdom of Vermont to spend time in a particular wetland there. He's been trapping since he was nine years old and figures he has rarely missed a season.

At the Fur Harvesters auction earlier in the month, 25,323 mink, 19,185 red fox, and 5,262 otter went mainly unsold. The last time fur coats were the height of luxury and fashion was in the 1940s, a time when beaver regularly brought in $45 a pelt. Now, major U.S. cities like Los Angeles, San Francisco, and New York have banned or are in the process of banning the sale of fur. As a result, the international market was saturated with unsold pelts.

I asked Tom once why he still traps and what it was about fur trapping he thought people misunderstood. "I love getting out. Every year, I learn something new." Trapping was something like a chess game between him and the animal: "I think like a mink. I know where the mink are going to go and I put my traps there." Trapping what are called "blind sets," without bait to lure the animal toward them, is an art to him; he compares it to the way dedicated fly fishermen tie their own flies.

"One grey fox, okay, one grey fox and go," the auctioneer begins. "Yes no gotta go...I've got one grey fox, who wants fur?" His voice rattles. I glance at my watch: The buyers worked so fast it took only 240 seconds for all four to examine the fur. Does Harlen need these fox pelts? I know he has prices and buyers lined up in his head. More than once he has told me that the biggest rookie mistake is to buy on looks; no matter how attractive the pelt, he never buys unless he already has a buyer in mind.

"Fifteen dollars, fifteen dollars and you have yourself a fox." The auctioneer's voice picks up speed. Suddenly Harlen interjects. "Twelve fifty," he shouts, the opening bid.

"Thirteen," counters Lee.

"Thirteen fifty," counters Harlen, his voice bold.

The auctioneer waits, just a pause, but there is only a leaden silence. No counterbid. He glances over to where the trapper stands, yellow paper in hand, eagerly watching. If he doesn't like the offered price he can shout "No sale" and his fur lot will be pulled out and dumped on the side for him to collect while the next batch of fur is thrown up on the table. He can take the fur home or send it to the NAFA auction next month. In the corner, the NAFA agent is standing by to take furs any trappers want to send up on consignment. There is no agent from Fur Harvesters here today. The trapper will get paid when and if his fur sells. The trapper must have signaled he'd accept the bid, for the auctioneer quickly shouts, "Sold for thirteen fifty to number five."

I glance over at Harlen, but if he is pleased I can't tell. His face is a mask, so still he often bids with just one eye, his trademark wink. The trappers from Connecticut are watching carefully, especially Al. At the sale last week in Connecticut, he had held on to his own fox. "I kept mine back," he tells me, his voice almost gleeful. "I'm going to get them tanned and make a red fox fur bedspread, grey on the sides and four tails on the four corners. Should look nice. I can't see killing a fox for six to seven dollars. I figure I need forty-eight, will take me about four years to get that many. Should look really nice." He nods his head, thinking of his future bedspread, which sounds awful to me, but this is clearly something he is going to dedicate himself to making and is proud of.

Next up is a pile of coyote.

We've got furs to sell, let's get 'em up.

Who's bidding?

I've got six coyote on the table, coyote here.

How about twenty, twenty for six, that's twenty.

Twenty-one. Twenty-two, twenty-three . . . and it's thirty-one and -two, -three.

The auctioneer's voice seems to flex and bend like an accordion, never stopping. When does he breathe? More numbers. Faster now.

And it's thirty, thirty-one, thirty-three.

Now he cracks the whip.

Okay now, we don't have all day, what'll it be?

Pause.

Come on, boys, these coyotes aren't going to walk off . . .

Sold to number five!

Now beaver is bringing nine dollars, ten dollars, then fifteen. Harlen takes them. I watch him grab the pelts, then almost fling them onto the growing pile of furs behind him. All day I will see the auctioneer take cues from Harlen, who is the most respected buyer at the sale. Once again, an unremarkable coyote is flung on the table, and after a pause, someone says, "One dollar." Tom Hart shakes his head. He's writing all the prices down. Harlen and the other buyers pass, but a man walks up to the table and buys the fur. He seems pleased. I am curious about who he is and why he bought such a mangy coyote and follow him as he walks to the office. "My daughter is twelve," he says. "She is really into nature shows. She'll love it." He just came to look, but then decided to register as a buyer once he saw the furs. But he is done now and heading out.

Another lot of fur is thrown on the table. I peer through the crowd and see four beaver. All the buyers look at the fur. Harlen shakes each one to check if the fur is loose and turns each over to see the leather side, then he says, "Nope," and pushes them away. The beaver are small, just yearlings, and have not been finished well. Later Harlen will explain that he passed on them because if the fur isn't finished properly the hair will start falling out and they will become worthless. "Sorry for all that work," says the auctioneer. The beaver is pulled off and put to one side. I look around the room and watch the crowd for a while, listening to the mesmerizing rhythm of furs thumping on the table, then the singsong of bids punctuated by the auctioneer's final call, "Sold!"

When I turn back to the bidding table, Harlen is turning coyote pelts over, running his hands through the fur. Harlen might be buying, Harlen might not be buying; his face is a blank. He draws the moment out. Across the table, the other buyers sit mute. The auction takes on this fast pace now, with everyone keyed up. After a dramatic pause, Harlen springs into action and the bidding starts. Sixteen, sixteen fifty, seventeen, seventeen fifty. Impatient now, Harlen shouts, "Nineteen."

Harlen remains still, but his opponent is animated, his face florid with emotion. Lee also chews gum, which Harlen considers a rookie mistake; Harlen insists he can read the pace of Lee's chewing and know exactly when he is going to fold. Lee also has a temper that Harlen likes to rile. More than once I'll watch Harlen pretend he really wants a particular set of fur and bait Lee with bids, then suddenly pull out, leaving Lee with overpriced fur. Harlen gets a kick out of doing this. Right now, he is his usual poker face, blank as white paper. The gum chewer is smacking his wad. John leans over the table, knuckles down, looking ready. They wait for the next lot.

"Lot number 45, here come the beaver," the auctioneer says, then jokes, "The real moneymakers." The crowd shuffles, laughter rises, but the buyers don't laugh, they don't even look up. Beaver pelts are lifted to the table. Harlen looks them over, runs a hand over the fur, pressing it back. He's looking for bites and scars in the coat. He's looking for the depth of the fur. He's looking at the color and to make sure it is not "singed," the hairs starting to curl. Is the beaver prime, meaning caught in winter when the underfur is most thick? When beaver are trapped early the fur tends to be light, and because the animal doesn't have enough fat, the hide takes on a deep purple hue. In contrast, prime beaver, caught when it is cold, have white or rosy-toned hides. Harlen is taking all this information in and calculating a price.

A voice in the crowd says loudly, "Twenty years ago that beaver would be sixty dollars." I hear murmurs of agreement. Meanwhile, Harlen pushes the beaver pelts to his fellow buyers. Two minutes have passed; they are studying this fur because it is large but not dark, complicating the question of its worth.

"Okay, let's go, beaver on the table," says the auctioneer, picking up on the hesitation.

"Five dollars," shouts Harlen. I don't see the gesture, but the auctioneer shouts, "I've got six." He looks to Harlen.

"Six fifty." The auctioneer shouts the number, looking quickly at all the buyers, focusing on Harlen, who placed the last bet.

"Seven."

"Seven fifty." Silence. But with that extra fifty cents Harlen has taken it. "Sold to number five." Off the beaver dollars go, whisked to the top of Harlen's growing stack of fur. Harlen doesn't even look to make sure the beaver is on his pile because he's already fingering the next lot. He flips each beaver hide over, then pushes the furs to his neighbor. He knows his price.

"How bout nine fifty to go," shouts the auctioneer. "Want to buy some?" Harlen cracks a smile. "No, I don't want to lose my hat, nine." Silence. "Sold for nine dollars to number five."

Again and again Harlen seems to set the price, or modify it, then outbid his competitors for the best furs.

I stare at the beavers. I can't believe the low prices. At that amount, the trapper was making maybe fifty cents an hour if you figured the time it took to catch the animal, skin it, then finish the pelt. I'm suddenly back in Herb's fur shack. A few months before, I had finally gotten up the nerve to try skinning a beaver. On the table was the yearling I had carried out that day from the line; Herb thought I should skin it. And I had steeled myself, and somehow I had finally managed to skin the beaver. But when I was done, I was overwhelmed by a confusing wave of emotions and felt such a rush of connection to the beaver that I had an urge to wrap the pelt around me, to cloak myself in that wild fur. Somehow skinning the beaver, as challenging as it had been, had put me into a new kind of relationship with the animal, and with myself.

I must have stood there gripping the thick beaver pelt—feeling it spill over my hands—for longer than I realized, because Herb had laughed, his eyes crinkling. Then he took the pelt from my hands and slowly nodded; he understood. But here on the table at the fur sale, the beaver pelts before me seem to have nothing to do with a live beaver; they are items for sale, commodities headed for the global fur market. These particular pelts, being slightly ratty, would be sold to clients who made felt for the best-quality cowboy hats and pool tables. Even so, it is clear that the fur trappers here aren't doing this for the money; they seek an authentic relationship with nature and a life not completely defined by dollars and cents.

Then the Amish guy walks in, dressed all in dark blue with a straw hat. He has a name, but everyone calls him the Amish guy. He is from Pennsylvania, and drove here with his grown son. They walk to the table, but only the father takes a seat; his son stands a few feet back, making it clear that only one of them is bidding. Now the Amish guy is buying up all the beaver, which keep coming. Ten lots, twenty. He's hardly looking. The hides are not great—some are light brown, some have bite marks—and he's still paying up to $24 apiece. Harlen seems content to let him win the bids.

"Why the hell would he buy that?" says Tom Hart indignantly, when we watch him take a lot of ten beaver that look particularly worn. He lowers his voice and adds slowly, "Harlen is dumping the fur on him." He nods, getting it now. "The Amish guy, watch, he's got an order and someone is bankrolling him so he doesn't care about the price. Now that he is here the prices are going to go up." Is the Amish farmer really buying for someone? Does he understand how second-rate the fur is? If anyone knows the answers to these questions, they are not saying. This is the fur trade, a world full of secrecy. Trappers did their best to hide traps from unsuspecting animals, then hid the location of their sets and where they trapped from fellow trappers; they hid everything about trapping from the general public, and at the fur auction, an unspoken code meant that you didn't pry into another person's business affairs. We watch beavers continue to sell for a good five to ten dollars more than they were an hour ago. Harlen bids, then retreats, and all but once lets the Amish guy get the beavers every time.

The auctioneer raises his hand and says it is time for lunch. Paul Johnson, who's been overseeing the administration of the auction since the start, comes up with two men who are pushing carts loaded with sodas and chips and paper plates piled with hamburgers. I walk up to say hello. I know not to try to talk to Harlen when he is working.

Harlen lingers for a moment, ginger ale in right hand, and turns a few opossum pelts still on the table with his left, still working. His stamina is amazing. He has been mentally focused, calculating prices and grades and outsmarting his opponents for over four hours, not sitting down once. But he clearly loves the auction.

"These are put up nice," he says, still fingering the fluffy grey fur. Harlen had told me once that he considers opossum to have some of the softest, most beautiful fur.

"Come, eat your lunch," says Paul, who pushes a burger on a paper plate toward him.

"Yes, sir," says Harlen, taking the plate. I nod and say I'll see him after, then step outside.

He's honest.

He's smart.

He's the real deal.

He never scalps—even when he is the only buyer he gives a fair price.

He knows what he's doing; he has to—he's the last one really buying.

He's good until he gets a hair across his ass.

Might as well pull up Harlen Lien's van and put all the fur in there at the start.

Harlen Lien knows everybody and everybody knows Harlen Lien.

He used to buy all over the East, hell, all over the West.

He's the last of the country fur buyers.

As a country fur buyer, Harlen works for himself; he takes all the profit but also all the risk. The year before, I had watched him in action in Toronto at NAFA, the North American Fur Auction. Fur buyers from China, Korea, Italy, Russia, Finland, and all across North America gathered at the NAFA auction site. In cavernous warehouse rooms, tens of thousands of furs were hung on racks for the buyers to inspect in the two days before the sale. Until I got used to it, the slightly sweet smell of rot had made me gag. In contrast, the auction was strangely sanitized of any connection to death. The actual sale was held in a large brightly lit room with seating that resembled a university lecture hall. But it was televised so you could watch it on the large LED screens positioned throughout the complex and uploaded online. Trappers who had fur in the sale could watch the proceedings in real time. Three men neatly dressed in dark pants and white button-down shirts sat behind a raised desk—the auctioneer, his co-auctioneer, and a third man who helped scout the audience for bids. While the sale was going

on, the buffet area served a continual spread of food, water, and coffee, and
buyers mingled. Once the auction began, the lot number, a brief description of the fur, then the selling price flashed on the screen. I sat next to
Harlen, who pointed out the different buyers in attendance. He seemed
to know them all, and they came from around the globe, particularly from
China, Korea, Russia, and Italy. I met a fur trader from Montreal who spe-
cialized in black bear and had accounts with the guards of Buckingham
Palace. The tall black hats worn by the Queen's Guard are made from *Ursus
americanus*, North American black bear. In the lobby was a thin, nervous
man who was bidding on expensive, top lot fisher and beaver to ship to
Williamsburg, Brooklyn, to a man who used them to make shtreimel, the
dark hats worn by Hasidic Jewish men. The day before the sale Harlen had
worked as feverishly as a pre-med student cramming for an exam, studying
pelts, then comparing them to lists of prices, making tiny, almost illegible
notes in the thick fur catalog. At the sale he kept the catalog at hand, but
shielded his notes from view, his large fingers spread over the page.

I can't cope with the idea of eating a hamburger in this room packed
with animal hides, so I walk outside into the fresh air and April sun. Herkimer is a one-street town with a gas station selling pickled eggs and lotto
tickets and not much else, except for Crazy Otto's Empire Diner, which is an
old-fashioned eatery in a silver train car. By the entrance, I meet a man I've
seen at the sale before; he cuts an elegant figure, long-legged and lean with
a hawk nose and slim face. He wears jeans and a yellow chamois shirt, and
his light brown cowboy hat is tipped over his clean-shaven face. But the most
striking aspect of his look is his tailored vest, which is made of otter and
glistens in the sun. His name is Frank Walter and he sewed the vest himself.
He is a retired engineer who worked for water systems, and often on his job,
which took him in and out of wetlands, he observed beaver, otter, muskrat,
and mink. As soon as he believes that I am actually interested to hear what
he has to say about fur trapping, and am not going to berate him for killing
animals, he talks easily.

"I started trapping when I was thirteen, about 1953 or '54," he begins.
"I'd take my bicycle and trap on my way to school. Shipped fur to Sears,
Roebuck—they'd send you a check or you could use the store credit to buy
things from the wish book. I never bought anything from that, though.

Don't tell anyone," he says with a smile, "but I grew up in New Jersey."
Frank's dedication to trapping reminds me of Herb Sobanski, who also
wasn't in it for the money, but as a means of encountering nature and somehow yourself within it. Then Frank grins. "I remember when fisher brought
two hundred and fifty dollars, now you might get forty! But I'm still trapping." Now he is laughing, "I'm a slow learner."

Frank mentions that anti-trapping sentiment is discouraging fur trappers, but I don't want to go down the rabbit hole of trapping politics.
Opinions vary about what is more humane—being trapped in a cage for
twenty-four hours then cudgeled to death or shot, or being stunned or
killed outright by the force of a body-grip trap that snaps closed like a giant
mousetrap. The American Veterinary Medical Association came out with
a statement in 2019 to the effect that death by drowning falls into the category of animal cruelty, but beavers can't drown because their lungs can't
fill with water: They asphyxiate or run out of oxygen in their lungs. A pro-
longed death is certainly a traumatic one. Perhaps the real answer to how
to trap beaver more humanely is to create policies that would allow trappers to live-trap and move beaver away from sites where their lifestyle was
creating problems for the local human population. But relocating beavers,
along with all other wildlife, is currently illegal in New York, Connecticut,
and Massachusetts.

Before I head back in I take a quick walk around the parking lot, which
is filled with trucks. At the far end, I pass two young men leaning against
a black Ford, loaded with fox pelts. The men make a striking pair, first
because they are not of the grizzled fifty-, sixty-, seventysomething crowd
that mostly fills the Veterans hall—they can't be more than thirty. One
man is tall and thin and wears jeans and a work shirt. His hair is a beautiful
auburn color and is plaited into two long braids that hang down on either
side of his slim face. The man's acquaintance is dressed like the renegade
cowboy Zorro: He wears black pants, a black button-down shirt, a black
cowboy hat, and black cowboy boots.

Tom Hart walks by and waves to us. He also glances toward the two young
men, but by now they have closed the back of the truck so the fox pelts are
no longer visible. If he is intrigued by their appearance, Tom does not show
it. I have been around fur trappers long enough to begin to understand

that as long as you are a fur trapper, you can present yourself pretty much any way you want. At the NAFA fur auction in Toronto, I watched one of the top fur buyers from Wyoming, working in the fur inspection area one day wearing nothing but a white lab coat, a bright blue T-shirt, bright blue hot pants, and bright blue high-heeled boots. Fellow buyers called him "Gorgeous George," but he was well respected, one of the top buyers and a sharp businessman. The next time I saw him at the auction, he was wearing a similar outfit, but bright red. He also sported flashy silver and turquoise bracelets clasped on each wrist; all he needed was a pair of ridiculous glasses and he'd look like a fur trapper version of Elton John.

Later, when I talked to him, he regaled me with funny stories, then brought out pictures of his fur trading depot in Wyoming, a long warehouse on which had been nailed hundreds of coyote skins; they were coyote he had trapped or bought from trappers that season. Nearby was a horrific pile of animal carcasses that he said would be rendered into pet food. He was like many of the fur trappers I had met, one paradox after another.

"Heading in?" asks Tom Hart.

"Sure," I answer, "just getting some fresh air. When is your lot up?"

"Soon, I think. I got here early so I could go early, but there was already so much fur."

I am curious to see what the fur buyers will offer and how Tom Hart will respond. He had said he and his fellow trappers were mostly on a field trip, but I know it's more than that because they drove a good four hours to get here.

As if on cue, Jim Koleman walks by carrying a rack of opossum. "I needed these," he says happily. He has just bought them from the back of someone's truck. Generally, parking lot sales are not allowed, but in this case the trapper had pulled his fur because he'd only been offered a buck fifty each. Jim followed him out and offered him three dollars apiece. Jim has a buyer who will pay him more than that, so he'll pocket the difference. And the furs are gorgeous, light grey fur soft as rabbit ruffles in the April breeze.

At the door, we stop to let a man pass by, his head barely visible above the load of raccoon skins he has slung over his shoulder, a great pile of grey and brown, the striking black ringed tails hanging down. Paul Johnson greets the newcomer and motions for where he can pile the furs. The man says he has more. Tom follows him out to help, along with a few other guys standing nearby. They don't need to be asked: Trapper credo reflects rural culture and you help your neighbor even if you don't know a thing about them. Soon three more loads of raccoon are piled on the floor. The man is on the younger side, his black hair greased back. He wears a yellow T-shirt, jeans, and work boots, but the noticeable thing about him is his huge grin. He has two hundred raccoons that demonstrate his prowess as a trapper this season.

So much raccoon has attracted attention. I hear someone murmur, "That's a lot of blue coon," but he keeps his voice low. When raccoon are trapped late in the season, the flesh side of the hide takes on a bluish tinge even after fleshing due to the animal's increased blood circulation in spring. Pelts taken late in the season when the weather has shifted into spring are not prime and the fur is never as thick or lush and often the hair has been damaged by then from being rubbed by ice and snow. Calling someone's fur "blue" is an insult. Underneath the jolly community vibe runs a steel wire of competition. Everyone wants to have brought in the best furs, the ones Harlen Lien and the other buyers will pay high prices for as top lot, and if quality is down, numbers matter. Seemingly oblivious to the commentary, the newcomer walks in slowly, looking around. I follow and we talk for a bit. He is friendly and curious. I learn that he just drove six hours to get here from east of Pittsburgh because he heard this was a good sale.

Over at the table the auction is in full swing, but while I was outside, there was drama in the room because a man started filming the auction with his iPhone. When Harlen saw the iPhone, he leapt up, angry, and the sale was stopped. Harlen is adamant about the no-photographs rule. I took a photo of him once and he immediately said, "What's that for?" Only when I explained that it was for my own research, not for posting or publishing, was he satisfied, but I never took a photo of him again. Who knows where those pictures will get posted, he tells me later. I don't want the government tracking me any more than they already do. Only when the man apologized and put his phone away would Harlen get back to bidding.

By 2:45, the Amish guy has left and the hall is only half filled with trappers. Grace sold her muskrat and was happy with the price and has left with her father and uncle. I turn to my left and start talking to a man I've seen before who tells me he raises fox as domestic animals. They each have distinct personalities, he says, and they are so beautiful, he really enjoys them. He can also sell them for as much as $1,000 each. He's had three litters, a total of thirty-five kits. I had thought fox were considered wildlife, meaning you can't keep them as domestic animals, but apparently like mink, they can be farm raised. I am making a note to research this when he tells me he has a dilemma because he has to choose two of his white fox to shoot because his cousin is having a medieval-themed wedding; she needs two white fox skins to make her wedding dress. I ask him if it is hard to kill the foxes he has raised and gotten to know and he says yes, "It will be hard to do, but I'll do it. I told my cousin, 'I got you covered.'"

A lot of raccoon is next. Tom fingers them and pushes them away. "Twenty raccoon," drawls the auctioneer. "Say three dollars and seventy-five cents, say four, say four fifty, five and fifty, now six. Sold!" There's a new buyer at the table, a small man wearing a big hat. The hat is a ten-inch cone of fur that sits on his head like a giant marshmallow with ear flaps; it is a replica of the traditional fur hats worn by mountain men. I recognize him. He and his wife, who is from the Oneida Nation, run a business making custom fur hats. They have several designs and use all kinds of fur, raccoon being the most popular. The last time I saw him he was dressed in a tan buckskin shirt and his wife was wearing a long buckskin dress. Both were heavily decorated with bone and claw necklaces. Today he wears jeans and a blue shirt and he seems to be on his own. He buys all the raccoon for six dollars each. He seems happy with his purchase and walks out with a spring in his step.

Next up are the large piles of raccoon from the man from Pennsylvania. Harlen looks bored; he is no longer leaning, knuckles down, staring keenly at the table. Now his arms are crossed in front of him, his hands hidden under them. I look at his posture—is this theater or is he not going to buy?

"We've got skins to sell," says the auctioneer, and the bidding starts. Before I know it, Harlen is leading the sale and buys the entire load of raccoon. The sale moves quickly from this point on. Harlen buys a bag of beaver castor for seventy.

Harlen won't tell me where his accounts for castor are, but says he has plenty of buyers. I've seen him buy about ten pounds so far; he pays about forty dollars a pound but can sell it at a good profit.

We watch a magnificent beaver sell for twenty-eight dollars. Harlen is the buyer. Tom Hart suddenly turns to me and says, "You know what? I think it's funny when antis are screaming at us about trapping but they are wearing mass-produced leather belts and shoes and eating hamburgers." He shakes his head. Tom often says things to me about animal rights activists. He believes I am one at heart. He's right, of course—I love animals, but I'm not de facto against trapping. In some instances, I can see it has a role, especially when the fur is harvested and utilized as it is here. "I don't see antis skipping McDonald's," he adds. I consider telling him that I know quite a few vegan animal rights activists, but let it go.

A few muskrats are up next. We are on lot number 868. In the past five hours, close to nine hundred lots of fur have been sold. Only a few left.

"Okay," says the auctioneer. Even he seems to be waning. "This is it, the final lot. Three rats here, three rats. Who will have them?" John buys them all. "That's the rap on rats," says a voice in the crowd, using the trapper nickname for muskrat.

The auctioneer leans forward to confer with the buyers, checking to make sure there are no lingering bids or anyone has changed their mind on furs thrown to the side during the bidding, no bids offered. Satisfied, he looks back up. The buyers stare in his direction. Then the auctioneer shouts, "Thank you, gentlemen. The fur sale is over."

It is 3:40 p.m.

Trappers start to amble out. Buyers move to collect their furs and settle up. In the back room, Shelley is still calculating the auction accounts as fast as she can. Paul is moving fast through the large room, saying goodbyes and making sure everything is running smoothly. Two men begin pulling the brown paper off the empty tables. They will clean the tables and sweep the floor before they leave. Harlen stands up and I catch his gaze. His usually animated face looks pale. He nods. We'll catch up later and go over the sale. He's been on his feet for the past seven and a half hours with only a thirty-minute break for lunch. He starts sorting through the furs and putting them in large white bags for transport. He will count each one and double-check the math, then write a check to the auction.

On my way out, I overhear two men talking about a "beast feast," and when I ask about it, they say they are heading to a wild game dinner featuring dishes made of beaver, venison, muskrat, moose, and possibly bear, depending on who has donated meat. The event is a fund-raiser for a rifle club near Little Falls, and they invite me along. It starts in an hour. While I'm grateful for the invitation, I decline; I want to watch the sale close down and talk to Harlen and others afterward. But the mention of Little Falls has caught my attention. I ask if they have ever heard of Dorothy Richards, the woman who lived with beavers and founded the beaver sanctuary she had named Beaversprite. One man gives me a blank look, but his companion's face brightens. "Oh sure, I grew up near there. You mean the beaver lady?"

"Yes," I say, a bit stunned that he seems to have heard of her. "She founded a beaver sanctuary and wrote a book."

"I think I met her," he says. "I was maybe eight. One day my dad took me along with him on a plumbing job. We visited this old woman. She had called my dad because I think the beavers had flooded her house or something. I remember going in with my dad—she was really nice and had us sit in chairs and wait for her to get something, and then this beaver came up and started pushing my dad's chair."

"Wait," I said. "You met her?"

"Yup."

"Beavers were in the house?"

"Yes!" he said, growing animated. "This beaver, I mean it was really pushing at my dad's chair, and when the woman came back my dad asked, 'What's it trying to do?' She just said, 'You are sitting in its path.' That was the path the beaver used or something. So my dad moved his chair and sure enough the beaver walked right where the chair had been and into the next room."

I couldn't believe my ears. This must have been the time the beavers dislodged the water pipe that brought water into the swimming pool Dorothy had built inside for the beavers to swim and play in. In her book she had called it "the Y." I ask if he knows anyone who worked for Dorothy or knew her. But he shakes his head. He doesn't know anyone who knew her. When I ask what her reputation was in the community, he gives me a sideways look and shrugs. When I push him, he says, "She was considered kind of crazy.

I mean, most people want to get rid of beavers who flood where they live, but she wanted them in her house!" Then he adds, "Her place is still there."

This news hits me with a shock. I feel as if I've just won the researcher jackpot. Her memoir, published in 1983 when she was still alive, mentioned that she had created a beaver sanctuary, but I had assumed it was long gone. No one I had met up until this point had mentioned anything about it, and Dorothy herself seemed to be part of a world that was now history. But he had met her and, more important, it seemed her place was still there.

As soon as I can, I make hasty goodbyes and head for the door. I had to set out for the Adirondacks. Dorothy Richards had been influenced by the writings of Enos Mills and Archie Belaney (Grey Owl), both of whom championed beaver conservation. Inspired by them, she had gone on to defy the gender roles of her time and to found the first beaver sanctuary in the country. My first stop would be the canalside town where she grew up, then I would find Beaversprite.

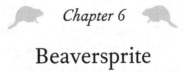

Chapter 6

Beaversprite

PART I: *Little Falls*

It is May, and I am off to find out what I can about the "beaver lady," Dorothy Richards, who at one point lived with fourteen beavers in her compact farmhouse in the foothills of the Adirondacks. They had names like Eager, Delilah, and Hunk, and they trundled back and forth through the small rooms, stealing kindling from the fireplace to wedge between chairs and table legs, and dragging her oriental rug across the floor toward the door that led to their indoor pool. One night, Dorothy woke up to find Delilah on her chest, staring down at her. Then the beaver ran under her bed and had a blast pushing up against the bedsprings with her large webbed feet, making them creak and heaving the mattress up and down so rigorously that Dorothy didn't get a wink of sleep.

Ever since I had seen the photograph of Dorothy Richards sitting in her armchair, a thin upright woman holding an enormous beaver, I wanted to meet her. In the grainy black-and-white photograph featured on the back of her memoir, the beaver seems to grin with the joie de vivre of a golden retriever, the strong legs and duck feet sprawled across Dorothy's knees in absolute trust and comfort. Her thin arms balance the beaver, but he leans back into her, lounging as he looks bright-eyed right into the camera. He isn't afraid of the person taking the photograph because it is Dorothy's husband, Al, who wasn't keen on having beavers move in with them at first, but then got used to them. This is Eager, Dorothy's favorite of the many generations of beavers that lived with her over the course of forty years. I copied the photo and pasted it on my wall. Who was this woman? What combination of circumstance and desire had motivated her to dedicate her life to the study, then protection of beavers in the late '30s, way before beavers were in the news? In the photograph, her long, narrow face opens into a beatific smile. This is a face that holds secrets; even her hair, pulled back severely, is further hidden beneath a scarf. By the time Dorothy Richards died at age ninety-one she had become famous as the "beaver lady." Two years before her death, she published *Beaversprite: My Years Building an Animal Sanctuary*, a memoir of her years creating a wildlife haven near Little Falls, the canalside town where she had grown up. I had fallen for the opening line: "I'm writing this with a sixty-pound beaver on my lap." She had died in 1985, and I assumed her memory had died with her and the sanctuary was long gone—until that day at the country fur sale, surrounded by beaver pelts, when I heard that her house and the beaver sanctuary still existed, right where she had founded it, on the confluence of two creeks just to the north and east of Little Falls, in the southern Adirondacks.

Little Falls, New York, lies in the low point between two proto-glacial lakes, the only break in the otherwise impenetrable ledges of rock heaved up during the Taconic orogeny, a series of geologic events that sound more like mythology than science. During the orogeny, a long volcanic island formed in the Iapetus Ocean and collided with what would become North America; from this collision the Taconic Mountains emerged. Then the Allegheny orogeny heaved up the great Appalachian chain. It was through that one low spot in the rock ledge, between two ancient lakes, that the Mohawk River pushed its way through.

The river runs east until just north of Albany, where it merges with the mighty Hudson and heads south through the Hudson valley, past Athens, then Hudson, where it broadens out into a silver expanse almost a mile wide. Near West Point, the river sweeps around the curve of Bear Mountain before making its final ascent down through the Bronx, around the west side of the island of Manhattan, and out into the open sea. During his years of traveling New York State in search of beaver and other furs, John Jacob Astor had journeyed this route in the opposite direction, traveling north along the Hudson, upriver by steamer to Albany, where he would have transferred to a large canoe and followed the Mohawk west toward Little Falls.

Little Falls was a Native American trading site. The river drops a hundred feet in less than half a mile; travelers carried their canoes on land to avoid the falls, made camp, and conducted trade. The land was neutral territory until the beaver wars brought on by the fur trade disrupted historic intertribal relationships, the balance of resources, and power structures. Intertribal trade had been an important aspect of Indigenous cultures for thousands of years before Europeans arrived. Following trade routes established on rivers like the Mohawk, obsidian from present-day Wyoming traveled east along with red ochre, pipestone, and turquoise. Copper from the Great Lakes made its way north and south and east. Flint from places we now call Ohio and Pennsylvania made its way north and south and east. And wampum, made by the Pequot and other Native tribes in modern-day Connecticut and along the eastern shore, made its way up the Atlantic seaboard, then followed rivers like the Mohawk west. Wampum was highly valued because it was believed to have spiritual powers along with great beauty.

This region we now call the southern Adirondacks was populated by Native people who called themselves "people of the long house," the Haudenosaunee. The early French traders would call them the "Iroquois Confederacy." The English would call them the "League of Five Nations": the Mohawk, Cayuga, Oneida, Seneca, and Onondaga. According to the local Indigenous tradition, the confederacy was founded by the prophet Aionwatha, more commonly known as Hiawatha. The confederacy represents one of the first and longest-lasting participatory democracies in the world. The early British and French explorers and fur traders didn't consider that they were encountering a well-developed political system; to them, the Indigenous people they met were Native tribes hungry for trade goods for which they would exchange ridiculously valuable beaver pelts. Most Euro-Americans learned of Hiawatha through Henry Wadsworth Longfellow's famous nineteenth-century poem "The Song of Hiawatha," a thrilling poem written in trochaic tetrameter and set along the southern shore of Lake Superior—and a complete cultural mishmash. Across the pond in Hastings, England, Archibald Belaney, later known to the world by his Ojibwa name as Wa-Shah-Quon-Asin, or Grey Owl, read and internalized this poem as a schoolboy.

For a good hundred years even before the European colonists arrived, the beaver wars incited by the fur trade had brought increased levels of war and violence to Indigenous life. The Dutch traders had come first and quickly realized that if they could control wampum production along the coast, especially among the Pequot who lived in the area we now call Connecticut, they could control much of the fur trade, especially with tribes like the Iroquois who had access to the sumptuous furs brought east from the Great Lakes region. Tribes that traded directly with the Dutch and later with the English and French (who came soon after and pushed out the Dutch), had access to guns that enabled them to dominate neighboring tribes with whom they had been in competition for hunting territories and other resources. As the French and the English battled for control of the fur trade and rushed to build colonies in the New World, Native tribes became embroiled. The Iroquois allied themselves with the French and the Mahicans allied themselves with the English, but soon the Mohawks were at war with the Mahicans. Traditional balances of intertribal power and methods for handling disputes were replaced by years of ruthless war.

The town of Little Falls was not officially founded until 1781, when European settlers, already feeling crowded in Massachusetts and New York, began to press north and west of the Hudson. By 1792, they had built a canal around the falls to make the river more navigable, but this was just a warm-up for the huge waterworks project that was to come: the Erie Canal, finished in 1825. When the canal was completed, it linked Little Falls with the manufacturing and business centers of Rochester and Buffalo, Albany, and New York City. For a time, Little Falls even became the cheese capital of the East; the price of cheddar was wired down to New York City. In 1867, a whopping sixty-eight million pounds of cheese were shipped out of Little Falls, including exports to England. Dorothy Richards remembered skipping rope on the sidewalks of Little Falls. That was 1902, still the tail end of the Gilded Age. Dorothy was still a Burney, the sickly middle child of Arthur Burney, owner of Burney's Hardware Store. And Little Falls was still a thriving canalside town. Dorothy had been a talented student, so ahead of her class that she entered high school at age twelve, but she never went to college. A severe bout with tuberculosis as a child had left her sickly, and her parents did not think she could thrive away from home. Instead,

Dorothy read, book after book after book, and after high school took a job at the local library. It was there that she met Mabel, whose brother was Al. Dorothy would eventually marry Al Richards at the age of twenty-six. Later, when Al lost his job as a forester during the Depression, they would return to their hometown and run a stationery supply business.

On this May morning, almost forty years after Dorothy published *Beaversprite*, the Mohawk River swells ominously, a deep chocolate brown that pushes up over the rock banks. Little Falls looks like a town thrown together as if by chance; houses seem to be half tumbling down both sides of a steep ravine, and the long Main Street, which runs parallel to the ravine, is a collection of mostly boarded-up shops. Where the ravine bottoms out, the usually quiet Mohawk runs alongside a long brick mill building long past its manufacturing heyday and now converted into a hotel, offices, and a small coffee shop.

From my room in the old mill building, which once produced cloth for the Union army, I see the dark water racing by, carrying a whole tree, which is soon snagged by something under the water. The tree rears up, its tall trunk, the limbs still leafed, waving in erratic circles. Suddenly the force of the current pushes the tree under, but it rears back up again, still caught by boulders and bits of tree hidden beneath the surface. The enormous tree is now flailing as if it were no more than a branch, half swallowed by the thick tongue of brown water. All night the sound of the river kept me awake, the loud rushing of the floodwater a stark reminder of the climate weirdness that was changing our world. I was still haunted by the memory of the February day when my mother died; that night spring peepers had come out, their haunting cries filling the woods a good month early. The apple trees had bloomed too early as well—although that meant I had been able to fill the church with their blooms for her funeral. An early spring was not unheard of in New England, but the new pattern of dramatic temperature swings was due to climate change. Then there was the rain. This May it has rained for twenty-two of the past thirty days and the usually tame Mohawk is a torrent. If beavers were still in the landscape as they were in the time of Beaverland would the Mohawk be flooding this high?

I am starting my day at the Little Falls Historical Society, where I hope to find out more about Dorothy Richards's early years. At eleven, I am meeting Paul Johnson, who I had watched run the Herkimer fur sale. Paul grew up just north of Little Falls and I am curious if he knows about Dorothy. But the highlight of my day promises to be my visit with Sharon and Owen Brown, who seem to be Dorothy's spiritual heirs. They run their own sanctuary as well as an educational website on beavers, and tomorrow we are going to see Dorothy's house. I give the river one last uneasy look and head down the stairs.

The Little Falls Historical Society is located in the white clapboard bank building, just one block up from the river and Main Street. With the help of a historical society member named Pat, who has dark brown hair and a ready smile, and an equally helpful member named Jeff, I am soon looking at a newspaper clipping dated January 10, 1879, with the dark headline "Prices Paid for Furs and Skins." The brief article notes that in its market report, the *New York Tribune* says that "the receipts of all kinds of furs and skins in that city are increasing, skunks being especially in demand." And it lists prices paid "for prime skins" only. Northern beaver, with the darker fur, are selling for 75 cents each, while beaver from the western and southern parts of the state bring only 50 cents. Prime black skunks are $1 each, as are mink. The top seller is the silver fox, going for a whopping $10. Muskrat, even the famed Montezuma muskrats from the western part of the state, bring only 7 cents. These prices seem ridiculous, until you factor in that $1 in 1879 was worth about $25 today. Beaver were thus selling for $12–15 a pelt, about twice what they sell for today. Skunks were selling for $25, twenty times what I had seen them going for at the fur auction last month. In 1879, fur coats, fur mittens, fur jackets, fur blankets for sleighs, and beaver felt hats were still in style, and the fur trade in New York City was thriving even though American beaver were not.

I can find no clippings about Dorothy Richards or Beaversprite. When I look up, Pat is standing before me. "Here," she says happily. "I found some articles about a fur trapper. There's a whole section of clippings on him in this book."

I look at the scrapbook. On the faded pages someone has pasted photographs from the newspaper featuring elegantly dressed young women in '20s fashion; their hair is bobbed short and pulled back with dramatic tiaras and headbands, and around their necks hang myriad furs and boas. Between these pictures are clippings about Nat Foster, the "Famous Fur Trapper." Apparently there is even a town-wide Nat Foster day celebrated each summer in nearby Dolgeville. "He is famous here," says Pat, then adds matter-of-factly. "He murdered an Indian, I think." The shock of her comment hits me with some force, but I have no time to talk about it now. I quickly photograph the pages to read over later and grab my bag to head out. I am due to meet Paul Johnson in ten minutes.

"Wait, we forgot about Louis," Jeff says. He turns to Pat. "You'd better call him."

"Oh yes," Pat answers, "she has to meet Louis."

"Who is Louis?" Both of them glance at me but say nothing.

"Did you get through?" Jeff asks.

"It's ringing."

"Try his other number."

"Who is Louis?"

"Try the other number." Pat dials. "Okay, he's coming right over," she says with a smile. I protest, explaining that I have to interview someone at noon. I hold up my watch, showing them that the time reads 11:50. I've given up on asking who Louis is, but it's clear I am going to have to meet him. Pat calls again and arranges for me to meet him at 1:00.

"Who is Louis?" I ask yet again. I wonder—are they connecting me with someone who knows about Dorothy Richards?

"Oh, he'll explain," says Pat. "Louis knows everything about Little Falls. He can give you the tour."

Almost a month has passed since I saw him at the Herkimer fur sale, but Paul smiles warmly when I walk into the warm café in the old mill building. "Howdy," he says. "I thought you'd like this place."

He is seated by a table by the window, already drinking a cup of coffee. He points to bookshelves full of secondhand books that fill one corner of the room. The place has a homey, country décor, but the Erie Canal towpath is not far, and canalside tourism is now big business. The entire five hundred-plus miles of the canal is now a heritage corridor with the towpath converted to a walking and biking path that runs from Buffalo to Albany. Paul is not a tall man, but he has the woodland look of a Paul Bunyan. Today he wears blue jeans and a red-and-black-checked flannel shirt. As usual, his black plastic glasses are shifted a bit low over his nose. Paul is clean-shaven, but his long face has a slightly guarded look as if he's waiting and watching, which I have learned he usually is. We talk about his work as an underground utility locator. His specialty is natural gas. He is proud of his reputation for finding gas lines when nobody else can. When we turn to the subject of trapping, Paul surprises me by saying that he only started when he was in his thirties because growing up, his parents forbade it. When I ask why, he shakes his head and answers sheepishly, "Well, they didn't like killing any animals."

"But you wanted to?" I ask.

"Yes," he answers. "I didn't see it the way they did."

I ask him how he felt the recent fur sale went last month. Paul thinks it went well. As usual they only just broke even, though he and his wife work mostly on a volunteer basis. They rent the hall for $400, but Shelley does the bookkeeping for a nominal fee or donates her time like Paul. After they pay for supplies and for help cleaning up after, there is not much left, but any profits are donated to the Fulton-Montgomery trapper organization.

Paul was upset because a journalist showed up and wrote an article about the sale that made it seem as if trappers were making large sums on coyote this past year due to demand from the coat company Canada Goose. "I didn't care about the article," said Paul, "but the fur buyers were upset. They said Canada Goose didn't like the publicity and they might lose those markets. Also, it exaggerated the prices. I mean, nobody is making any money at this. We do it because we love it and to keep the animal population under control."

On that note, I ask him if he ever heard about Dorothy Richards when he was growing up. What did he think of her work with beavers? I can feel Paul sizing me up, as if he knows something but is wondering if he should say it. I press him, and he finally admits, "She was kinda nutty, wasn't she? I mean, she kept beavers in her house...She kept them imprisoned. Those beavers didn't want to be there, and she wouldn't let them out!"

Paul's comment raises an unsettling thought I'd had myself; did the beavers really want to be living with Dorothy in her small farmhouse? In her memoir, she described one beaver that dug a hole through the basement and ran away. It was clear from the many photographs of Dorothy with her beavers how much some of them felt completely at ease with her. They looked happy. But were there perhaps other less cheerful accounts she had left out of her story? Dorothy's practices would most certainly not be allowed today. When I point out that she had a permit from the state to keep the beavers, Paul nods. It is not his way to disagree with anyone. When I ask if people knew about Dorothy locally, he says, "Well, sure, we all knew she was there, but no one really knew what she was doing. Living with beavers, I guess." He sighs. It is clear he isn't impressed. Paul has never read her book, but he thinks the sanctuary was a good idea, especially as it supplied trappers with beaver when the young went in search of a location to start their own lodges. He continues, "Local trappers knew of it and didn't mind it one bit. Means there's a lot of beavers coming out of there..." He pauses, then adds slowly, "The thing is...I mean, I help people out when beavers are flooding their basement...Or I help them get wildlife out of their house, if it's a skunk or something, but she, well she *wanted* beavers in her basement. And other animals too." He shakes his head. "I think it's nutty."

The first thing I see when the door of the small blue hatchback opens is a pair of long legs in khaki trousers. "Here, I brought something to show you," comes a sprightly voice. A tall man in a blue jacket with a shock of white hair emerges. Louis has a face made for smiling. But he is a man on a mission. He shakes my hand and walks quickly to the back and opens the hatch, then attempts to pull out a large piece of white foam core on which articles and photographs have been pinned. But the board is so large it snags against the sides of the car. The two of us wiggle it out and Louis stands the board on the ground. "This," he says proudly, "tells the story of my father, who snowshoed all the way home from his trap line in the Adirondacks, about twenty-three miles north, when he was only seventeen.

That was February 19, 1930. I heard you were interested in fur trapping. My father was a great outdoorsman. He was the great-grandson of Nat Foster."

"Nat Foster?" I ask. "You mean the trapper I saw articles about in the historical society?"

"Yup." Now it's my turn to grin. Is this why Jeff and Pat wanted me to meet this guy?

"Do you trap or hunt?" I ask.

"No, not at all," Louis says. "I don't like the outdoors."

We manage to stuff the display board back in the car and Louis gives me a tour of Little Falls, starting with the site of the original old canal, then we drive to lock 19, which he points out is the highest lock in the world apart from the Panama Canal. Like beavers, we have always sought to harness waterways, and the canal, with its controlled flow, is quiet. The sun comes out and the still dewy woods above the ravine light up like a flare. Birds chatter and we talk companionably. I let him guide me here and there because I am curious to see what he wants me to know about his hometown.

Louis Baum is a retired businessman who grew up in Little Falls, raised a family here, and now lives across town from his two grown sons and their families. I am grateful for the tour, and by the time our hour is up I have a sense of the layout and atmosphere of Little Falls, and I've seen the library where Dorothy Richards worked. But when I ask about Beaversprite, he has no idea who Dorothy Richards was and knows nothing about the sanctuary.

"Little Falls is a great town," Louis says cheerfully. "They even made a movie about it called *A Perfect Place*." Later I will google this movie and discover it's actually a John Krasinski horror film called *A Quiet Place*. The tour has been a delight, as has meeting Louis Baum, but I am no closer to learning anything about Dorothy Richards except the depressing fact that it seems her life's work was not considered important by the keepers of this town's history. When I look up information about Nat Foster (1766–1840), I will discover that he was a renowned pioneer trapper and hunter widely accredited with being the model for James Fenimore Cooper's character Natty Bumppo in the *Leatherstocking Tales*. In 1834, Nat Foster was also famously tried for murder after killing a Native person against whom he held a grudge, but he was acquitted.

My mood only lifts as I drive along the narrow road, bordered by scenic farm fields. I am headed toward Dolgeville, where in 1932, Dorothy and Al Richards found a run-down farmhouse by the confluence of two creeks and decided to rent it. Fifty-three years later, two scientists from the Syracuse area heard Dorothy Richards lecture and made a pilgrimage out to meet her. That meeting would change their lives.

Sharon and Owen Brown located jobs in the area, then bought land close by. They visited Richards weekly to help at Beaversprite and learn from her. When she died in 1985, they worked to ensure that her sanctuary survived and now publish a biannual newsletter, *Beaversprite*, in honor of Dorothy. A few years later, they founded Beavers: Wetlands & Wildlife, a nonprofit organization with the mission of continuing Dorothy's life's work to educate the public about beavers.

PART II: *Sanctuary*

The path leads down the hill through a stand of pine. Gradually we see water through the trees. Owen strides on ahead, carrying a white canvas bag filled with five pounds of cracked corn. The bag swings from his right shoulder. His long legs cover the ground quickly and the saplings he is pulling behind him scrape the ground. I follow, dragging my own load of poplar saplings. Sharon is behind us with another bag of corn and a handful of raspberry canes. The sun is beginning to set. We speed up, passing over several boggy areas where we walk along planks laid over the dark mud, before jumping over a narrow stream. Our goal is to get to the farthest pond and hopefully arrive in time to see the beavers that are now living there.

At the next bend, Owen is waiting. "This is our big pond," he says, pointing to the expanse of water I can now see through the trees. "It's about sixty acres now; the far pond is maybe fifteen. The beavers made both of these ponds the first years we were here." Then he strides ahead. Owen is a tall, lanky man with a grey ponytail, mustache, and short grey beard. He disappears into the trees. I wait for Sharon, who is coming along more slowly on account of an injured knee. Soon I see her, a petite woman in white cotton pants and a long-sleeved white shirt. Her long white hair is half hidden under a light brown sun hat with a low brim. When she catches up to me she smiles; she has one of the kindest faces I think I have ever seen.

"Is this your daily ritual?" I ask.

"Pretty much," she replies simply. Sharon doesn't waste words, and although she speaks quietly, her voice is clear and confident.

I offer to take the cloth bag of corn she is carrying on account of her sore knee, and she doesn't protest. I sling it over one shoulder, enjoying its comfortable weight, and we continue along the slender path. Soon it dips down into a grove of white pines, then rises up onto a level area that opens out into an expanse of water—the pond. Owen stands by the bank and throws handfuls of corn onto the ground, then he flings more handfuls into the edge of the water. Behind him, two deer emerge from the trees. I see their long brown faces, the huge brown eyes and quivering black noses. They stand calm, not yet nibbling at the corn, but curious, waiting. They are so close to Owen that he could reach out and pet them, but he ignores the deer and keeps throwing down handfuls of corn, making small piles along the bank. Behind him is a small wooden building that has been built into the bank so that it extends out over the water. A ramp leads from the shore to the door of the building, which is sided with large windows now bronzed with sun.

"That's our viewing platform," says Sharon as she walks up. "It's warm and it's great when the flies come. Or when Ben is too curious." Ben is the resident black bear, who also likes corn, although he prefers the black sunflower seeds they spread on a platform near the house for the birds in winter. I glance toward the woods, wondering if Ben might be curious today, but Sharon says, "He hasn't been around much lately." She takes the bag from me and motions for me to follow her to the right where there is a small cove. "See the lodge?" she asks when we are standing by the water. I can't miss it. Off in the distance, where the pond curves to the right, a gorgeous wigwam of sticks rises up from the water. It looks like something from a beaver fairy tale; the symmetrical lodge is a good ten feet high, the sides formed from a latticework of saplings and sticks from which the bark has been stripped clean.

Sharon starts throwing handfuls of corn into the water. "Just beyond

that is the first dam," she explains, "then there is another farther back." I
see the deer, moving closer now, nibbling at the corn, but mostly watching.
Then, in a rush of wings and a great splash of water, Canada geese land on
the water near the beaver lodge and start swimming toward us.

"Shall I call them?" asks Owen, whose bag is now empty. Sharon says yes.
Before I know it, Owen has cupped his hands around his mouth and his
strong voice is echoing over the water. "All right!" He pauses. "All right!"

"This is how Dorothy always called the beavers," explains Sharon. It is
clear from the tone of her voice that this is their homage to the woman who
inspired them to dedicate their lives to protecting beavers.

Owen's voice carries over the water, then it is still. We wait.

"Do they always come at this time?" I ask. I am suddenly so excited by
the tension of waiting, I feel almost giddy. I've been reading about beavers,
and talking to people about beavers, and thinking about beavers, and last
month I had my fill of seeing beaver pelts at the spring fur sale, but it had
been a long time since I'd seen a beaver even swimming in the distance
across our pond.

"Usually," says Sharon simply, "but we didn't come last night, because
of the rain, and it's been stormy, so they might not." We stand together in
the evening light, feeling the coolness descend, listening and waiting. Then
Owen's voice breaks the silence: "Here they come!"

And they do come, first a squadron of brown noses that break the water
into that telltale, rippling V. They move toward us like a chevron of geese in
formation, swimming steadily, then when they are about ten feet from the
bank they dive down and disappear. Sharon moves back toward the house,
but I stay where I am near the bank, and it isn't long before a beaver shows
up, first a brown hump, then, like some kind of jack-in-the-box, a head
pops up and stares right at me. Her expression is quizzical, calm. I hold my
breath. Will she flee? She is so close I could reach out and touch her blunt
nose, but I am a stick, holding myself as still as I can. The beaver slips under
the water, then comes back up. Now she is half sitting in the shallows, her
front paws cupped as if she were a squirrel holding a nut. In those jet-black
fingers, I see bits of yellow; she has a handful of corn and now she moves it
to her face, takes a bite, moves her hands back down so she can keep looking at me, and starts to chew the corn. All I can hear, beyond the thumping

of my heart, is the gentle rustle of water, and the beaver crunching corn. She's eating steadily now, studying me all the while. The intensity of her stare is unsettling; for a moment I wonder if she is going to leap out of the water and rush at me. But this is not the hard stare of a predator after prey, nor is it the alarmed look of a nervous herd animal; this is the stare of a beaver that is, in this moment, completely at ease.

Soon there is a brown undulation and a second beaver pushes its head out of the water. Now two beavers are eating corn. This beaver, slimmer and darker than the others, looks away, glances at me with a nervous expression, glances back, then swivels her neck to look all around, watchful. In contrast, the first beaver continues to have no qualms. She cups a handful of corn in her hands, takes a bite, then quickly looks back up at me, chewing, staring right at me. She is so close I can hear the swish of water when she thrusts her hands down to find some more. I wonder what I am to her: a shadow, or a new shape? She can smell me better than she can see me, so perhaps it is all those odors that intrigue her: Little Falls, my car, the café, maybe the bag of almonds I ate on my way here.

More beavers surface; the water is now moving with the shapes of many slick brown bodies. Whales swim in pods, wolves travel in packs, crows descend in a murder, while owls form a parliament, but there is no word for groups of beaver because they are rarely seen together like this. The beavers dive down for corn and surface, often bumping into one another in the process, and they have begun to talk, a stream of chirping, mewling sounds. A few Canada geese are swimming by them, also dipping their beaks down into the water to find corn, but the beavers ignore them. Dorothy Richards remarked that she observed beavers to be very affectionate, and to spend a lot of time grooming one another with their small black hands. Archie Belaney (a.k.a. Grey Owl) described Jelly Roll, the beaver who kept him company in a small cabin as he wrote his book *Pilgrims of the Wild*, as often staring up at him like a fat little Buddha. But the beavers here today are as winsome and busy as elves; they reach their dexterous black hands under the water for corn, then bring the corn up to their mouths, or dive under and around one another, as if in play. Herb Sobanski and most fur trappers I met looked at the fur of beavers they trapped and, seeing bite marks and nicks, emphasized how territorial and aggressive beavers were.

But within this beaver lodge, which I'll learn, houses three generations of one beaver family, there seems to be no fighting over food.

Suddenly a Canada goose begins swimming fast toward the beavers, neck extended snakelike, hissing, clearly ready for a fight. There is a great honking and flapping of wings as the other geese are driven away. The beavers dive down quickly, black tails flipping up like rudders. But soon enough they resurface, and the goose swims off looking for other geese to fight. The beavers are back up now, with more handfuls of corn, or they have begun to nibble on the leaves of poplar and raspberry cane, and bits of apple that Owen also flung into the water at the edge of the pond. A sharp whistle breaks the stillness.

"Here come the wood ducks," says Owen. Soon a pair of wood ducks have landed, their colorful heads alert as they swim over. The deer, meanwhile, have moved close to the water and now nibble bits of corn. I feel as if I am standing in a scene from a nature movie, but the entire cast has not yet arrived. Owen points across the pond to a brown shape swimming toward us. "I think the muskrat is going to join us today," he says and chuckles. Both he and Sharon clearly love this.

"You can tell it's a muskrat because they swim a bit slower," says Sharon explaining, "There are binoculars in the house. Let's go inside."

But I can't move a muscle, even when the mayflies begin to hover and sting. The sky goes neon. The water is a purple bruise. I am locked to this spot, almost afraid to breathe. All these weeks and months I have missed the sight of beavers by our house, and even when I did not see them, the question—would they appear?—would arise, and now here I am, closer to a live beaver than I ever have been before, and when I stare at her, she stares back. What is it about her face that seems so familiar? And it hits me: I've seen this look of trust and curiosity before. I am hurtling back in time; I am waist deep in the pond, and Coda, my old dog, is swimming on the far side, too far, I think, and when I call her she veers around right toward me, and I am back to that moment, staring at her retriever face, beaming love.

A mosquito drills into my cheek, then another. Still I do not move. Then finally, a sudden itch burns my cheek so badly I can't help myself and give it a slap. The beaver dives at the noise and the spell is broken. Coda had died last summer, but for fourteen years she had been my ambassador to the world of animals. She was the first to see the beavers and led me to so many other discoveries as we roamed the woods. What is it about interspecies connection that enables us to feel that our world has suddenly expanded to something so much larger than what we could know on our own? My eyes sting and I feel slightly stunned as I turn away from the beavers and walk over to catch up with Sharon and Owen, who are already in the house.

Why do we love some animals and dislike others? For an animal behaviorist like Hal Herzog, who wrote the classic *Some We Love, Some We Hate, Some We Eat*, the reason is clear; we like animals that resemble human babies, with large heads, prominent ears, and big eyes. That makes sense; as primates, sight is our most highly developed sense, and the eyes reveal emotion, which you need to understand if you live within a complex social order. Herzog goes further in developing a diagram that has to do with need. We also like animals that have use to us and don't like animals for which we have no use. Then there is the issue of legs. We are fussy about legs. We don't like animals with too many legs, like centipedes, but we also don't like animals with no legs at all, like snakes. We tend to like animals that we can relate to, so when a beaver (or a dog) sits up on its two legs to look at us, we feel a rush of connection. Of course, there are exceptions.

In his bizarre documentary *Fast, Cheap & Out of Control*, Errol Morris profiles four people so good in their field they approach the level of genius. One of them is a man who has spent his life researching naked mole rats that live in East Africa. This man adores naked mole rats. He doesn't seem to notice that they are the most awful-looking animals you could imagine, with long hairless pink bodies, short legs, and pointed heads that end in curved white teeth that stick out like tusks. He calls them by their nickname, sand puppies. When this researcher talks about naked mole rats, cupping one in his hands, his voice grows wondrous with admiration, and it is clear that he finds the wizened creature now biting his finger to be endlessly fascinating. His eyes gleam when he speaks about the ways they are mammals that live like insects. They organize themselves underground into huge colonies similar to bees with one queen and castes of workers organized into jobs like soldier, tunneler, and forager. Only the queen reproduces, and when the colony lacks food they kill older mole rats to ensure food for the young. The more I learned about these sand puppies the more I was sure

I'd run if one came near me. On the other hand, now that I have seen the beavers up close and listened to them—and one beaver in particular seems to have stared right into my soul—I can barely drag myself away. I think of how Dorothy Richards, Enos Mills, and Archie Belaney insisted that certain beavers were their friends.

Sharon and Owen are trained in wildlife rehabilitation and seem to maintain a bit more distance. Once she is inside, Sharon sits down to start making notes in the book she keeps there. Owen sits in a wooden folding chair by the far window and scans the perimeter of the pond with the binoculars. When I step in, Sharon points to the stool by the sliding glass window that looks out onto the other side of the pond. I take a seat and witness two, no three, no four beaver busily swimming around branches of poplar. More beaver swim out. Now I count nine.

"I was worried they might not come today," Sharon muses.

But Owen snorts, still staring through the binoculars. "Of course they would come."

Suddenly one beaver takes a branch and starts swimming away with it and another follows.

"They are taking the branches to the lodge," says Sharon simply, "probably for the kits. We had two litters last year and there are kits now." She adds that they have three lodges on the pond. "After the kits are born they seem to like to build a new lodge," she explains. The beavers will alternate between these lodges. Even if beavers are not in them for a season, the lodges will be used, for muskrat and otter and even mink have been documented living in abandoned beaver lodges.

Soon I see a beaver with reddish fur move toward the poplar branches floating in the water just off the bank, then she begins to eat. She nibbles a few leaves, then does something I have only read about. She uses her hands to grab for a few leaves, then rolls them like hot dogs and places them in her mouth. I'm astounded—there is so much deliberation to her eating, such delicacy and ordered purpose. Soon she has stripped the end of a branch and she bites off the tiny twig. Again, those magic black hands come up and she gnaws off the bark as if she is chewing a cob of corn. Once the twig is stripped, she drops it and continues on to the next. There is method to her madness. Within a few minutes the entire branch is stripped of leaves and small end branches and all that is left is a pole. Now the beaver takes the sapling pole in hand—I can see those small black fingers under the clear water moving back and forth over the sapling, feeling it like a merchant smoothing cloth. What is she feeling for? She continues this way for a few minutes, handling the sapling as deftly as a conductor, then decides to bring it out of the water toward her face and starts gnawing. The soft sound of beaver teeth razing bark now joins the other noises.

"See that large one with the slit on her tail?" says Sharon, and points to a beaver whose tail has such a large nick in one side—it resembles a large arrowhead. "That's the mother. The smaller ones are the yearlings, they are helping care for the new kits."

I learn that they call her Reba, after the singer Reba McEntire.

Sun glints through the trees. After what seems like a month of rain, the world has turned pearl. We listen to the sounds of birds in the trees, the gentle rippling of the water when the beavers dive, and the occasional hiss of geese. Suddenly a beaver flaps its tail and dives close to the bank.

"What was that about?" I ask.

"Not sure," says Sharon. "They didn't like something."

Now we see small shapes in the water. The kits have arrived, adorable as kittens, and about the same size with their small alert heads and miniature flat tails. Each swims bright-eyed toward the other beavers, then bobs around. They have only recently learned to dive, and don't try going under the water for corn. They look at us curiously, but keep their distance. Soon the three kits are bobbing around the three yearlings that are trying to get some of the poplar leaves. A blackbird flits over, but the kits keep on mewling and bumping into the yearlings, then diving under them. The timbre and pattern of soft cries sounds remarkably similar to sounds made by human newborns. But these kits are little scamps, for one attempts to dive under a yearling but only gets a little way under before thumping into her side, chirping merrily, then the kit starts pulling at the leaves the yearling is chewing. The yearling is patient and ignores the kit, but now the kit is making a game of swimming into the other yearlings and bumping them while they try to eat. The babysitters have had enough—one grabs a branch of poplar in her mouth and starts swimming back toward the lodge. As if on cue, the other yearlings do the same. The three kits immediately follow them. I watch the ensuing parade: big beaver, big beaver, then little beaver, little beaver, little beaver, with the third yearling bringing up the rear. That one pulls along a branch of poplar.

On the periphery, five geese silently swim, hovering like big white blimps, or sentries. When the beaver parade approaches them, they glide away, then circle. Meanwhile, the older beavers, Reba and presumably her mate, keep feeding by the bank and completely ignoring the departure of their kits. The scene is so peaceful, comic, and heartbreakingly beautiful.

Shadows begin to fall across the woods and the peepers start up, that sonic marker of New England spring. At first we hear just a few lone calls, a shrill twist of sound here then there, but soon it is as if lights are flicking on through the woods, and the trilling of tiny woodland frogs is everywhere. I glance at my watch. 6:50 p.m. Finally, Sharon says, "Shall we go?" and Owen answers with an emphatic, "Yes, I'm hungry." We walk back to their house through the trees, hurrying against the fading light. The deer follow us for a while, then disappear.

In her memoir, Dorothy had described their joy one June day when they first saw the small farmhouse located at the confluence of two creeks. It was 1932 and Dorothy and Al had recently returned home to Little Falls to live with Dorothy's family after Al lost his job with a lumber company. Like many Americans then, Al and Dorothy were struggling to put a new life together in the wake of the Great Depression. Dorothy wanted to find a place in the country; ever since her bout with childhood tuberculosis, doctors had prescribed fresh air. Al and Dorothy had heard about an abandoned house on the confluence of the Little Sprite and Middle Sprite creeks, and one June day they put their two Boston terriers, Bugsy and Goldie, in the car and drove out to look. The minute she saw the spot, Dorothy loved everything about it—the swaybacked roof, the rotted beams, the way jewelweed and ferns were growing up all around it, and most of all, the way the house perched on the wide island formed by the creeks on either side. Al wasn't nearly as enamored, but the rent was only $4 a month and Dorothy insisted. Better still, it was only eight miles from Little Falls, so they could go back and forth easily. There were no beavers yet, just the quiet of the woods and the sound of the creeks slipping by, rushing down toward the Sprite River, then on to Canada Creek and the Mohawk River, and eventually the mighty Hudson. Dorothy knew immediately that it was where she wanted to be.

The first night they could not sleep on account of the bedbugs, but Dorothy was completely in love with the spot, and when she inherited some money from her mother the following spring, she bought the place plus one hundred acres. There were no beavers in her woods yet because beavers had not yet returned to the southern Adirondacks. When Dorothy was growing up in Little Falls, beavers were gone; by 1890 there was only one known colony still living in the state, near Saranac Lake. In 1904, the state brought in fourteen beavers transported from Yellowstone Park and distributed them throughout the Adirondack Park, and by 1932 this beaver restoration effort had resulted in a growing population.

Dorothy would discover beavers by chance as a result of this beaver restoration program. In 1935, three years after they moved in, some of Al's friends from the state conservation department called to say that they were looking for a good location to release two beavers. Al and Dorothy said yes. That September, two men arrived, each carrying a burlap bag with a beaver inside. They hiked back through the woods up along the Little Sprite where the creek was slower and thus better suited for beavers than the fast-running water near the house. Dorothy remembers the beavers stepping out, shaking their fur, and slipping into the water. She didn't think much about them until two months later when she and Al hiked back to check on them. In her book she describes her amazement at the transformation of the creek into a stunning woodland pond. The beavers had built a dam, and a small lodge.

That winter Dorothy and Al worried that the beavers might starve because they had not had time to collect a feed pile. They began to tromp down through the snow to visit the beaver pond, leaving apples and branches of poplar by the lodge. As much as she could, given the snow, Dorothy made it part of her day to spend time at the pond hoping the beavers would appear. The food disappeared. By summer, the beavers began showing up when Dorothy was there and grew comfortable enough with her presence to start eating the food she had brought in front of her, then eventually to take food from her hand. They named the beavers Samson and Delilah.

For the next two years, Dorothy went to work at their stationery store, then spent all the evenings she could taking carrots and apples to the beavers and sitting with them. In her memoir, she mentions that she had struck a deal with Al: She would play cards with him once a week in Little Falls, but in return he would help her with the beavers. She recounts the way Delilah in particular formed a bond with her, often bringing her kits to Dorothy each spring to show them off. My favorite photographs of her from this time show her sitting on the banks of the pond with a row of beavers lined up along her outstretched legs. The beavers sit on their haunches like a row of pet Pekinese, each of them clearly so pleased with where they are and the bite of apple grasped in their front paws. Dorothy looks right into the camera and beams. In another photograph she sits in the flat-bottomed boat she used to explore the pond, her companion a curious beaver who has come along and peers over one side. Looking at the many photographs of Dorothy with the beavers surrounding her, it is hard to remember that they were wild animals that she had befriended.

Then one early March day, Dorothy and Al were braving the wind to visit the beaver pond when a dramatic event happened. As soon as they reached the pond they saw that the top of the beaver lodge was caved in. Then they looked at the water surging around the lodge and saw what looked like a piece of driftwood. The wood kept breaking the surface in the same place, then disappearing, only to surge back up again. Then they realized what the flotsam was—the bit of brown wood was a beaver's nose! One of the beavers was being held by something below, swimming up only to get its nose through the water and take a breath before it was pulled back down. Without hesitating, Al tore off his coat and plunged into the current. Soon the water was swirling around his hips, then his chest. Near the beaver he plunged his arms down into the water and heaved up a log to which a steel trap was attached, and in the trap was a beaver. Al managed to get both the beaver, still attached to the log and the trap, to shore. They recognized the beaver as Delilah. As soon as Al released the trap, she fell over unconscious. Al still had to get her across the creek. Taking the fifty-pound beaver in his arms, he waded into the swirling water. At one point it was completely over his head, and Dorothy remembers screaming, "Go back, go back!" because Al could not swim. Somehow, Al found his footing and made it to shore.

Dorothy wrapped the beaver in Al's coat and he rushed her back to the house. Dorothy searched for other traps, then hid in the bushes in case the trapper returned. As she recounts it, she waited by the pond with "murder in my heart."

That night, they wrapped Delilah in wool blankets, put her in an unused upstairs bedroom, and, exhausted, went to sleep, hoping she would make it through the night. About midnight, Dorothy woke to hear banging and clattering, then a crash. When she opened the door, she saw the beaver busily moving furniture. The beaver had chewed the legs off a mahogany dresser, which had crashed over, and was working on a desk. To keep an eye on the beaver and prevent more damage, Dorothy slipped into the guest bed in the room. Before she knew it, Delilah had waddled over to the bed, climbed on a nearby box, and was staring at her. "She looked deep into my eyes," wrote Dorothy, "which were on a level with hers where I lay. Her expression and manner were so gentle that I lost my initial apprehension. "

Not content to just look at Dorothy, Delilah soon decided to climb up on the bed and sit on Dorothy's chest. According to Dorothy, the beaver then explored the room. She crawled under the bed and, finding the steel springs, pushed on them so that Dorothy rose up and down as if on a trampoline. The beaver then found the new water pump lying on the ground ready for installation and began giving the pulley a push to see the wheel twirl. She busied herself dragging rugs and shoving chairs, generally rearranging the furniture in the room. Only then, her desire to modify her environment satisfied, did the beaver climb back up on to the bed and curl up next to Dorothy so that she and Dorothy lay back-to-back. Then Delilah fell asleep.

"I think it was the trapping of Lilah that motivated me to devote the rest of my life to beavers," wrote Dorothy when she recounted that dramatic event. The next year she would write, "By the time the November ice closed the pond I had been led step by step to a life I'd never dreamed of."

They returned Delilah to the pond the next day, but she didn't stay. The whole lodge clearly believed the site was too dangerous, and soon the entire family left. Dorothy recounts feeling despondent at the sight of the empty pond and the loss of her evening companions. Not long after, when Dorothy was forty-six, she became gravely ill with an abdominal infection and was carried out by stretcher to Little Falls, where she spent months in the hospital. It was during this time that she discovered the writings of the Canadian beaver champion, Archie Belaney, who called himself Grey Owl. Inspired by him, and especially by his descriptions of raising beaver kits, when Dorothy finally recovered, she wrote to the conservation department asking for permission to adopt two beaver kits and raise them in captivity for study. They agreed.

Dorothy's rationale for raising beavers in captivity was to extend her research and create opportunities to share it with the public. That April she finally roused herself from her sickbed, and made her way down to the pond. To her utter astonishment and joy, she found Delilah there with a new family of kits.

They took two of Delilah's kits from the pond and brought them indoors. There were mishaps. The first pair of kits died, but Dorothy and Al learned from their mistake, which was that very young beavers can pick up colds from humans. When they took in the next pair, they carefully wore surgical masks around the kits for the first weeks. These kits survived, and when they reproduced after a year, it was the start of generations of beavers that would fill Dorothy's house until she died. Initially they provided a swimming area for the beavers in the basement, then they built an addition with a five-by-ten-foot pool. In her memoir Dorothy describes the increasing amount of time she spent with the beavers. "That winter I spent most of my time in the cellar, practically being another beaver. I helped them build, wrestled with them, talked with them and was accepted as one of them."

One of Dorothy's great influences was the writer Archie, a.k.a. Grey Owl, whom she had read intently when she had been bedridden for ten months. Born in 1888, Archie was a man who was but wasn't. Always perfectly dressed in handmade buckskin clothing, his dark brown hair dyed black and braided in two plaits, he looked the part of the role he meant to perform—an Indigenous person fresh from the Canadian wilderness. With his handsome chiseled face, framed by a headband and a few eagle feathers, he fulfilled audience expectations for the noble Native person who through his life experience and cultural history has the authority to speak for the wilderness. And while, looking back, it is hard not to wince at such an overt performance of the trope of the "noble savage" (which has a long history in Western culture), or to forgive his shameless appropriation of Native American ethnicity, the irony was that this new identity enabled Archie to reach a far larger audience than if he had attempted to speak and write on behalf of the wilderness as an Englishman. In many ways, Grey Owl was a fiction that gave authenticity to his very real cause.

Archie Belaney was not the first to appropriate Native American ethnicity. While Archie was in Canada, Chief Buffalo Child Long Lance was creating a sensation with his public appearances in Buffalo Bill's Wild West Show. Only after his death was it discovered that Long Lance had been born as Sylvester Clark in North Carolina and was not a Sioux chief but rather a biracial man with brains and determination. Unlike Grey Owl, who used his Native American platform to promote conservation, Long Lance adopted this ethnicity to escape racism, for given the 1 percent rule of the Jim Crow South, he would have been classified a Black man. Long Lance also made a lot of money as Chief Buffalo in his own right.

The more I read about Archie's past, the more I felt as if I was opening a set of Russian dolls. Photos of Archie from Hastings, England, depict a respectable middle-class British schoolboy; his hair is slicked back and his purebred collie stands at attention by his side. But Archie was living with his elderly aunts back then, and while he looked respectable, his father had been a drunk and a philanderer and his mother a hapless child bride. They had abandoned young Archie when he was a baby. The dog wasn't even his; it belonged to his aunt, who raised collies. There was a family history of philandering men that went back generations. It wasn't hard to see why young Archie, smart and desperately lonely, would have spent much of his childhood and teenage years reading about the American West, or that by the time he was sixteen he felt the way forward was to board a steamer for Canada and never look back. Or why, once he arrived, he would reinvent himself. He worshipped the Indigenous cultures of North America, and no one knew him, so when he took up living with a group of Ojibwa, he began to adopt this culture for his own.

It was impossible to excuse the lies and the complicated sense of privilege involved in appropriating Native ethnicity as a white man from England, but the more I learned about Archie, the more it seemed he was deeply troubled. But Dorothy did not know the truth of his identity when she first read *Pilgrims of the Wild*, and his writing so inspired her that she had risen from her sickbed.

Dorothy must have loved escaping into the thrilling rhythms of his adventure tale set in the Canadian wilderness. Archie's book weaves a romantic tale of adventure, and the central drama is the conversion of a wilderness trapper to a beaver advocate. When Archie traps and kills a beaver, he and his Ojibwa wife, Anahareo, hear the baby kits in the lodge crying. Anahareo insists that they must raise the beavers for they have killed the mother. Archie objects, but Anahareo is adamant and they bring the beavers into their cabin, feeding the young kits by dipping slender twigs in condensed milk, and later by spooning them porridge. Inevitably the beaver kits would end up snuggling into their shirts, and Archie was soon amazed by their cries, which he described as sounding like human infants. In the following chapters, Archie regales the reader with lively descriptions of their lives, now filled with the antics of two growing beavers, whom they named McGinty and McGinnis. He writes of being in constant amazement at the beavers, which he had previously only known through his trap lines. "These beasts had feelings and could express them very well; they could talk, they had affection, they knew what it was to be lonely—why they were little people!"

Archie would go on to write and publish prolifically for a number of years under the name Grey Owl. Interestingly, his conservation message blended wilderness preservation with what could be called the "wise use" practices that Theodore Roosevelt had promoted. Like Roosevelt, what he abhorred was the overexploitation of those resources through greed. He would write, "I do not think hunting should by any means be abolished, but that...the methods used in trapping should be less cruel & that the Wild Life should not be made a burnt offering on the altar of the God of Mammon." Ever since the near death of Delilah, Dorothy had become rigorously opposed to any trapping, and I wonder if it had been reading the descriptions of Archie's months in the cabin with a new beaver kit he named Jelly Roll that gave her the idea of writing to request permission to raise some beaver kits in her house. She wrote in her memoir, "Every word he had written increased my desire to know more."

Born on two different continents, eight years apart and separated by a deep gender divide, on the face of it, Archie Belaney and Dorothy could not have been more different. Placed side by side, the trajectories of their lives seemed to move in opposite directions, except that in the end, both were dedicated to wildlife conservation and beavers. In many ways, Dorothy can be considered a part of Archie's conservation legacy.

Next morning, we are up early. Owen has already downed three cups of coffee, and he is ready to go. All he needs is a lab coat and he could pose for the mad scientist, which he sort of is, given his years studying and teaching chemistry. Sharon is his opposite, as quiet and watchful as a little brown wren. We jump in the car and soon we have arrived. Before me is Beaversprite.

As soon as we step out I hear the two small streams named Little Sprite and Middle Sprite that Dorothy had described in her book. The house has weeds growing up along the sides, giving it a bedraggled look. In one area they reach the bottoms of the windows. The place that Dorothy had kept as an outside pond by the house has dried up and is also full of weeds. Dorothy had come up with the name Beaversprite from the names of the two creeks. The site with the two creeks and the woods beyond is so idyllic, I can see why Dorothy fell in love with it and wanted to move right in.

I peer in through the window and my first thought is that I am looking at a shrine—there is Dorothy's high-backed armchair and the small table where she had lunch with Eager. Through the doorway is the small kitchen and the stairs that lead to the upstairs bedroom where Delilah had raised a rumpus then slept by her side. If I am on a pilgrimage then this is my axis mundi, but the only revelation I have is my second thought, which is that the house seems so small—how in the world did Dorothy live there with fourteen beavers? I remember Paul's comment about his sense that the beavers had been imprisoned here, but despite this unnatural environment, they had thrived. Eager lived for nineteen years, and many of the other beavers lived equally long lives. In the wild, beaver life span averages only ten years. I think Dorothy would have documented being bitten or attacked by a frustrated beaver if it had happened. And Sharon and Owen, who spent more time with her than probably anyone else, never observed signs of beaver aggression. But the fact that Dorothy was observing beavers not in the wild but in a house puts a question mark on the scientific value of some of her observations. Clearly, when beavers live in a human environment, they adapt. Hunk was so attached to Dorothy that he slept in her bed a good deal of the time. Eager, like a good kit mirroring her parent, tried to copy what Dorothy was doing in the kitchen when she cooked, and followed her everywhere.

I stare at the high-backed armchair where Dorothy was often photographed with beavers in her lap, or standing up on two legs on a stool by her chair, paws resting on her knees like a child as they waited for her to fish out an apple. She kept a wooden bowl of popcorn near her to use as beaver treats. By the chair is a small wooden drum given to her by a man who was half Iroquois and visited often. Owen had recounted how the place was often a joyful pandemonium, with beavers teasing Dorothy by pulling at her rugs and pulling the furniture about to get her attention. Dorothy was clearly close to them, for when Eager died she called Sharon in despair in the middle of the night.

"It's sad to come back here," Sharon murmurs after we have been at the house awhile. I ask if we can walk to the place along the creek where the first two beavers had been released. We set out walking down the road, but soon we aren't sure of the path. Sharon explains that since the land trust took over following Dorothy's death, they hadn't come back much. We pass an area being quarried on the left and signs of logging. Sharon looks glum. There have been problems with the land trust, and they hope that the new stewards, the Utica Zoo, will take better care of the property.

We try to set off down into the woods, but the path is overgrown. I had wanted to see the beaver pond Dorothy had sat beside day after day. I had hoped it might even be once again full of beavers. But Sharon and Owen look so depressed, I don't have the heart to insist. We turn and head back to Dorothy's house. In the front yard is an empty bird feeder, the top tilted like a windmill. Owen walks over and adjusts the top so it is level, then we all get in the car and head out.

Dorothy published her memoir at the age of eighty-three. She had struggled with writing it and only accomplished the task with the help of her friend the wildlife illustrator Hope Sawyer Buyukmihci, who had visited Dorothy years earlier and been so inspired that she had returned to New Jersey to found her own wildlife sanctuary. But Beaversprite would become part of a continuum of books about beavers written by self-taught nineteenth- and twentieth-century American naturalists. Not since Lewis Henry Morgan or Enos Mills had someone studied beavers so intently over such a sustained period of time. Dorothy would share the insights she learned through lectures, and she opened her home to visitors. Word spread and people contacted her to arrange a visit or just showed up for the daily nine-to-five visiting hours. Sharon, who has taken on the role of Beaversprite archivist, estimates that over the years one hundred thousand people visited.

Since taking up the mantle of Dorothy's work, Sharon and Owen have been at the forefront of a growing number of beaver enthusiasts who now call themselves "beaver believers." Members of this group are citizen scientists, environmental consultants, engineers, and researchers. They work for the Forest Service, or for the National Oceanographic and Atmospheric Association (NOAA), or for state fishery and wildlife departments. They are college professors in geomorphology and wildlife biology. Their common goal is to educate the public about the ways beavers can help address environmental problems, particularly those accelerated by climate change—wildfires, diminishing biodiversity, drought, and flooding. Since the 1990s, beaver believers have been gathering in southern Oregon at a biannual conference called State of the Beaver but generally received little attention. Then in 2018, Ben Goldfarb, an environmental journalist, published *Eager: The Surprising, Secret Life of Beavers and Why They Matter*, which took readers through a fantastic overview of beaver believer projects throughout the country. The following year, filmmaker Sarah Koenigsberg released her engaging documentary about the movement titled *The Beaver Believers*, which featured beaver-inspired projects in Oregon, Washington, Colorado, and California.

"Beavers are hope," commented Koenigsberg when I called her one day to ask about her work. "We are watching the West burn and the East Coast float away. Climate change is here. We can either moan and groan or make things better." Both Koenigsberg and Goldfarb have joined the beaver believer movement, which now includes a number of national organizations, including Worth a Dam in California; the Beaver Coalition in Portland, Oregon; and the Beaver Institute, headed up by Mike Callahan, here in New England.

Initially, the West Coast led beaver restoration efforts, but more recently, environmental restoration projects making use of beavers have been on the rise here on the East Coast and in the Midwest. One of the most ambitious is being developed in Milwaukee by Bob Boucher, who founded the Milwaukee River Keepers in 1996. In the nine hundred square miles that comprise the Milwaukee River watershed, Boucher and fellow researchers found that the habitat could support an estimated 4,563 beavers. The plan would be to release beavers into the best habitat of the upper reaches of the river's tributary system, where they could build ponds and wetlands. It would take about twenty-five years for the beaver population to recover, but their dam building architecture could store 1.7 billion gallons of water annually. This storm water storage is valued at 3.3 billion dollars by the Milwaukee Metropolitan Sewage Department.

Boucher's plan for the Milwaukee watershed is outlined in a 2021 study titled *Hydrological Impact of Beaver Habitat Restoration in the Milwaukee River Watershed*. The thick study is comprehensive—including extensive data collection, hands-on field work, and storm modeling—and took nine months to complete. Boucher worked with two scientists from the University of Wisconsin—Qian Liao, who is a civil engineer and hydrologist, and Changshan Wu, the chair of the geography department—and contributors from various environmental groups as well as the Milwaukee Municipal Sewage Department, which helped provide funding. The researchers modeled the hydrology effect that fifty-two beaver dams would have on the peak flood levels. The results are significant, with reduced peak flood levels of 37 percent in Milwaukee. Their findings outline that beavers can create water storage at least 100 times cheaper than an engineering project. Additionally, the Milwaukee watershed contains 961 bridges and 1,027 culverts; by lowering peak flows and thus lowering intense flood pressure, Boucher estimates that this project would extend their life span by 20 percent, saving additional millions in repair and construction costs.

"When you have a hurricane," says Boucher, "you build shutters to keep the windows from flying off. In our current climate, putting beavers in the landscape is like putting more two-by-fours in your roof: It is storm prevention, and it is also water cleansing and increased biodiversity. Most of all, you have to remember that each of those wetlands functions like a storm water detention pond." His analogy of storm shutters resonates. You put shutters on before a storm to keep the windows from blowing out; you put beavers in the landscape before a storm because their wetlands serve as huge sponges to absorb floodwater.

Boucher's plan draws on research conducted by Glynnis Hood and others. Hood, a wildlife biologist at the University of Alberta in Canada who studies aquatic mammals, summed up her research in her 2011 book, *The Beaver Manifesto*. In it she identified the many ways that beavers could be put to work as "water superheroes." By examining aerial footage of wetlands in the boreal region of east-central Alberta from 1948 to 2002, she identified that beavers increased the amount of open water by ninefold in times of drought.

If she were alive today, Dorothy Richards would be thrilled to learn of Hood's research and restoration projects like Boucher's vision for the Milwaukee watershed. She also made an impact on one of the country's leading naturalists and wildlife photographers of the time, Edwin Way Teale. Teale had visited Dorothy in 1943 out of curiosity, but was so influenced by her work, he went on to befriend the beavers that came to his own woods. Although I don't know it yet, one fall day I will find myself standing at the edge of Teale's pond while a crew attempts to install a pond leveler and enable Teale's beaver colony to remain.

Chapter 7

Lewis Henry Morgan and the Great Beaver Dam

They were bushwhacking through a boreal forest, spruce and hemlock and maple and aspen giving way to a wide canopy of pine, then to the twisted shapes of tamarack. At the front, a line of men cleared the underbrush with great swipes of their machetes, the rest following in single file. They made good time despite their heavy loads of provisions, tools, tents, theodolite and stadia measuring rods, and boxes of fragile photographic equipment. The ground underfoot was rocky glacial drift and outwash, slow going, but mercifully dry under their thin boots even in the mist and slight rain. Best of all, unlike the previous weeks, when they had fought a miasma of biting deer flies and mosquitoes, the Michigan forest that morning was cool and without pestilence.

They had left the mining town of Marquette the day before and camped their first night at the Lake Superior dam, the last stop for the fledgling Marquette and Ontonagon train line. The men were well rested and in good spirits. The sun was still an orange orb rising up from the far rim of the lake to the east. Soon it would hit the cliffs of Precambrian metamorphic bedrock that rose up along the shoreline, lighting up the massive boulders and outcroppings. Eons earlier, tectonic forces had shifted the continental plates, grinding them into one another with such incremental force that rock from earth's deepest core had been thrust upward, forming the fantastic cliffs and outcroppings that ringed the shoreline. On that October morning, the wind was unusually calm and the vast surface of Lake Superior was a sheet of glass, glazed dizzying shades of blue.

It was Wednesday, October 1, 1862, and Lewis Henry Morgan—America's first anthropologist and Iroquois specialist, an acclaimed social theorist, a railroad lawyer, and an industrialist—was on a mission. He was determined to photograph what he had called "one of the most perfect and artistically formed structures in the Lake Superior region"—a beaver dam. For the past seven years, since his first visit to Marquette in 1855, studying beavers and in particular documenting their dams, lodges, canals, and ponds, which he collectively called "beaver works," had been Morgan's burning passion.

Morgan was determined to photograph what he considered the finest beaver dam he had yet encountered. He had learned of it from Captain Daniel Wilson, an experienced fur trapper who along with two local Ojibwa trappers had been providing Morgan with a great deal of firsthand information about beavers in the Lake Superior region. Earlier in the summer, Morgan had made a quick trek out to the site with Captain Wilson and together they had spread a tape measure along the dam, measuring it at over 488 feet—almost one-tenth of a mile. Morgan had marveled at its pristine condition and perfectly formed walls of interlaced sticks. He was eager to photograph it before the railroad extended its line any farther; it was the practice of railroad engineers to break the dams and drive the beavers out. Much of the railroad track had been laid down in beaver meadow, low-lying areas of flat land that beavers had cleared of trees and built dams to flood, then abandoned so that the pond receded into swamp and finally particularly fine meadows where field grasses grew thick and fast.

The question of how beaver colonies sustained huge dam networks for decades, even for as long as a century, burned with special importance for Morgan. Beavers, classified as "horrendous morsus" due to their ever-growing incisors, were rodents, the fifth-lowest order of Mammalia according to Georges Cuvier's classification of living creatures in his iconic *Animal Kingdom*. Beavers might be the largest rodent in North America, but their brain-to-body-weight ratio is extremely low.

Beavers are the only animals apart from man that radically transform their environment. They build their dams across the narrowest points in a small river or stream, and if they are trying to dam an existing pond, they always locate a pinch point, where the water is easiest to cut off. Similarly, when beavers dig canals to connect one pond to another, or to create waterways on which to float wood back to the pond from areas where they are harvesting it deep in the woods, they exhibit geospatial understanding: They dig these canals at the shortest distance between the two ponds. The ability to chew, carry wood, and respond to the sound of running water by building a wall of mud and sticks may be instinctual, but beavers seem to exhibit levels of what Morgan and others assumed was "reasoning," if not intelligence, in the decisions they made.

Morgan hoped to understand whether beavers could reason. And he was fueled by a sense of urgency, for he knew his time to document historic beaver dams and ponds was limited before human activity in the Marquette area, specifically the mining industry, destroyed them. When Morgan began his study, the railroad connected only the three principal iron locations. Morgan's party could take a train to the Lake Superior mine station, twenty-three miles from Marquette, but then had to hike in the remaining six miles to the dam. By 1865, at a cost of $1.5 million, the line would reach all the way to Lake Michigamme, many miles to the west.

As a railroad lawyer working in Rochester, New York, Morgan had heard of the new speculation in iron ore mining in Michigan. In 1843, a two-ton copper Ontonagon boulder had been delivered to Detroit, and two years later the first mine opened in Negaunee just west of the city of Marquette. So began an industrial triangle that would eventually link Marquette with Detroit and Cleveland, Ohio, then eastern Pennsylvania. Mines in the Upper Peninsula produced one of the nation's chief sources of iron. Of the three great UP iron ranges, the Gogebic, the Menominee, and the Marquette, the Marquette range was the first to be discovered. Morgan soon became an investor.

Studying beavers had not been on Morgan's agenda when he first visited Marquette; he discovered them quite by accident. Back in Rochester he had become friends with Samuel Ely, whose family had recently founded the Marquette and Ontonagon railroad line. Morgan became an investor and later a member of the board of directors. In 1855, when Marquette was still a two-street town with one church, Morgan went to visit. Soon after his arrival, Samuel Ely arranged a trout fishing trip for Morgan, an avid fly fisherman. What would amaze Morgan, however, was not the plentiful trout but the great beaver works he would witness along the Carp and Escanaba rivers. Everywhere they went, they had to stop often to portage across great beaver dams. Morgan stared in awe at the perfect teepee shapes of the beaver lodges, some rising twelve feet above the water, and began to wonder about the extensive engineering of beaver canals that seemed to interlace the entire woods. He came back from the trip professing to have been transformed from a "trout man to a beaver man." For the next twelve years, as soon as spring lifted the snow from the Michigan woods, he journeyed from Rochester to Marquette to spend the summer months exploring the surrounding forests; everywhere he went he found an ecosystem shaped by beavers.

Lewis Henry Morgan would join the line of great American thinkers, politicians, and intellectuals such as Benjamin Franklin, Thomas Jefferson, and Henry David Thoreau, who had no formal scientific training but who nonetheless conducted rigorous studies of the natural world. Before he was a naturalist observing beavers, Morgan was an ethnographer, conducting studies and writing papers that earned him the title of America's first anthropologist. He was fascinated by the Iroquois Nation of central New York, studying their culture and language with a ferocious dedication and publishing *The League of the Ho-De-No-Sa-Nee* in 1851. This book, the first serious ethnographic study of Iroquois culture, established Morgan's reputation as an anthropologist. (He was, however, seemingly unmoved by the plight of the Native American in nineteenth-century America, the deforestation of the East, and the near-extinction of the beaver, bear, and wolf in the region.) He was part of the business establishment in Rochester, eventually serving as a Republican state legislator. He married well, entered genteel society, and was grounded in the exceptionalism of Anglo-American culture. In 1843, he founded the ritualistic fraternal club "The Grand Order of the Iroquois," a group of white men who met regularly to don pilfered regalia and sing songs. Morgan's secret name was Skenandoah, and later he took the name Tekarihogea, which means "supreme chieftain." From his anthropological work, he proposed the concept that the earliest human domestic institutions were based on matrilineal clans, not patriarchal. He developed a unilinear theory of evolution—a social theory that traced humans from stages of hunter-gatherer to agriculture to a final level of civilization in which writing was developed. While that theory is now widely discredited as Eurocentric, he remains the only nineteenth-century American to have his anthropological work cited by the most revolutionary thinkers of his time: Darwin, Marx, and Freud.

Morgan's peers were surprised and confused by his decision to commit twelve years to studying beavers. But his resulting book, *The American Beaver: A Classic of Natural History and Ecology*, published in 1868, was the first authoritative work of its kind. Before Morgan's book appeared, beavers were often the subjects of cultural fantasy. They were part of the great news hoax of 1835, in which the *New York Sun* ran a completely fabricated series on the discovery of life on the moon. The third day of these discoveries featured lunar beavers that walked on two legs and held their children in their arms.

Keeping with a nineteenth-century emphasis on taxonomy, the book opens with a discussion of beaver anatomy. But Morgan's true interest is in studying, naming, and classifying types of beaver-made dams, ponds, canals, and lodges. With tremendous care, he identifies the types of dams he encounters: *grass bank dams, solid-bank dams, spring rill dams, high dams, low dams, lake outlet dams, dams in gorges, river bank dams*. Morgan pursued the central paradox of the beaver—its ability to conduct complex feats of engineering with little brainpower. The apparent social cooperation of beavers had propelled Western imagination for some time. In his eighteenth-century treatise *Rusticatio Mexicana*, the Mexican Jesuit humanist Rafael Landívar saw in beavers a reflection of a utopian society. In Book 6, he described their labors: "Then they fill with branches and bark the great storehouse built as a collective enterprise, and giving up sleep, they arrange the food neatly, so that their comrades may have easy access to the gathered food."

In the beaver world imagined by Landívar (no doubt influenced by Virgil's bees), "No impetuous discord ever invades their homes...But rather these tranquil citizens enjoy nurturing peace."

Morgan was not one bit interested in considering how beavers might teach us valuable lessons in social justice, but he was one of the first to recognize that they are in fact the only animals apart from man that deliberately and continually transform their environment. To conclude his book, he dedicated a chapter to animal psychology and encouraged readers to better respect the beaver and value the role they played in the landscape. While he knew of Darwin's controversial new work on evolution, he chose to ignore these ideas and summed up his thinking on beaver intelligence with a vague statement: "Each animal is endowed with a living and a thinking principle."

By midmorning, Morgan's photographic expedition was still carving a way through the final half mile of dense woods to the dam, and he was concerned that they would not arrive in time to take advantage of the good weather. He kept pushing the men to go faster, then reminding them to take care lest they damage fragile equipment. In his party that day were eleven men, two of whom were amateur photographers: Mr. Walter Kidder and Reverend Josiah Phelps, the rector of St. Peter's Church in Marquette. Morgan had invited the rector because he owned "an excellent instrument" and was adept in its use. The two men had carefully overseen the packing of photographic chemicals and instruments.

Finally, they arrived at their destination, and, Morgan was careful to record in his book, "without accident to the materials." The dam was indeed magnificent, a picture-perfect construction, as Morgan had remembered from his brief glimpse of it earlier that summer with Captain Wilson. The dam itself spread out in a beautiful half-moon shape, a sinuous crest that made up most of one side of a twenty-five-acre body of water. Along the skirts of the pond dead trees rose up sepulchral, like great forest bones, while along the banks the underbrush had been freshly cut back, stashed under the water as the beavers' winter feed pile. Morgan noted how on all sides the woods surrounding them were otherwise thick with cedar, spruce, and tamarack, and where the ground was lower, dense with aspen and willow, which beaver rely on for their nutrient-rich bark. Morgan knew immediately that he was looking at a work "resulting from the labor of many years bestowed by many successive generations of industrious beavers." The dam itself was massive, a great construction of sticks and poles "interlaced and arranged in every conceivable way." The lower face measured ten feet above the water, while the upper face measured four feet nine inches. Canals had been dug along the shoreline creating waterways that spread out like arteries throughout the woods so that the beavers could safely travel farther into the surrounding forest to harvest trees.

Morgan had found larger dams in his treks through the Lake Superior woods, but the perfection of this dam had greatly impressed him. The sticks, each carefully peeled of bark, measured from a half inch to an inch in diameter, while the poles, also stripped of bark and branches, were cut to a uniform length of two to three feet. The beavers had interlaced the sticks and poles into such a complex yet uniform construction, consistent in height and thickness, that from a distance overlapping poles seemed to create a pattern of repeating chevrons, as if the dam was a wall of woven twill.

Due to its size and the solidity of the mud foundation that had been formed in part from layers of packed mud and long-rotted sticks, Morgan figured that the dam might be over a hundred years old. One or two generations of beavers, even with five kits each spring, could never have built—or, more to the point, have maintained—such a large dam structure. Morgan had reason to be excited. He was looking at one of the last remnants of what has come to be called Beaverland, the time when the great forests of North America were still being shaped by beavers. The North American beaver we see today, *Castor canadensis*, has been part of the landscape, creating waterways and cutting down forests, since the last glaciation, some eleven thousand years ago. Because of Michigan's Upper Peninsula's reputation as an inhospitable wilderness, settlers had largely avoided it in their migrations west. Until the mid-nineteenth century and the discovery of iron ore in the region, the great boreal and northern hardwood forests had been left undisturbed. Morgan was looking at the landscape of precolonized North America.

Morgan was proud of the beaver dams he had located in the Upper Peninsula. He would later write that "their works in number and magnitude are not surpassed by those of any other beaver district in North America." But first he had to photograph them so that an engraver could make plates for his book. If readers could see beaver dams in their full glory the way he was seeing them, Morgan was convinced that they would understand the beaver's true intelligence.

Photographing the first dam required first cutting back trees for the camera's sight line, then building scaffolds upon which Morgan planned to place the camera. They had calculated that to capture as wide a section of the dam as possible, each scaffold would need to be sixty-two feet back from the edge of the dam. At that distance they could capture a fifty-foot length in each ten-inch photographic plate, meaning they would need to take seven or eight shots. Morgan's men set to work right away. By evening, in addition to making camp and setting up the dark tent to process the photographic plates, they had the first scaffold built, had cut a triangular sight line between it and the dam, and had managed to remove a band of the forest ten feet wide between the first scaffold and the next.

As the soft rain let up and rays of setting sun broke through the forest, lighting up the rain-soaked ferns, the woods filled with a brief frenzy of birdsong that abruptly stopped as soon as evening shadows set in. Morgan then recounted a great and wonderful silence. In his usually matter-of-fact account of the day's events he took a few lines to rhapsodize about the grand mystery of the scene, humans camped by a magnificent dam dating back to a time before human settlement. Beaverland.

The next morning opened clear and bright and Morgan had the men rise early. Because of the angle of the morning sun as it filled the trees, dam section two was photographed first, then they moved on to take plates of sections one and three. These plates went well and Morgan was satisfied with the images, but section four would prove so difficult that they would try four times before giving up and calling it a day. They spent the remaining hours of light continuing the chopping and clearing.

Morgan had been wise to push the men hard the first day. By ten o'clock that night the weather had clouded up and soon turned to wind and rain. Morgan went to sleep worried, and with good reason, for the next day opened with mist but soon turned to driving rain, which only let up toward evening. They were now into the fourth day of the expedition and only had the following morning to finish three more plates. It was Friday and Morgan had promised the rector that he would get him back to Marquette on Saturday night so that he could fulfill his obligations on the Sabbath.

By midnight sheets of rain gave way to thunder and lightning. Then the winds began. At daybreak, what Morgan described as "gale winds" began whipping and twisting the trees around the camp so hard that before long tamaracks began to crack, crashing down around them. Morgan had the men gather up the fragile photographic equipment and huddle in the open space by the beaver dam, figuring that at least there they would be safe from falling trees. Finally, the rain ceased, and miraculously, the wind lifted the clouds away. As soon as they perceived the emergence of sunlight, Morgan and his team set to work and in quick succession took the final three plates, all of which they managed to process successfully. To the great relief of Rector Phelps, they made it back to the station just in time for the last train back to Marquette.

In the final book, Morgan's great pride was the number of beautiful engravings and the pull-out map, which carefully listed the exact locations of sixty-four dams, each numbered and labeled along with ponds, canals, and waterways. The seven photographic plates they had worked for five days to complete were printed and placed side by side to create a photograph of the dam that measured nine inches high and thirty-six inches long. As soon as he returned, Morgan conveyed these photographs to the engraver, who began work on a stunning illustration that would become plate VII in the final book.

We are driving through what remains of the boreal forest, sun bouncing off the bright yellow leaves of aspens and maples, the tamaracks and great stands of spruce and hemlock and pine. I am following Lewis Henry Morgan's steps to see if I can find beaver pond number 19, the slim oval he had outlined so carefully in his pull-out map. Above all I am hoping that something of the magnificent beaver dam he had photographed so painstakingly might remain. If it is still there, it will be one of *the* oldest intact beaver dams in North America. If beavers are living on the pond, it could be one of the oldest continuing beaver colonies, well over two hundred years old.

My guide on this quest is Jeff Koch, a slim young man with extensive experience in the Upper Peninsula woods.

Jeff works as a field scientist at the Superior Watershed Partnership, one of the largest environmental groups in the state. He spends much of his time monitoring environmental conditions in the Lake Superior watershed, including collecting water samples from groundwater, surface water, and wastewater from the remaining mines still operating in the region, testing for heavy metals. By law the mines now have to clean heavy metals from the wastewater before releasing it back into the watershed.

Castorioides ohioensis (Giant Beaver), Minnesota Science Museum. (1a)

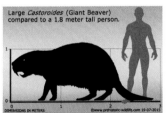

Giant Beavers roamed North America throughout the Pleistocene, which lasted 2 million years. (1b)

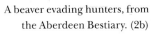

Aberdeen Bestiary, Scotland,
thirteenth century. (2a)

A beaver evading hunters, from
the Aberdeen Bestiary. (2b)

Salisbury (Harley) Bestiary, thirteenth century.
"When hunted, the beaver escapes with his life
by biting off his testicles. If he is hunted for a
second time, he shows his incompleteness and is
spared." (2c)

Manāfi'-i ḥayavān, thirteenth century, Margheh, Iran. Ibn Bakhtīshū', 'Ubāyd Allāh ibn Jibrā'īl. "Two beavers in water swimming toward hunter wearing headdress." (3)

Beaver depicted by Konrad Gesneri in *Historia Animalium* (A History of Animals), 1551. (4a)

"The Beaver" from *Hortus Sanitatis* (Garden of Health), printed by Johann Pruss in Strasbourg, 1497. *Hortus Sanitatis* was a popular encyclopedia of knowledge and folklore on plants, animals, and minerals. (4b)

Figure of a beaver from the (supposedly) earliest known engraving in Canada, dated 1685. The image was used by Horace Tassie Martin in his 1892 classic, *Castorologia*. (4c)

Portrait of Henry VIII by Hans Holbein the Younger, 1538–47. The king displays power and prestige through clothing richly adorned with furs. (5a)

Coat of Arms of the City of Oxford, as seen at the entrance to Headington Hill Park, 2005. A festive beaver with a blue-and-white checked tail and green fur stands opposite an elephant. (5b)

FORTIS EST VERITAS

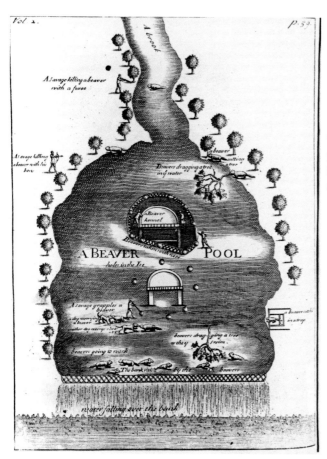

"An engraving of a beaver pond indicating the prime hunting and trapping spots," 1703. (6a)

Detail of "Beaver Hunting in Canada," an engraving in *Middleton's Complete System of Geography*, Chiedel, 1775–1825. (6b)

The Cataract of NIAGARA, some make this Water-Fall to be half a League while others reckon it no more than a hundred Fathom.

A View of ye Industry of ye Beavers of Canada in making Dams to stop ye Course of a Rivulet. in order to form a great Lake. about wch they build their Habitations. To Effect this: they fell Large Trees with their Teeth. in such a manner. as to make them come Cross ye Rivu let. to lay ye foundation of ye Dam: they make Mortar. work up. and finish ye whole with great order and wonderfull Dexterity. The Beavers have two Doors to their Lodges. one to the Water and the other to the Land side. According to ye French Accounts

Detail from Herman Moll's Map of North America, 1715. Moll imagined beavers as a line of workers near Niagara Falls. (7)

Portrait of John Jacob Astor, by Alonzo Chappel (1763–1848). Originally published in *National Portrait Gallery of Eminent Americans: Including Orators, Statesmen, Naval and Military Heroes, Jurists, Authors, Etc., Etc.,* 1862. (8a)

Engraving of a Chinese furrier, 1799. The Chinese consumed vast quantities of furs, supplied by the United States and Great Britain at Canton and by Russia via Mongolia. This image is from *The Costume of China*, by George Henry Mason, 1800. (8b)

Hudson's Bay Company beaver tokens. In the 1860s the HBC began minting brass trade tokens in denominations of one-half, one-quarter, and one-eighth "made beaver." (8c)

North American beaver (*Castor canadensis*), lithograph, c1849. John James Audubon made this painting for his famous *Viviparous Quadrupeds of North America*. (9a)

Colin Fraser, a Hudson's Bay Company trader at Fort Chipewyan, in Alberta, Canada, sorts fox, beaver, mink, and other precious furs, c1890. (9b)

Herb Sobanski Jr. on his trap line, c2017. (10a)

Laboratory assistants feed young beavers, c1950, at the Voronezh State Nature Biosphere Sanctuary and Beaver Breeding Center, founded in 1926, Russia. (10b)

Native people of the North Red River area, probably in the vicinity of old Fort Douglas, now Winnipeg, Canada, hunting beaver. "Indian Spearing Beaver," by Peter Rindisbacher, 1821. (11a)

Stacks of purchased "beaver dollars," fox, raccoon, muskrat, and other furs piling up at the April Wild Fur Sale, Herkimer, New York, 2018. (11b)

Idaho conservation officers preparing Geronimo for the beaver parachute drop, 1948. (12a)

Idaho, 1948: Two beavers on the way. (12b)

Archie (aka Grey Owl), a British-born conservationist, feeding his pet beaver, Jellyroll. (13a)

Dorothy Richards having lunch with Eager, 1950. (13b)

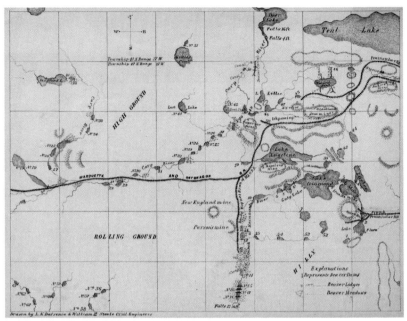

Map of beaver damming complexes included in Lewis Henry Morgan's classic *American Beaver and His Works,* 1868. (14a)

SECTION of GREAT BEAVER DAM. GRASS LAKE.

Plate VII, "Section of Great Beaver, Dam Grass Lake." This was the beaver damming complex I most hoped to locate when I traveled to the Upper Peninsula with Lewis Henry Morgan's map in hand. (14b)

Beaver damming complex in the foothills of the Rocky Mountains on Blackfeet territory in northwestern Montana, along the Canadian border, where spring floods wash out the vast majority of the dams on an annual basis. This photo is a high-resolution orthomosaic created from drone footage by Jordan Kennedy, summer 2018. (15a)

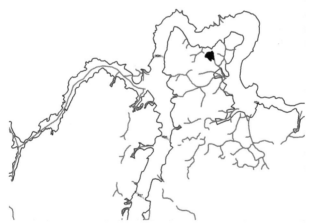

This color outline of the beaver damming complex shows the extensive canals and trails made by beavers by the end of summer. (15b)

Sharpe Wildfire, Idaho. In this wildfire in 2018, 64,000 acres were left completely charred save one area that researchers were stunned to discover had remained green because beavers were living there. This is a good example of the critical "refugia" beavers provide even during mega wildfires. (16)

I ride shotgun in a silver SUV, staring at the houses, strip malls, and stands of forest whipping past, feeling a strange kinship with Lewis Henry Morgan. If I sat across the dinner table from him, I'd no doubt be arguing with him endlessly; I couldn't forgive his nineteenth-century paternalism or the cognitive dissonance of his era that professed to love the natural world while participating in its wholesale destruction. But his passion for observing, recording, and theorizing about this weird rodent was something I could understand. The moment I retrieved the faded yellow pull-out map from his book, I felt both admiration and something close to jealousy; Morgan had been able to witness beavers living as they had in precolonial North America. Those days were long gone, but wouldn't it be fantastic if something of the landscape he had described so carefully in his book remained?

It took Morgan and his party a half day to travel to the Lake Superior mine where the M&O train line ended, then a full morning to beat through the woods to the beaver pond. We've only been on the road for thirty minutes, but already we have passed the town of Negaunee and are coming up to Ishpeming. I glance back down at the map and put my finger on the spot where Morgan had drawn the location of the dam. We are speeding west on Route 28, a road that today runs roughly parallel with the train line Morgan had followed. No doubt Morgan, who predicted in his book that Marquette would become a lively city, would get a kick out of this route today. We pass a big sign for Da Yoopers Tourist Trap, which has an enormous replica of a chain saw out front with the words "Big Gus" painted on it in blue. Already we have seen a sign advertising the iron ore museum. The magnificent Upper Peninsula forests Morgan had traversed from 1855 to 1867 now support tourism.

Morgan's dedication to the study of beavers coupled with his industrialist attitude toward resource extraction, a practice that would end up almost destroying the beaver's habitat, was a haunting paradox. Only five months before Morgan's trip, on a windy April morning in 1862, Thoreau had stood on the steps of the Congregational church in Concord to read his now famous words *In wildness is the preservation of man,* calling for Americans to stop destroying the forests before it was too late. But for most of the country, nature still seemed so abundant that progress—meaning wealth for those who could harness nature the fastest—was the ethos of the day.

Soon, the legacy of the iron ore industry becomes visible. I stare at what looks like a range of foothills, only each ridge is perfectly square as if someone had laid down a line of gigantic dominoes. "That is overburden rock from the open pit mines," Jeff says quickly, anticipating my question, and goes on to explain the open pit mining process, in which the earth's surface is literally scraped off, leaving huge basins, often as large as a mile wide and over one thousand feet deep. The tons of removed topsoil and rock—the overburden—is systematically stacked by enormous machines, thus the symmetrical line of man-made foothills. This was the control of nature on a vast scale—awe-inspiring, and environmentally tragic. When some of the mines closed in the 1960s, the open pits became huge lakes, toxic with heavy metals. They are still visible from the air, along with the enormous rust-colored waters of the tailings ponds. By the 1960s, mercury used in the mining process polluted Lake Superior to the extent that even today, over fifty years after most of the mines have closed, eating more than four fish a year from the lake is a well-publicized health risk. And the atmospheric deposition of pollutants from other sources has become a major concern.

I see wave-ruffled water to my right and the words on the next sign hit me with a jolt. *Teal Lake.* Book and geography now merge. We are driving right past one of the lakes Morgan outlined so carefully for his map, carefully naming it in his thin elegant script. I sit up, mines temporarily forgotten. "We're almost there," Jeff says and turns onto a small road. The dense forest of hemlock, spruce, and pine that Morgan described his men hacking through all morning is now a pattern of sloping manicured green, the Wanaconda golf course.

We've knocked at the house on the land adjacent to the pond, greeted by a black cloth witch tied to the front door in preparation for Halloween and a husky who began to howl from deep inside the house. Confident that he has done due diligence to contact the landowner, Jeff drives on to park on the side of the old M&O railroad line, which has been converted to a recreational trail for walkers, ATVs, and snowmobiles. Through the trees I can see an open patch of meadow, then a stretch of silver water, and on the far side of the pond, rising up from the water, grey-white spires of dead trees. Clear signs that beavers have been here, if not recently, then within the past decade. It is a good omen. I walk forward quickly and stare down at a muddy track leading from the edge of the meadow down to the water. No doubt about it, this is a beaver drag, a well-traveled path used to venture back and forth into the woods. I look along it for tracks, but the mud is strangely smooth. Then I remember the terrific rainstorm of the day before; any tracks would have washed away. I walk back to the water and study the shoreline as Herb had taught me, looking for small mounds of mud that beavers will make to mark their territory, spraying it with their distinctive beaver trademark, musky castor oil. No beaver mounds. I study the shallow water by the slide looking for small brown balls, beaver poop. Beavers only defecate in water. Still, I am amazed by the size of the trail.

Herb had shown me plenty of beaver drags and paths in the Connecticut woods, but even the heavily populated beaver ponds were not half this size. This trail looks like beavers the size of small bears have been dragging saplings and branches up and down. Jeff comes up and we walk the path back into the woods. Beavers could have made the slide some time ago; the only proof that they are still living on the pond will be to find signs of fresh cutting, saplings or bushes chewed at the base. If there is no wood available, beavers can sustain themselves on pond grass, ferns, cattails, and water lilies, but this pond is too deep for water lilies, even around the edges.

Soon we see a grouping of young birch and aspen among the conifers. Beavers don't like conifers, which are too sticky with sap, but they love birch and especially aspen with its sugar-dense bark. Sure enough, when we look down, we see a ring of chewed stubs that were once saplings. But the points are grey and weathered; months or years could have passed since the time the beavers anchored their incisors into the bark and began to chew. It is when I push through a stand of browning tamarack that I see it: a ring of chewed saplings and bushes, each end bright yellow and moist with sap. Freshly cut wood. Jeff pushes back some underbrush to reveal more cut saplings.

We both stand speechless. Morgan's nineteenth-century beaver pond seems to have survived. And even Morgan had noted its antiquity when he first discovered it in 1855, wondering at how long it had been there.

From Google Earth we had seen a serpentine bend extending along one side of the pond, the outline of what looked like the remains of a beaver dam, but it wasn't clear how much of the construction remained. At the edge of the pond I notice a narrow strip of earth that separates deep pond water to the left, and on the right and downward side a slight drop toward a swampy area. Lewis Henry Morgan's beaver dam. Tall clumps of grass rise up from what would have once been the top of the dam. I push through them and step out onto the slippery footing. My feet sink into soft mud, cold water soon filling my sneakers, but I find traction by stepping from one tuft of grass to the next. It is hard going. I remember Herb's advice when we were crossing swamps and dams: Never trust the footing, check the depth of mud and water before you step by poking ahead with a stick. I reach down and from the downside of the dam grab a weathered length of sapling, chewed on one end to a point. Walking stick in hand, I am more confident and make my way carefully toward the center of the pond.

The dam is more of a dike now, weathered sticks and rotting poles interlaced on the downward side, but it has survived. Water runs over the top of the dam in tiny streams or pushes through holes, so that it leaks like a sieve. But there was fresh beaver chew. The sounds of trickling, gurgling, splashing water are beaver cues to mobilize. Researchers have played tape recordings of running water to penned beavers and observed them immediately rush to grab sticks, carrying them in their mouths and between their chest and forepaws to the spot where the recording was hidden to begin building a wall.

So why are the beavers not maintaining the dam? I walk on.

A feeling of exhilaration fills me as I look out across the sheet of silver water, a pond so tranquil it seems from another time. Out across the pond I see a stand of dead trees, and beyond them the woods begin. Beavers will move on if food is depleted, but I am looking at a whole forest of beaver food. It is when I am at the midpoint that I see the glimpses of yellow on the downward side of the dam. I walk toward the site and peer over the edge. Lengths of freshly cut wood, each end chewed to a perfect point, the entire length stripped of bark, have been pressed against a particularly large hole in the dam. Water is still pouring out, but the repair has begun, or was halted midway. Either way, beavers must have been living here this fall.

It only takes us a short hike along the shore to find more proof of life, a beaver lodge. It is small as lodges go and slightly squat, built into the bank by a stand of conifer trees that tower over it. Across the top are numerous lengths of freshly stripped saplings and, more curiously, bunches of pond grass so that the structure seems to be dripping with green hair. I've seen all kinds of beaver lodges—once, at the edge of a cornfield, a lodge made almost entirely of cornhusks and stones—but I have never seen a lodge coated with fresh pond grass.

"They were just working on this," Jeff observes, picking up a bunch of grasses to examine the scissor-like precision of the gnawed ends. On the trap line, Herb was always looking down for beaver signs, but then he'd look up and study the trees, the sky, the far side of the swamp or pond we were in, taking in the big picture. An osprey nest in a dead tree told you something about how long beaver had lived there; wildlife biologists now state with certainty that the older the beaver pond the larger its wildlife diversity. The wide pond tells me only that it seems about as large as when Morgan first discovered it, a good twenty-five acres even today. I look back down. This is a small lodge, most likely the work of juvenile beavers who moved in recently. But the fur trapping season here in Michigan hasn't started. I haven't seen any trapping sets, and I've been looking; unless there is a feed pile showing signs of current activity, the beavers that had been here recently could now be gone. It wouldn't be the first time that beavers were hunted or trapped out of season. Jeff looks up from his phone where he has been reading measurements. "I think the dam is about five hundred feet long," he says. Morgan had recorded the dam to be 488 feet long; it has endured.

If beavers are living here now, there will be freshly cut branches sticking up from the water not too far from here. Jeff and I find it at the same time, near the bank where the tips of branches are sticking up from under the water, almost hidden by thick pond grass. A beaver feed pile! One hundred and fifty-seven years after Morgan photographed it, the "great grass lake dam" has survived. And beavers—perhaps the fifteenth generation to live here—are still in the pond.

Now Jeff has a surprise for me. That morning before heading out, he looked again using Google Earth, and he thinks he has found another remaining beaver work from Morgan's book, dam number 23, on a tributary of the Carp River. We head off along a rutted dirt road and are soon driving into an area owned by the paper company. Jeff parks by the side of the road. On our right a large pond is visible through the woods. Once again, it isn't hard to find the dam, this one just as beautiful, a perfect half-moon holding back a body of water that extends far into the woods. I walk out along it for as far as I can safely go but see no signs of recent beaver activity. Across the pond about halfway toward the middle, however, I see the classic cone shape of a large beaver lodge; it rises a good eight feet above the water. Still, as in the pond we saw earlier, it is strange to see just one lodge on a pond this large, and a robust population of beavers would be keeping the dam maintained. People must be limiting the population, trapping or hunting or both.

In 2014, Carol Johnston, a scientist from the University of Minnesota, conducted a study of beaver ponds in this area by comparing Morgan's 1868 map to satellite imagery of the same area. Her results were surprising. Despite changes in land use—mining, new development, and roads, all of which have dramatically reduced beaver habitat—forty-six of the sixty-four dams and pond sites identified by Morgan, 72 percent of them, were still discernible. She does not mention either of the beaver dams we have just found. Pretty much the entire bottom of the map, dam sites 10–15 to the south and east, have been filled in by mine tailings. Still, a remarkable number of beaver sites remain.

Back at the shore I borrow Jeff's camera to use his zoom lens to get a closer look at the lodge and study it for signs of freshly chewed saplings. Suddenly Jeff taps me on the shoulder. "Stay still," he says, "really still, and can you slowly hand me the camera?" Across the pond where the land juts out into a small peninsula an enormous black shape has emerged from the woods. A bull moose. Jeff eases the camera out of my hand and starts taking photographs. Even at this distance it is clear that the moose is huge, his rack of antlers so large it looks like he is carrying a candelabra the size of a bicycle on his head. I wonder at how he can even move under that weight, and then I see the powerful neck and shoulders. He ambles toward the water, reaches up to rip branches from a small tree, chewing methodically while staring across to where we sit. Two more moose step out from the woods, both smaller and lighter in color. Neither have antlers. The smaller of the two walks directly into the pond until it is half submerged and begins to graze, the great head submerging, then reappearing, strands of pondweed still draped across its enormous flat nose. Jeff motions to me not to speak. I have no trouble remaining silent; in the face of such wild beauty, what is there to say? We sit and watch while the bull moose, on guard now, head with its enormous antlers raised and terrifyingly still, stares across the pond toward us while his companions continue to graze.

Jeff keeps photographing at a rapid pace, his excitement visible. Finally, the bull moose turns and the other moose near him immediately follow as if pulled by invisible strings. They disappear into the woods.

Jeff and I head back to the SUV, but not before we spy a truck parked just down the road also on the side of the dam. Soon the truck pulls up and idles alongside us. The window on the passenger side rolls down. We see two men dressed in outdoor garb—plaid shirts, tan Carhartt jackets, bill caps. Full beards cover their faces. The atmosphere is suddenly tense. Jeff isn't sure who they are or why they have stopped. A rack of guns is visible behind the seats. The man on the passenger side stares at us, engine idling. Then he leans out the window, his arm on the side of the car, and his voice breaks the silence. "Yah, how about that!" he says in a voice alive with excitement, his strong UP accent rounding the sounds.

"Yes," Jeff answers, visibly relieved. "Incredible."

"Yah, they like that spot," the driver continues, leaning over. "You see all three, the calf and mother, yah?"

"Yes!" Jeff answers excitedly, then thinks to ask: "You see moose here often?"

"Oh yah," the man answers, his Michigan accent thickening. "We always see them, yah, right there. We drive especially over to see 'em."

Then a thought occurs to me. I wait to see if Jeff is going to ask about the beavers, but he is silent.

"It looks like someone might be trapping beaver here." Silence falls over us. The men stiffen. Trappers can be secretive. Then they turn their heads to look at me slowly, and stare, clearly surprised. But they are becoming relaxed with us now as we are with them. We've all sized each other up. "There's a good-size lodge down below," I continue, "but looks like someone's been harvesting the beaver. This big of a pond, seems like there should be more than one lodge...Any idea who is trapping here?"

"Oh yah, that's my cousin!" the man at the wheel bursts out, breaking into a grin as he looks out the window and points emphatically toward the pond. "We all trap, yah, but he traps here, oh yah...every year since I can remember. Always beaver, nice ones..." He turns back to look at me again and nods slowly. "Saw a beaver right there, yah, a big one...running right across the top of the lodge this morning."

In the 1860s when Morgan was researching his beaver book, fur trappers were still harvesting half a million beavers annually across the country. Then, by 1900, they were gone. Now, due to a combination of factors—luck and wise environmental policies, wildlife restoration efforts and the beaver's innate resilience—beavers were coming back, bringing other wildlife with them, and the fur trappers were some of the first to know.

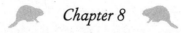

Chapter 8

Kitaiksísskstaki and the Story of the Beaver Bundle

PART I: *Beaver Bots*

For twelve years, from 1855 to 1867, Lewis Henry Morgan had bushwhacked through the Upper Peninsula of Michigan studying beaver constructions to try to understand how beavers could pull off such massive feats of engineering. He even made four trips out west, traveling two thousand miles up the Missouri River through Montana to observe beavers at work in the very different landscape of the Rocky Mountains and northern plains. But apart from his increasing sense of awe at the ability of beavers to create massive waterworks even in arid landscapes, he gained no insight into his central question—are beavers smart?

I had come back from Michigan curious to pursue Morgan's questions about beaver intelligence, but I soon discovered that most researchers today are more interested in measuring the beaver's environmental impact. Throughout the twentieth century, European ethologists, doctors, and researchers made periodic attempts to measure beaver intelligence. One of the most interesting was a study undertaken by a team of Russian and Polish researchers who set out to test if beavers could extrapolate, or make predictions based on experience. For the experiment they made use of fifteen Canadian (*Castor canadensis*) beavers and twenty-three European (*Castor fiber*) beavers. The Eurasian beavers and the Canadian beavers that populate North America are considered cousins, because they look similar and are monogamous herbivores with similar damming skills. But the two species cannot interbreed as they have different numbers of chromosomes. Most of the beavers collected for the study had been raised in captivity, although some of the Eurasian beavers were from the wild. The experiments were conducted at the beaver nursery of the Voronezh State Reservation in Russia and the field station of the Polish Academy of Sciences. They found that most of the beavers (85 percent of the Canadian beavers and 65 percent of the European beavers) showed an ability to problem solve, in this case, to anticipate the movement of a food bowl that they could not see, based on experience. The resulting paper, titled "Experimental Study of the Intellectual Ability of European and Canadian Beavers," was published in Moscow. The researchers had proved that beavers could extrapolate, which is considered a basic facet of intelligence. The Italian-Swiss neurologist Giorgio Pilleri of the Institute of Brain Anatomy at the University of Bern had become interested in the Canadian beaver and had written an important paper on the morphology of its brain in 1959. Then, years later, he began to measure beaver intelligence by studying aspects of the way they build. He published a series titled *Investigations on Beavers* in 1983. But these studies generally supported what people already knew from observation— beavers can build very well; how they did this and why the first beaver began to make dams in the first place remained a mystery.

Intellect in animals is directly related to increased size of higher brain regions, increased diversity of neurons, and more complex interactions between them. The frontal brain and especially the neocortex of beavers is more developed than in other rodents, but you won't find beavers following a maze, figuring out puzzles, or pulling on levers like a Norway rat. Part of the problem in studying beaver intelligence is logistical. Beavers live mostly underwater, are clumsy on land, and can barely see. They are also nocturnal. Jacques Cousteau made one of the first documentaries about the Canadian beaver in 1975, an evocative film in which his son and the crew of *Calypso* donned scuba gear and dove under the ice in Saskatchewan to try to photograph beavers in their winter lodges. But they only found one rather frightened juvenile beaver; the rest had swum off.

Then I found a news clipping about a talented doctoral candidate in material science and mechanical engineering at Harvard who has begun to crack the mystery of beaver intelligence by thinking about beavers in a radical new way; when she studies beavers, Jordan Kennedy thinks about termites, an animal so tiny it has almost no brain at all. Yet termites, which are smaller than a grain of rice, work collectively to build termite mounds that tower up to twelve feet. The human equivalent would be people living in skyscrapers over a mile high. According to Kennedy, the reason Lewis Henry Morgan and the twentieth-century scientists who came after him could not answer the question of beaver intelligence was because they were asking the wrong questions. "You are trying to get answers by looking at the individual, when the intelligence of it and the engineering comes from collective intelligence," explained Kennedy when I reached her by phone in her office in Cambridge. "It comes from a collective, from hundreds if not thousands of beavers working independently on a waterway, and the end result looks very intelligent. The beaver dams Morgan was studying took generations of beavers to build."

Kennedy's face breaks into a quiet smile when she mentions her childhood helping her family ranch cattle on the Blackfoot reservation in north-central Montana, where her father is an enrolled member of the *Amskapi Pikuni* southern Piegan, Blackfeet tribe. Kennedy has blonde hair and blue eyes from her mother's side of the family that came from Sweden, but she grew up surrounded by Blackfeet culture. "The beaver has a very sacred place for us," she said. She then went on to mention one of the most important sources of Blackfeet ritual, the Beaver Bundle. "Within Blackfeet culture the Beaver Bundles are like history books, for each bundle contains objects, each of which holds a song or a story. When you receive a bundle, you learn all the stories and the knowledge." She went on to explain how the Beaver Bundle was like a library, with the physical manifestations of knowledge literally wrapped up in a bundle and passed down.

At Harvard, Kennedy is a member of the Soft Math Lab led by Professor L. Mahadevan. Mahadevan has received numerous awards for his work, including an Ig Nobel prize in physics as well as a MacArthur Fellowship for his work in applied mathematics. The renowned Soft Math Lab brings together the fields of mathematics, physics, engineering, and evolutionary biology to study phenomena in the natural world. Another of Kennedy's former advisors, now at Princeton, Professor Radhika Nagpal has leveraged previous research on social insects in the field of biology to develop kilobots—a robotic system for advancing the development of "swarms" of robots that can be programmed to perform collective tasks.

"I originally started thinking about how beavers build in the context of being exposed to how ants and termites build," explained Kennedy. "Termites got me really thinking about it. The insects that begin making a termite mound are not the ones to finish it. And arguably, individual termites are really not that smart. A single termite isn't going to solve complex problems, but if it works in a collective and operates through a simple set of rules—like I'm going to build here because my friend built here—it can build structures thousands of times bigger than what the individual could."

Termites and ants and bees (and as Kennedy's new research now indicates, also beavers) do not organize themselves around a central authority figure; instead, they build by following simple rules that are initiated by environmental cues—a form of behavior called *stigmergy*. The French biologist Pierre-Paul Grassé coined the term in 1959 to describe the way termites leave traces in the environment (piles of dirt or pheromones) as clues for fellow termites; these act as signals for other termites to build in that location so that the termite mound grows. Kennedy now believes that beavers also exhibit stigmergic behavior, and she has an idea of what at least one of those environmental clues might be. Kennedy found that beavers began to build their damming complexes in response to the volumetric flow rate of water, the current. Kennedy had deliberately chosen beaver damming sites that were in areas that washed out each spring. Because the beaver population on the reservation is robust, young mated pairs setting out on their own are forced to build in subpar sites where spring flooding means their dams will wash out.

"I didn't want to look at generations-old dams like Lewis Henry Morgan," explained Kennedy, "because I wanted to see where and when beavers built in a new location." What she found was that when the volumetric flow rate of the river diminished to 250 liters per second, the beavers sprang into action, building dams, canals, and overland trails in order to forage and collect building materials. Once she graphed her data from a season of weekly scans on all her sites, Kennedy saw that beavers began building in direct inverse proportion to volumetric flow rate. Until Kennedy's study, the prevailing hypothesis of when and where beavers build was that they are cued to build by the sound of running water, and the louder the water the more they will build. While Kennedy's work does not disprove this, it does suggest that the cues to build are more complex than just an audio signal, which makes sense because beavers don't try to dam up places like Niagara Falls where the audio cue to build would be the loudest. "We don't know what beavers are thinking," said Kennedy. "But this makes sense from a mechanical standpoint; the dam will fail if the shear rate is too high."

Kennedy did not set out to study beaver intelligence or even their behavior. When it came time for her to put together her Ph.D. research topic, she decided to conduct a study of the beaver dams near where she grew up, on the Blackfeet reservation. Blackfeet reservation lands in north central Montana include much of Glacier National Park, which is leased to the U.S. government. This meant that the damming complexes Kennedy set out to study were located in one of the most important watersheds in the world. Triple Divide Peak, located in the Montana portion of the Rocky Mountains, is considered the "hydrological apex" of North America. Water from the divide flows down three different river systems to empty out into three different oceans.

Kennedy initially set out much the way Morgan had a century and a half earlier, aiming to document, map, and photograph beaver dams within a specific region. But while Kennedy surveyed the area first on foot to identify sites (encountering grizzlies and wolves along the way), her plan was to fly drones to photograph the beaver sites throughout the summer. From these photographs she would reconstruct three-dimensional images of the dams through photogrammetry, the technique of using point clouds to establish locations and stitch photographs together.

"When I started out I was very interested in the dams as a mechanical engineer," she explained, "how you could have a biologic system built in a fluid environment out of subpar materials to make a mechanically robust structure. Even as humans we are not very good at that." Throughout the summer, Kennedy flew drones over twenty colonies within a range of a hundred square miles. "It was once I was in the air that my thinking changed," she said. "I saw how vast the scale of the damming complexes was. The dams were actually tiny; what was most impressive were the canals."

To make her point, Kennedy sent me one of the images from her study, taken on Milkwood Creek. The image of the damming network was stunning. The creek was so enlarged and extended by canals and the surrounding land so intersected by the overland trails of the beavers that it had become a labyrinth; each damming complex was an extensive oasis of green in the otherwise expanse of arid brown landscape.

Kennedy's findings address interesting questions, such as just how large can a stigmergic system get? Beavers appear to successfully operate in a decentralized way on a scale much bigger than termites. In theory one could create an algorithm based on the simple rules of building that beavers follow, or the simple rules they follow for successful overland navigation, and use this information to program robots. Might we one day see a fleet of beaver bots? A group of beaver-sized robots working together could become something quite useful for humans. Kennedy is clearly excited by the implications her research could have for robotics, but she is also interested in the practical ways that the study of beaver constructions can help us better manage our waterways, especially by gaining resiliency against flooding through improved dam design.

"People say beavers can't stop flooding," said Kennedy, "but in my sites they do. Let beavers build canals and they can stop even a major flood." In addition to designing canals into our damming systems to help manage floodwaters, Kennedy believes we can also improve on current dam design by imitating how beavers build—beavers never make just one big dam, they create multiple tiers of dams that increase the dam system's resiliency. "Also worth thinking about," she added, "is the value of cyclic failure. Beaver dams persist, then fail in cyclic ways that dump out nutrients for fish and wildlife and plants. Designing dams to release on a cyclic basis offers another way to manage our waterways."

Looking to the future, Kennedy would like to see her study extended by adding a GPS component in order to track the movements of individual beavers within the damming complex while it was being built. "What are individual beavers doing within this collective? Who is doing what? Are they distributing work? People ask me what were the beavers doing and I have no idea, and this is a major oversight in my study." In fact, throughout her entire study, Kennedy, who was flying drones during the day, never saw any beavers at all. She had initially planned to track beavers as part of her study, but one of her advisors discouraged it, pointing out how time-consuming and labor-intensive it would be to live-trap the beavers, somehow attach transponders (beavers have no neck on which to affix a radio collar), or microchip them.

In 1973, Professor Peter Busher at Boston University was the first U.S. scientist to attempt to track beavers with GPS. He attached a radio transmitter to the beaver's tail by securing it with nylon webbing. But he found the process so time-consuming that he stopped. Busher oversees what is the longest-running study of a beaver population in the country; since the late 1960s scientists have been conducting a yearly census of a population of beavers that lives on the Quabbin Reservoir in central Massachusetts. The Quabbin is of interest to the state because it provides most of the water for Boston. Every November, Busher partners with a group of organizations and volunteers to walk the area and count the number of active beaver lodges.

Although Europe is twenty years behind North America in the reintroduction of the beaver, which in Europe they call "re-wilding," it has become a center for beaver research, although as in the United States, the focus of most beaver research now is on beaver management and utilizing beavers for environmental restoration. A Bavarian wildlife manager, Gerhard Schwab popularly called the "Johnny Appleseed of beavers," spearheaded much of the reintroduction of beavers throughout Europe. In the United Kingdom, Derek Gower and fellow researchers, along with organizations like the Beaver Trust, have been at the forefront. The United Kingdom and Europe committed to river restoration as part of a green deal some years ago, and increasingly beavers are part of those efforts. Most current research in Europe is being conducted in Norway at the University of South-Eastern Norway and at the Norwegian Institute for Nature Research (NINA) in Telemark. Frank Rosell, of the University of South-Eastern Norway, is one of the foremost beaver scientists in the world. He's published hundreds of papers and is now leading research teams to track Eurasian beavers using GPS via ear tags and microchips. By putting antennae near the entrances to the lodges, his research teams have begun to collect data on the movement patterns of individual beaver. In one of their most recent studies, published in 2022, they attached accelerometers and GPS systems to thirty-three Eurasian beavers and observed that beavers dive less often than previously thought, make shallower dives, and actually stay underwater for much shorter periods than had been understood.

As for when and why the first beaver started to make the first dam, Jordan Kennedy, who also studies logjams, has a theory. In north-central Montana, logjams also happen when the volumetric flow rate of a river is 250 liters per second, the same flow rate that cues beavers to start to build. Perhaps ancient beavers were drawn to the pools of water formed upstream from logjams, discovering a new abundance of vegetation and safety, for the deeper water protected them from predation by bears and wolves. Then one day a beaver added a stick to the logjam and the rest was history.

"No one builds like a beaver," Kennedy added before we ended our call. "Not on the same scale, anyway." Several species of animals and fish nest and burrow, both of which are types of building. Pufferfish create fabulous mandalas in the sand to attract mates, and we now know that at least one type of octopus in Australia builds the equivalent of a walled medieval city that researchers have dubbed "octopolis." But the longest known beaver dam, located in Alberta, Canada, is the largest animal-made construction, visible from space.

PART II: *Tree Biter*

"In the Blackfeet language, when you talk about a tree, a rock, a buffalo, a beaver, you are talking about another person," Kennedy had said at the outset of our phone conversation. "The way you grammatically conjugate these nouns has the same weight as if you are talking about another person." She paused, then added, "When you lose your language you lose that worldview, because language impacts the way you form thoughts and the way you interact with the world."

In the Blackfeet language, the word for beaver, *ksísskstaki*, means "tree biter." The Blackfeet, who are descended from Indigenous people who have lived in the northern plains for millennia, learned the environmental knowledge of their landscape. They understood ethnobotany, the plants, and especially the high-protein species of fescue grass that supported the richest buffalo ecosystem in North America. They understood the bison ecology, enabling them to hunt successfully, and they learned how to live in an arid environment. Most of all, they understood the critical role that beavers played in maintaining water in a drought-prone landscape. And they learned a great deal of this, according to Blackfeet cosmology, from the beaver, *Kitaiksísskstaki*, who even helped the Sun, whom they called Napi, Old Man, when he set out to create the world.

> In the beginning there was water everywhere; nothing else was to be seen. There was something floating on the water, and on this raft were Old Man and all the animals. Old Man wished to make land, and he told the beaver to dive down to the bottom of the water and to try to bring up a little mud. The beaver dived and was under water for a long time, but he could not reach the bottom. Then the loon tried, and after him the otter, but the water was too deep for them. At last the muskrat was sent down, and he was gone for a long time, so long that they thought he must be drowned, but at last he came up and floated almost dead on the water, and when they pulled him up on the raft and looked at his paws, they found a little mud in them. When Old Man had dried this mud, he scattered it over the water and land was formed.

The Story of the Beaver Bundle

During *sto-ye*, the "closed" season of winter, a human who had been shamed by his community and forced to leave was invited by *Kitaiksísskstaki*, the beaver, to spend the winter in their lodge. He went down into the underwater world to live for a winter with the beaver people. When winter was over and the human returned to his people, he brought with him the knowledge and lessons transferred to him from the supernatural world—the water world of the beavers. He brought back knowledge of how to plant, cultivate, and harvest *piistaahkaan*, native tobacco. He brought songs through which to charm the bison, bringing them near to ensure a successful hunt. And he brought back sticks that the beavers had given him in order for him to begin to count time. He was called the "beaver man," and his first obligation was to build a "Beaver Bundle" of objects that represented the lessons and knowledge he had learned from the beaver. These objects, which initially are said to have contained the hides and skins of all the animals and birds, correspond to songs and movements and rituals. And it was through the opening of this bundle that the beaver man transferred the supernatural power, the *saam*, or medicine, of the beaver to humans. The Beaver Bundle is the oldest ritual from which all other Blackfeet rituals emanated.

In her 2017 book, *Invisible Reality: Storytellers, Storytakers, and the Supernatural World of the Blackfeet,* Rosalyn R. LaPier, an enrolled member of the Blackfeet tribe, describes how the Blackfeet believe in two types of knowledge: knowledge gained from experience in the empirical world, and knowledge gained from alliance with a supernatural ally. Both are important. Through the Beaver Bundle, beavers transfer some of the power of the waters to humans, but through this exchange a compact is formed and in return humans must fulfill their obligations to the beaver. Historically, the Blackfeet people, along with other peoples of the northern plains—an area which includes almost all of the grassland east of the Rocky Mountains and north of the Canadian border—upheld strict prohibitions against harming and eating beavers. Among other things, religious stories involving beaver reflected an understanding of the beaver's role in conserving and maintaining the critical resource of water. The ways in which the cosmology of the Blackfeet and other peoples of the northern plains led to the conservation of beavers had environmental underpinnings similar to the Hindu protection of the sacred cow. In India, another arid landscape, the traction power of cattle and the usefulness of their dung as fuel outweighs their value as food. Gradually Hinduism began to stress that refraining from killing and eating cattle was a sacred duty.

Traditional stories such as the Blackfeet story of the Beaver Bundle portray beavers as protectors of humans, and the archeological record of the northern plains shows that the people living there did not hunt them. Even the anthropologist George Bird Grinnell, who in 1915 collected and published many Blackfeet and Cheyenne stories (about twenty years after he founded the first Audubon Society), observed a connection between the ways that beaver was revered through the stories of the Blackfeet and other northern plains peoples and the important role beavers played in the arid landscape stabilizing surface water. While the stories of Great Beaver from

Algonquian cultures celebrated *Ktsi Amiskw* as powerful, he was also mischievous toward humans and had to be reprimanded by the creator. In contrast, *Kitaiksísskstaki* was a powerful protector and generous teacher who gave the humans knowledge critical to their survival. In her fascinating book *Beaver, Bison, Horse,* the anthropologist R. Grace Morgan posits that Indigenous communities of the woodlands, such as the Algonquian peoples of the Northeast who faced an overabundance of beaver up and down the Atlantic seaboard, saw the beaver in more ambivalent terms because at times beaver flooded grazing areas and habitat for the animals and birds they needed to hunt for food: deer, elk, moose, wild turkey, rabbit, and grouse. Woodland peoples tended to allow the hunting of beaver as long as the beaver was honored by caring for the carcass.

The Blackfeet considered the beaver so powerful, all their rituals emanate from the Beaver Bundle. In the Northwest, there is a people who call themselves the Beaver and believe that beavers are a fallen race of men. The Cherokee, Algonquian people, including the Ojibwa, and many other Indigenous people traced their origins to the beaver. Throughout North America when it was still Beaverland, the inhabitants had many restrictions or outright prohibitions that protected against the overhunting of beaver. Yet in the face of pressure from the fur trade, eventually all of these beliefs would, at least for a critical period (long enough to almost exterminate the beaver), become forgotten or deliberately abandoned. In the northern plains, early-nineteenth-century accounts of traders almost uniformly complain that they could not get the Blackfeet or their neighbors, the Gros Ventre, the Blood, and the Piegan, to bring them beaver. To the south, similar complaints were made by fur traders about the Cheyenne, the Hidatsa, and the Crow. The Indigenous groups living there would bring wolf and fox and bison, but resisted bringing the beaver pelts that the fur traders made it clear they wanted. But gradually this opposition to hunting beavers turned to cooperation, as most Indigenous groups eventually participated in the European fur trade.

In his landmark book *Keepers of the Game: Indian-Animal Relationship and the Fur Trade,* Calvin Martin put forth a convincing and disturbing explanation for why many Indigenous people abandoned their worldview of honoring the beaver people and began to participate in its slaughter. Using the

Cree, Ojibwa, and Chipewyan people as an example, he pointed out how in their worldview, nature was made up of societies: Every animal, fish, and plant species functioned in a society that was parallel to that of mankind. And each species had its leaders, called "keepers of the game," or "animal bosses." These leaders were generally bigger than the other animals, like *Ktsi Amikw,* Great Beaver.

If a hunter angered an animal boss by disrespecting his people— through overhunting and, in the case of the beaver, not caring properly for the carcass—he ran the risk of having his next hunt ruined, or of falling ill. According to Martin, when the Ojibwa and many others began dying as a result of the many diseases that came to North America via contact with the first Europeans, the Indigenous people blamed the beaver for bringing so much illness, believing it was some form of punishment. The response was rage; if the beaver would so abandon them, they would abandon their traditional protocols and hunt them without limit. Generalizing about a people is always suspect, as is the assertion of any monolithic Native American culture, which most certainly does not exist. Before Europeans arrived, North America was populated by the hundreds of different tribes that still live here, each with distinct languages and cultures. And there were the other pressures, such as the usefulness of many of the trade goods themselves and the ramifications of not trading, which meant having no access to guns, which soon became necessary for self-protection.

"We've been in a state of crisis since the turn of the century," Kennedy had commented matter-of-factly. "We are still dealing with the long-term effects of what colonization has done to the tribe, and there are still a lot of negative impacts of living within the bounds of the reservation. The ecology of the reservation is well preserved, but it was still designed as a prison. We are dealing with culture loss and language loss. Now there is a big push from an ecological standpoint of trying to regain knowledge that was lost."

Some of that knowledge is now coming back, once again via the beaver. In a forward-thinking environmental project on reservation lands called the Ksik Stakii (Beaver) Project, a broad partnership has begun installing "beaver dam analogs," called BDAs, and planting vegetation along riverbanks. The idea is to mimic the impacts of beaver dams in slowing and retaining water and repairing damaged streams in places where there is not enough vegetation (at least not yet) for beavers to thrive. A corollary aim is to engage Blackfeet youth with their people's deep Indigenous environmental knowledge regarding the ways they have always lived with and learned from *Kitaiksísskstaki*, the beaver.

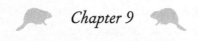

Chapter 9

The Underwater People

PART I: *The Yale Forest, Union, Connecticut*

Dr. Denise Burchsted studies the shapes of water—more specifically, the way rivers move through and transform landscapes. "At dinner parties I say I study rivers," she explained on the phone when I reached her in her office at Keene State College in New Hampshire, "but when I am in a room full of scientists, I am a fluvial geomorphologist. I think there are about twelve of us in New England." To her, rivers are the sinews that connect our landscape, and their current state of degradation is a pressing environmental issue, not just here in New England but throughout North America and the world. Ironically, her research on water has led her to places where there is none—at least no visible moving water. Her research on New England rivers led her to beaver meadows, which is what first excited me about her work. "Beaver meadows are the beaver dam that is but isn't," she explained on our first phone call in June. "They are incredibly helpful and incredibly understudied."

When she learned that I was researching a beaver site in northeastern Connecticut, just eight miles from where she had done her Ph.D. research in the Yale-Myers Forest, Dr. Burchsted offered to show me the sites in her study. She had not been back for ten years and was curious to return. I couldn't believe my luck; finally I had found a researcher working on beavers here on the East Coast.

Water was in the news. Too much rain in one place was causing extreme flooding, while too little in another was causing extreme drought. Meanwhile, rising sea levels from melting ice were shifting coastlines. Water entered the watershed as rain, but then it traveled through the land and was either captured or washed right back out to the sea through the river system. To understand water, one must understand rivers, not as that handy metaphor for the passage of time, but as the hydraulic system that keeps everything on the continent that was living alive.

All of this begged the question: Could beavers be reintroduced along the Connecticut River watershed and reduce the threats of flooding in cities like Hartford? One of the most revered deep time stories of the Algonquian people, who have inhabited the Northeast since the end of the Pleistocene, involved that rascal Great Beaver. *Ktsi Amiskw* had flooded an area that began at the top of New Hampshire and spread all the way down through Vermont, Massachusetts, and Connecticut. The Algonquian people understood the power and importance of beavers to the larger environment, and their impact on the landscape.

Connecticut was the fourth most densely populated state in the country; could beavers effectively help restore rivers here? Fur trappers were excited to see beavers back and worked hard in many ways to help preserve their habitat, but their priority was a "sustainable harvest" of beaver fur. For the most part, the highway department in my town, as in most towns throughout the state, still considered beavers a "nuisance" animal. I was thrilled to think that finally I could show my beloved beaver site down the road from my house to a geologist, engineer, and ecologist who also happened to be knowledgeable about beaver meadows.

Follow Dr. Burchsted into the woods and as soon as she spies a brook, a stream, a creek, a river, even a patch of water resting between the trees, her usually gentle brown eyes take on a determined glint. Before you know it, she's pushing back the undergrowth or crashing right through even the most intimidating thickets of green. Thick stands of hobblebush, ostrich fern, underbrush tangled with thick vines of wild grape, sharp blades of sawgrass, even bayberry prickers do not hold her back once she's following a path of forest water. "I just love bushwhacking," she said on a hot August day when we both stood looking into the Yale-Myers Forest. With her earthy good looks and beaming smile, she looked like she had just stepped out of a Patagonia catalog, although her clothes did not sport fancy labels. I smiled weakly, so exhausted and hot my legs felt like rubber. Every time I half toppled into a boggy spot, or tripped on vines, I wished I had brought a walking stick, or better yet, a machete. At each brook she studied the size and shape of rocks in the water's channel, then stepped in (in summer she explores the woods in socks and Tevas) to feel the water's temperature. She'd lean down to feel the rocks for slime, a sure sign of nutrient-rich slower water upstream, often due to a beaver dam. More than once she grabbed handfuls of dirt from the side of a stream to let it slip through her fingers. She can feel the difference between fifteen-thousand-year-old glacial outwash and soil deposited later through erosion.

Initially trained as a civil engineer, Dr. Burchsted had been working for several years on dam removal design for river restoration projects when she decided to get a degree in geology. The goal of environmental restoration is always to return a damaged ecosystem to something closer to its natural state. But Dr. Burchsted had begun to ask a simple question: What is that natural state? Literally billions of dollars are spent in the United States annually to restore rivers, but until recently we have been restoring them to an unknown reference condition. We could not know what rivers in North America really looked like because we'd been studying rivers already degraded over the course of three hundred years without beavers to manage them.

Geologist Dr. Ellen Wohl, who studies beaver meadows and river systems in Colorado, calls the years from 1600 to 1900—essentially the three hundred years of the fur trade—the "great drying." Once beavers were gone from forested headwaters, and everywhere else, not only did the wetlands dry up, but the very shape and function of riverine systems changed. Scientists now estimate that more than 80 percent of the riverside marshes, swamps, lakes, ponds, and floodplain forests of North America and Europe have disappeared. We have only to think of Beaverland, that time when sixty to four hundred million beaver lived in North America, to understand. A population that large would mean that on any given river, one could find at least one beaver colony every three miles. At that density, beavers would have inhabited every single watershed throughout the continent. No one knows exactly how many beavers live in North America today. The estimate

is something like six million, less than .05 percent of the estimated population of beavers that for thousands of years had once lived here.

Historically, river restoration in the United States has focused on dam
removal, with engineers like Dr. Burchsted researching how best to safely
remove these human-made blockages. Much of Dr. Burchsted's research
focuses on studying so-called river discontinuity, what she calls the "myth
of the free-flowing river." When she first mentioned these terms on the
phone, I had circled my notes with a big question mark. Wasn't the very
definition of a river, a stream, a brook, even the tiniest creek, that place
where you saw running water?

Geomorphology is the study of landforms, their genesis and history. A
fluvial geomorphologist studies the physical shape of rivers, the way they
transport water and sediment, the landforms they create as a result, and
more generally how this water movement interacts with the landscape.
Here in the United States, as in the rest of the world, river restoration is
both a pressing issue and big business. River flooding causes loss of life and
billions of dollars of damage to cities, towns, and infrastructure annually;
it also damages the larger ecosystem and our ability to grow food. Each
year, a staggering amount of topsoil is washed down degraded river systems
and ends up in the ocean. To say that rivers are the sinews that connect our
landscapes is an understatement; when I pulled out a map of the five major
river systems in North America, they looked more like the continent's arteries, lines of water branching from a main tributary into a series of thinner
and thinner lines, directly or indirectly feeding everything—plant and animal, including human—that lives along them.

Historically, we have relied on rivers for transportation, for irrigation,
for energy, and to develop industry of all kinds. But we have a long tradition
of abusing them because we have not understood our dependence upon
them for the health of the larger ecosystem.

As a Ph.D. student, Dr. Burchsted had not set out to study the impact of
beavers on the river system. "My master's degree advisor had given me an
article on beaver meadows," she said, "and I thought that was interesting
and they were quirky, but it was really my husband who helped me put the
pieces together." Just when she was at the point of defining her doctoral

research, her husband came back from kayaking one day on Branch Brook in the Yale-Myers Forest area with an interesting report. He couldn't get any distance along the watercourse without having to carry his kayak over yet another beaver dam blocking the current. His experience confirmed her initial discomfort with the emphasis in river restoration on connecting rivers by removing dams.

"The classic narrative of river restoration is that people have built these big dams and we need to take them out, they are the problem...but there is a whole bunch of grey area." She paused. "We tend to think in a binary way—dam is bad, so no dam must be good. But the reality is more complex." Dr. Burchsted then began to ask, what if our vision of rivers in the Northeast as free-flowing was based not on the river's natural state but on years of study of rivers that were already degraded? In other words, rivers that for almost three hundred years—ever since the fur trade had knocked them out—had been a river system without beavers? She wanted to know what rivers had looked like before the beavers were gone.

In 2010, Dr. Burchsted coauthored a paper for the journal *Nature* that challenged the prevailing emphasis upon fluvial connectivity in river restoration. Using the research she conducted at the Yale-Myers Forest in Union, Connecticut, she and her coauthors argued the opposite, that "fluvial and riparian discontinuities" were key to the health of a river system, especially those created by beaver dams. To understand what geologists like Dr. Burchsted and others mean when they mention "discontinuities," you need to imagine your local brook or stream after a torrential rain, or a cell storm event such as Hurricane Ida. (Ida dumped seven inches of rain in less than twenty-four hours in New York City and southern New England, flooding the New York City subways and causing loss of life.) Bits of branch, leaves, and grasses washed down by the fast current of the floodwater are snagged along the banks, or the water was so fast and high that it rushed over the banks, scouring an area. Perhaps a tree limb has become snagged in the streambed and is now the structure for a mini logjam of branches, leaves, and anything else picked up by the force of the current. Maybe the water now runs to the right and left of that object in the middle of the streambed, the flotsam creating a temporary island. What was a clearly defined stream has become a disheveled mess with water running over the banks, creating multithreaded channels. In their paper, titled "The River Discontinuum: Applying Beaver Modifications to Baseline Conditions for Restoration of Forested Headwaters," Dr. Burchsted and her three coauthors argued that "for sustainable ecologically based restoration, models of first orders must include pre-colonial fluvial and riparian discontinuities including those created by beavers." In other words, they argued that to properly restore a river system you needed to stop focusing on the restoration of flow by removing human-made dams and think in more integrated ways. You need to examine how and where the water has become temporarily blocked, especially by beavers.

What Dr. Burchsted had documented was hopeful, revealing the extent to which in the eighty plus years since their reintroduction to Connecticut in 1914 beavers had begun to radically reshape the river system. What she was documenting here in the Yale-Myers Forest was that even in densely inhabited Connecticut, rivers could restore themselves with the help of a relatively small population of beavers. In less than a century, the Yale-Myers Forest beavers had reshaped the rivers to something close to what they would have looked like in the time of Beaverland.

Within this partially restored river ecology, not only was one-third of the entire river system impounded in beaver dams, but another third of the system took the form of beaver meadows. In other words, while one-third of the river was still flowing freely, most of the moving water had actually been dammed up, blocked, diverted, slowed down, and generally dispersed throughout the forest. And within this highly beaver-worked river system, a great deal of water was actually being stored in beaver meadows, which at first glance appeared dry, but as Dr. Burchsted and many other scientists have gone on to discover, actually work like wetlands, serving as giant underground sponges that can soak up and hold large stores of water. When flooding occurs, beaver meadows serve to absorb the floodwater, lessening the force of the current and thus its ability to scour the landscape, washing critical soils away. When there is no rain and rising temperatures cause plants and trees to lose even more water through transpiration, resulting in severe drought, beaver meadows serve as secret caches of water that keep a river system from completely drying up.

Back in 2010, these insights about the ways rivers needed in-channel heterogeneity, including beaver dams and logjam debris, for hydraulic function—and the role the beaver meadows of New England played in the larger river system—were considered surprising news. In fact, those single-channel streams were an artifact not of the river's natural morphology but the result of the human manipulation that began with European colonization. For three hundred years, from the late 1600s up through the early 1900s, dams and races were used to run sawmills, iron forges, furnaces, and mining operations throughout the country. In this corner of Connecticut and parts of Massachusetts, by 1840 there were over 12,000 mills. Every stream in New England had some kind of dam on it.

When the scientists studied the sediment, they found a top layer of fine sand, silt, and loam that had been laid down since the mill dams went in, about three hundred years ago, but underneath was a deep layer of soil rich in organic matter dating from much earlier in the Holocene. This trapped hydric (wetland) demonstrated that by washing down sediment, the mill dams filled in areas that had once been wetlands. In other words, before European colonization, the streams of New England were not single-channel, but rather smaller, branching channels within a system of extensive wetlands. These wetlands (which, as Dr. Burchsted's work would reveal, included beaver meadows) not only stored and slowed down a great deal of water, preventing soil loss through erosion, but also stored substantial amounts of organic carbon.

I think it's this way.

   Maybe up there?

   No, it's not this way. Sorry, we have to circle back.

   Here?

   Hmm, not sure, maybe.

   Here?

   No, I don't remember it being this way.

   Over here?

   No, let's try looping back.

   Here?

   Maybe.

Here?

Not sure...

How about up there?

Wow... It's so overgrown since I was here last...

I looked up, dazed with the heat and the effort of pressing forward. Dr. Burchsted, flanked by Andy Fallon, a current graduate student in the Department of Earth Sciences at the University of Connecticut, was up ahead, looking for one of the sites where ten years ago Dr. Burchsted had documented a series of beaver dams and a large woodland pond. Andy had a map pulled up on his phone and was studying their location. Even though they were only a few steps ahead, the forest seemed to have sealed up after them. But while I couldn't see them, I could hear their cheerful banter. I began to realize that getting lost and going around in circles might be part of the process. Instead of trying to figure out where we were, I shifted my gaze down to my feet and tried not to think about all the deer ticks. Once jostled from a leaf or stem they were brilliant at finding their way down through fur or clothing to bite our waiting skin. I felt like I was walking through William Blake's green curtain, but as I trudged forward, slapping mosquitoes and gently releasing the barbs that kept snagging my legs, I was struggling to see the forest as anything close to divine. Then ahead, I heard a hoot.

"That's it!" Dr. Burchsted shouted, her voice rising in excitement. "There it is, that's the river." I quickly pushed forward and soon was looking at the two of them, staring at what looked like an oblong patch of meadow wedged into the forest. I did not see a river. I didn't see any water at all. "Lots of things blow my mind," Dr. Burchsted said happily, "but this is it. This *is* the river. See all this green stuff?" She took a stick and lifted the grass away, revealing a trickling line of water. "This isn't a meadow, it's the river!"

"This is a river?" I asked, staring at the area where she and Andy were now bent down, feeling the water with their hands.

"Yes, you have to remember that word doesn't mean anything," Dr. Burchsted explained. "A river, a stream, a brook, a wash, all that means is surface water with some flow."

As soon as I took a step forward I began to understand. Water swamped my sneakers. Soon both feet were covered in a cool bath of water and mud.

When I bent down I saw that hidden under the grasses, water was pooling up while in the center, a current was rippling, catching the light in gentle twists.

"Look at that." Dr. Burchsted grinned, pointing to where the water was running through the roots of a tree. "We are on the cusp of the second drought of the summer and what this beaver work here is doing is holding the water that fell here. If it weren't for all the dams that the beavers have along this part of the river it would be just a trickle by now. This is so valuable for amphibians and other creatures."

Andy and Dr. Burchsted began talking shop. Water velocity, groundwater storage, carbon and nitrogen cycling, nutrient exchange. I perked up when they start talking about the nitrogen cycle. Dr. Burchsted pointed down to a small pool of brownish water. "This will be full of microbes that can't live in oxygenated water," she explained. "If we go downstream where the water is running, oxygen will be entering it, but here it is an anaerobic situation so when nitrates enter the pool the bacteria that live in low-oxygenated water start what is essentially a two-step cleansing process." Nitrate pollution from chemical fertilizer was a huge pollution concern, but what she was describing was the ability of wetlands to cleanse water of nitrogen.

"Same as your local water processing plant," said Andy.

"Or sewer treatment system," added Dr. Burchsted. "There is a whole lot of nutrient cycling and water cleansing going on here."

Beaver dams alter the biogeochemical transformation of nitrogen. Bacteria living in wetlands such as beaver ponds and small pools can remove as much as 80 percent of the nitrate load that enters them. Not only do they conduct a great deal of metabolic processing, but the stream that continues to run through the beaver pond becomes a watery highway in which dissolved organic carbon nitrogen can be conveyed downstream.

Dr. Burchsted continued on. When she stopped to look back her face was framed by a broad smile. "Knew I'd find it," she said. "This right here is a cold pool of water."

Andy and I walked down to look, and sure enough, tucked into the ferns were beautiful scour pools. Through the clear water I could see the gravel bottom; this was where, when it flooded, or in times of heavy rain, the water was funneled through a low spot, creating a swirl of current that over time had washed the upper layers of soil, fallen leaves, and other detritus away.

"Would you call this a small beaver pond?" I asked.

"This looks more like a foraging zone," Andy replied.

Dr. Burchsted agreed and bent down to examine the dam. The structure was holding, but there were no signs of recent activity.

"Let's walk back up there," Dr. Burchsted said, pointing up the woods where the land rose. Through the trees I could see a brown rim of dirt, then the white spikes of sticks gnawed clean of bark and weathered.

Soon we stood on a narrow beaver dam looking over a large expanse of water, a beaver pond. Ten years ago, Dr. Burchsted had documented beavers living and working here, although there was no active sign of them now. Since the dam was intact, Andy noted the GPS on his phone to look at satellite imagery later to see if there was a lodge perhaps around the corner. From this slightly higher vantage point we clearly saw the path of the water as it moved down, sometimes visible, sometimes hidden under the lush growth, here and there pooling into a series of brown pools each held by a mud and stick dam.

"The beavers did all this," said Dr. Burchsted emphatically. "It's not surface water and it is not groundwater—it is a river—its own thing." As if to answer the perplexed look on my face, she explained again, "There is no real difference between a river, a stream, a brook, or a creek—in terms of fluvial geomorphology, each of them is groundwater made visible."

Springs bubble up, bringing this groundwater to the surface, usually all along the length of a watercourse, not just at the source. Over time, the moving water cuts grooves through the soil, revealing rocks as the sediment is washed away. But then a lot of other forces come into play to shape a river system, including, as we were witnessing here, beavers, who block the streams, creating ponds but also places like this that were essentially the stream spread out over such a wide area that it was like a slow-moving sheet of water.

We were looking at the shape of the river systems of Beaverland—diffuse, messy, spread out, flexible at times, and most of all incredibly dynamic. A river system that was constantly moving across the land, hydrating everything like a great wand of moving water. I felt like laughing out loud: For millennia beavers had been at work like modern suburbanites, constantly watering their lawns to make them spring up green. But a better analogy was to think of beavers as the world's first hydroponic farmers, creating wet areas where the aquatic plants they liked to eat could grow.

PART II: *In the Beaver Meadow*

By the time we made our way out of the Yale-Myers Forest and drove the eight miles to Pulpit Rock Road, all that remained of the sun was a hot band across the trees. We stood on the bridge looking over Taylor Brook and the beaver meadow and listened to the insects drone. The whole area was yellowing, the grasses drying after days of sun and heat, the brook shrunk down to an afterthought, an almost invisible thread meandering through the tufts of grass.

In the far back where the beavers had built their second lodge, I saw blue-green spires of phragmite, that invasive weed causing havoc in the Northeast by pushing out the more nutritious cattails. What remained of that once glorious body of water was a small turbid pool from which a large angular boulder rose up as a jagged tooth. Around the boulder, a few water lilies were blooming like stranded dandelions. I noticed how brush and shrubs had grown up along the sides, forming a puffy edge of vegetation. My first thought was that all that new growth, those tender branches, were good beaver food. But I couldn't help a second thought, that the meadow now looked slightly ridiculous, as if ringed with a feather boa, an image that only confirmed my sense of it as a place of worn-out beauty—my beaver pond as an aged beauty queen still wearing her tiara. I felt a wave of protectiveness. Before I knew it, I was describing how the water once stretched so far back into the woods you could not see the far end from where we stood, and how the water was deep enough for the beavers to build and maintain two iconic teepee-shaped lodges. I told them how I'd seen otters swimming and chattering by the bridge and once a muskrat had swum right up looking like a brown loaf of bread. How I'd seen wood ducks, mallards, herons, wild turkey, bobcat, and coyote by the pond, then how some winter days I'd see so many animal tracks crisscrossing and looping around that I often hooted out loud; I had come upon the footprints of so many different kinds of feet, moving in so many different ways, at so many different speeds, it was as if I'd walked into a great after-party. The Nipmuc, along with other Native American tribes, often traveled along the tops of beaver dams, incorporating them into their extensive path systems that spread out like a great spiderweb across the woods of southern New England. The road behind us, now named Pulpit Rock Road, had begun when the first colonists followed an existing Nipmuc pathway. Before the European colonists arrived the Nipmuc may well have used the dam as a natural bridge within their pathway system.

Dr. Burchsted nodded, then leaned over to peer into the culvert and reported that there was about a foot of water covering the bottom that ran under the road, providing a passageway for the stream to follow the downward slope of the land, heading south and east. "That is pretty good flow considering that we are on the cusp of the second drought of the summer." Then she was gone, disappearing into the woods by the side. Andy and I waited on the bridge. I was still nervous, but her curiosity seemed a good sign. I had wanted her opinion of the site after all. As beaver meadows go, how did she rank this one? Most of all I wanted to know if it still seemed a good site for beaver, because if that were the case, perhaps the beavers would return.

When Dr. Burchsted climbed back up she said simply, "I see plenty of food. Look—there's even a willow tree here... There are a lot of edible grasses, not just sawgrass, which no one eats, and other plants with bulby roots—those are all yummy things for beaver."

"I'd say this is a pretty great beaver spot," added Andy. He pointed to the hills that rise up on either side, forming a small valley. "The topography is perfect for making a pond, and you have the brook running through, so continuous water."

"When did you say beavers left?"

"Going on five years now."

"That is strange... the meadow is healthy. There's plenty of food," mused Dr. Burchsted. "I've seen meadows with nothing much growing and you can tell beavers won't return, but there is a lot of food here."

"Do you think they will come back?" I asked, trying to keep the hope from my voice.

"The trouble is everything is so site specific, it is hard to generalize." Dr. Burchsted looked again across the meadow. "In my experience, though, when they move back to beaver meadows I see them build small dams, goofy, funky things. They tend not to really remake the whole pond."

In other words, what Dr. Burchsted was reporting was that the beavers might bring enough water back to create an area in which aquatic plants can grow, but not necessarily enough water to thrive. Water lilies, a main source of beaver food here in the East, needed three feet of water to grow, sending a long taproot down, but they did not need that much water year-round, and duckweed, another beaver favorite, merely floated on the surface. Michael Callahan, of the Beaver Institute, who spends most of his time in and out of beaver sites in Connecticut and Massachusetts, had seen places where beavers were surviving on ferns and smaller grasses until winter.

"You have to remember," added Dr. Burchsted, "that the longest dam in the world is just groundwater seep. People find a pinch point and build a maximum-sized dam there, the highest dam they can, but beavers work in an opposite way. What I've witnessed is that they move into a spot and they build really low. They want to start low and they don't mind building long. They'll find a spot like this one"—she points to the stone wall by the bridge—"where there is something they can take advantage of."

I understood what she was saying. I'd seen a picture of a beaver dam built around a pickup truck that had been abandoned in the woods. But as if to rethink what she had said earlier, Dr. Burchsted looked out across the meadow and added, "Still, I'm seeing a great location, water, and food. I'd say if beavers have not come back at this point there is a human reason."

Her words fell like stones. *A human reason.* I thought of the time I had found a three-legged beaver dead in the beaver pond and sent pictures of it to Herb Sobanski, who also became interested in the mystery of what had happened to it. I thought of the many times Coda had leapt off the trail to find a deer, shot but abandoned in the woods, and of the time I found a headless coyote in the field above the beaver dam. Some were sloppy, unethical hunters. I explained that our neighbors just down the road, whose property included a huge wetland with a beaver lodge, had trapped those beavers some years ago. One night on my way home, I had seen a large beaver walking up the road near that wetland. As I stared at the beaver, caught in the glare of my headlights, my head buzzed with thoughts of how I might catch it. If I could kidnap the beaver and drive it to Taylor Brook, maybe it would settle there and, if it had family members, hike back to get them; we had a perfect spot for beavers and it was just over the hill. If only I had a piece of burlap. But I wasn't sure I could grab a beaver barehanded, much less by wrapping it in burlap for a short ride.

I still thought of beavers as slightly dangerous, and in any event, how would I ever navigate that weird rubbery tail? Even if I managed to get the beaver into my car and over the hill to the pond, would she stay? State laws prohibited the relocation even of problem beaver due to fears of spreading disease. But our site was so close, you could argue it was within the same stream system, the water just having been diverted on either side of the drumlin that rose up between the two streams. While I sat behind the wheel, plotting, the beaver rose up on its hind legs and leaned back on its tail as if straining to get a better look at the great light coming its way. Then it whipped around and scuttled to the edge of the road where the stream ran by. I heard a splash as it fled into the darkness. Still, I went home in great excitement, thinking that if beavers were just up the road, one drumlin over, it was only a matter of time before one of them found the great beaver real estate now waiting on the other side. But beavers never showed up. Starting in 2016, we began hearing target shooting near that end of the road by the wetland where the beavers lived, then Sunday afternoons became punctuated by rapid-fire rifle shots, hideously loud. When we started hearing the shooting after dark we called the state trooper (our town had no police department), but they said it wasn't against the law; our neighbor was within his rights to shoot on his property. Historically around here, shooting beavers was a country pastime, like shooting rats at the town dump.

"Too bad you can't bring a beaver here," said Andy, interrupting my thoughts. "Of course it's against the law, but it looks like a place they should be."

Dr. Burchsted said nothing. It was clear she was considering the role the meadow played especially now, holding water despite the drought.

"It would be interesting to get some rebar and poke around," she said. "We call it checking for 'refusal,' just poke around and see how deep the mud is and what is going on in the streambed. I bet you are going to find that it's bedrock."

Back in the Yale-Myers Forest, Andy had described his current research. His geomorphology research lab was studying sedimentation patterns in beaver sites in Connecticut to try to determine not just the ways beavers have shaped the river system but how long they have been here. Andy's team was collecting sediment cores from beaver sites to analyze them for grain size and organic content. The cores were also being subsampled for geochemical analyses including radiocarbon, lead, and cesium-137 in order to date the sediment. In 1963, peak fallout from nuclear testing in the United States left traces of radioactive particles everywhere. (If cesium-137 is detected in the sediment you know it was laid down in 1963.)

While in places like Oregon, California, and Washington, scientists have been able to deduce a great deal from studying the sedimentation in beaver meadows, it is more difficult here in the northeast. Overall sedimentation in the northeast is highly variable due to glacial history. When the glaciers retreated north beginning 21,000 years ago, the landscape was scoured, scraping away much of the surficial sediment and leaving behind mostly glacial till, a poorly sorted mix of sediment sizes. In addition, there is a long history of anthropogenic land use, including deforestation and the damming of rivers for mill power, further scoring and complicating the sedimentation throughout the watersheds. This complex land use and glacial history makes for highly variable sedimentation patterns. And the mountain ranges in the East, the Adirondacks and the Catskills, are much older than western ranges such as the Rockies.

Andy's team hopes to identify how long beavers have been actively building dams here in Connecticut and extend our understanding of the role of beaver meadows in river systems. Until recently, most people, including scientists, have tended to skew toward valuing the beaver pond over the beaver meadow. By transforming from pond to meadow, the beaver site allows for grasses, then shrubs, then trees to recolonize the area—this disruption brings vitalization, and creates habitat for creatures like rabbit, grouse, moose, and deer that need dry land. Only now when we better understand the complexity of the forest, the way trees communicate, and the value of dead wood to the fungal networks that operate as the world wide web of the forest, are we beginning to understand the fuller value of the work beavers do.

I was guilty of this. I still missed my beavers down the road, the fact of them moving between their world and mine, the pond's messengers, surfacing when they felt like it. The Algonquian people called the beavers the "underwater people," acknowledging both their connection to and distance from humanity. I thought of beavers as an enigma, a constant reminder that there was a world under that water I could never fully know.

If I imagined hard enough, I might be able to see beneath the meadow's grasses and sedges, the wildflowers and ferns, bringing to mind a world of microorganisms now happily looping and twisting, curling and unwinding or holding in the soil—an ocean of life only recently discovered and that scientists had named the *soil biome*. But to even begin to see those microorganisms I'd need a powerful microscope.

Before we left, Andy and Dr. Burchsted started talking casually about how if they dated the sediment layers, they might well find evidence of beavers living here back through the 11,700 years of the Holocene. Just the mention of that word opened a gate in my mind and I was soon thinking of those ancient bear-sized beavers that lived alongside mastodons in the late Pleistocene. Those megafauna beavers had died out in the fifth extinction at the end of the last great ice age, but given the geology here, it now seemed even more plausible that *Castor canadensis*, the more modest-sized later species of beavers we see today, had indeed been living here right in this perfect valley between the drumlins not just for hundreds of years, but for thousands. Beavers were here long before the first ships left Europe, initially in search of cod banks, then beaver fur, way back before the discovery of so much beaver fur, those round pelts, which launched the transatlantic trade that instigated the beaver wars that destabilized, then almost destroyed, the culture and economies of the Indigenous peoples living here, to become the currency of this newly colonized land, those "beaver dollars," which ignited the first great engines of American capitalism. Take back three hundred years and right here on this road we would be standing in North America at the time when the mythic Great Beaver and Gluskap—the man who came from nothing and often stood in for the creator in chasing Great Beaver—were knocking about the forest. Before 1600, all of the continent from west to east, save a few desert sections, had stretched out as one great Beaverland. Could beavers now help us restore some of that natural resiliency?

A few weeks later, I meet Dr. Burchsted on Zoom so she could show me slides of one of her current research sites on the Ashuelot River near Keene, New Hampshire. In 1940, the federal government moved people out of a wide area on the Ashuelot, a tributary of the Connecticut River, in order to create a flood control zone. In the eighty-two years since people moved out, beavers have moved in. In a grainy black-and-white photograph of the river dated from 1940, it moves through the land as a serpentine thread. But in the next slide, an infrared image of the river from 2002, I see many thin lines of water, running everywhere, swelling into oblong pods then seeming to disappear altogether before popping out; the area was a series of beaver ponds, strung along like beads on a chain.

"This is what the river would be doing if people weren't here," said Dr. Burchsted excitedly. "You don't see a single brook going through meadows; the brook disappears into the landscape instead." I thought of what we had seen in the Yale-Myers Forest, the Branch Brook watercourse hidden beneath a low-lying canopy of grasses. *A beaver meadow is a dam that is but isn't.* This was Dr. Burchsted's point made vividly clear: The Ashuelot was still running, but so spread throughout the land that there was no longer any visible channel.

In the United States, as in most countries, billions of dollars are spent yearly to manage rivers, mostly through engineering solutions like building and maintaining dams. And, as in most things, science is not without fashion. According to Dr. Ellen Wohl, a fluvial geomorphologist based at Colorado State University, connectivity has been the current buzzword in river restoration for some time (dating back to the river continuum concept).

But that vision of connectivity has historically been longitudinal—and ignored thinking of the river as an ecosystem interdependent with and connected to its surrounding floodplains and drainage basin. Dr. Wohl has written extensively on the need to create a different kind of connectivity, one that considers a river system in lateral terms, as a watercourse connected to its banks and floodplains and larger ecology. Here in Connecticut, which is divided by one of the largest river valleys in the world, the Connecticut River valley, that means thinking of the Connecticut River as integral to the land spreading out on either side. In her book *Disconnected Rivers: Linking Rivers to Landscape,* Dr. Wohl points out the ways in which rivers are not static but instead are impacted by weather and geology and inevitably adjust, becoming less and less that classic vision of a single rushing channel of water. Rather, left to its own preferences, a river naturally widens, flattens out into a series of braided channels as sediment deposits—carried down especially in times of flooding to create, over time, a series of islands around which the water must flow. Thinking of a river as an ecosystem means not just connecting the channel to the land through which it flows, but taking into consideration the needs and health of the organisms that live in the various zones of the river, particularly the photosynthetic organisms like algae and bacteria as well as the less famous protists, all of which serve as the basis of the food web.

It doesn't take much scientific knowledge to understand the gravity of the situation. No algae, no insects. No insects, no fish. And no amphibians, either. No frogs or fish means no mammals like bear, raccoon, fisher, bobcat, or birds. No insects, no frogs, or fish, or birds, or mammals, no food for humans. No food for humans, no humans.

But ecological connectivity is not the aim of most river management, which historically has focused on trying to get rivers to behave like canals. The reason is simple: Look on a map of the continental United States and along each of the five major river basin systems—the St. Lawrence, the Mississippi, the Columbia, the Colorado, and the Rio Grande. The land is a grid of cities, towns, and roads. The Connecticut River, which flows 410 miles from its source in a pond called Fourth Connecticut Lake in northern New Hampshire and ends in Old Lyme, Connecticut, is controlled by sixteen dams on its main waterway, plus another thousand dams slowing the waters of its tributaries. In his now classic work *The Control of Nature,* John McPhee tells the tragicomedy of one of our most famous environmental fiascos, historic attempts to control the Mississippi. And North America is not alone; today the world has dammed or diverted most of its major rivers. It is pretty obvious that we have far too much infrastructure in place in the form of cities, railroads, factories, and roads for us to enable most rivers to return to their fully natural state. To take a local example: Where would the city of Hartford, built along the banks of the Connecticut River, go?

Dr. Burchsted believes that beavers can still play a valuable role in overall river health, particularly beaver meadows. She explains, "A study in the Adirondacks calculated that beaver dams there gave way after four to ten years, but the beaver meadows last a lot longer. This means they can provide a lot of small storage along a river system. All those small areas of storage can add up."

"So beavers can play a role in helping control flooding?" I ask.

"The problem is that we have built cities where the water goes," she answers slowly, "so asking if beavers can control a flood is maybe the wrong question." She flips off the PowerPoint and her face suddenly fills the screen. She is grinning. "What we saw in the Yale Forest was baby stuff. You need to see a place where beavers have really made a river move around. If you are up for a drive, I'd like to show you one of my research sites in the White Mountains."

Chapter 10

Beavers in the White Mountains

It will be a full year before I can take Dr. Burchsted up on her offer. When we finally meet at a rest stop along the highway south of Keene, New Hampshire, we will both still be wearing masks. We will still be living through the pandemic that has left us all with a new sense of anxiety and fear, but, newly vaccinated and hopeful, we jump in Dr. Burchsted's car and speed north. Our destination is the Hubbard Brook Experimental Forest, a 7,800-acre expanse in the White Mountains established in 1955 by the U.S. Department of Agriculture as the primary hydrological research facility in the Northeast.

The research center lies at the top of a dirt road, fourteen hundred feet above sea level. During the drive up, Dr. Burchsted and I were almost giddy to be on the road, in the company of a person outside of our Covid "pod"; the Delta variant is yet to come. Dr. Burchsted's research projects are still on hold due to the pandemic, but the center is now reopened and she wants to revisit the Zig Zag Brook where she and a team of graduate students had been marking dying or dead trees to document the rate at which the trees rotted, and eventually fell, and once they fell, how they served to create blockages along the river.

What excites her about where we are going is that the Forest, managed by the National Park Service and funded by the federal government through the National Oceanic and Atmospheric Administration, is so remote and has been undisturbed long enough to give researchers a picture of what North American paleo-rivers once looked like. These are the rivers of Beaverland.

The plan is to first pick up Dr. Scott Bailey, the lead scientist for the Hubbard Brook Ecosystem Study located there. Then we will hike in together.

The entire forest is watershed for Hubbard Brook, a tributary of the Pemi-gewasett River. As we pull up, Dr. Bailey steps out the door. He is a large, jovial-looking man dressed like a park ranger in a tan long-sleeved shirt, dark pants, and boots. His open face is framed with curls of brown hair. A knapsack is slung over one shoulder, his socks are pulled up over his calves, and he carries a walking stick; he is ready to bushwhack and jumps in the car.

We drive up a steep, winding road. At a curve, Dr. Bailey points out the window and jokes, "That's it, that's where you should genuflect—that is where it all started, where watershed studies began and they discovered acid rain." I peer into the woods. In 1963, one of the biggest discoveries in environmental science occurred here when three Dartmouth professors set up a radical research project to study the water flow of a particular water-shed and in doing so discovered acid rain. This rain is so toxic to plants and trees that entire forests, particularly spruce, began dying. The professors went on to document without a doubt that acid rain was formed when fossil fuels, primarily oil and coal, are combusted, emitting sulfur dioxide and nitrogen oxides into the atmosphere. Some of these gases are converted to acids, which fall back to earth with the rain. The researchers assessed the damage that acid rain was doing to forests throughout North America. The situation was extreme enough for Congress to enact two critical pieces of environmental legislation, the Clean Air and Clean Water acts, which put in place federal regulations to reduce emissions.

The Hubbard Brook Ecosystem Study continues to this day, funded by the National Science Foundation. And in 1988 the area was declared an LTER, a Long Term Environmental Research site. Over sixty scientists con-duct research there, including Dr. Denise Burchsted.

Bug spray on, water bottles packed, we are off. The plan is to follow the Zig Zag Brook and locate some of Dr. Burchsted's research sites along it, then head along Hubbard Brook to find more research sites before loop-ing back here to the car. Dr. Burchsted has a plan and a map in her head of where she intends to take us, but I have no idea yet where exactly that is. Soon we are wading through ferns so tall they almost brush my neck. Dr. Burchsted leads the way, followed by Dr. Bailey. They move quickly, cer-tain of their destination although I don't see any path. Each step is spongy with thick layers of forest duff, moss, and leaves. I can't believe how lush the forest is. Images of acid rain come to mind, those wasted grey spires of great spruce and the lines of maples denuded in early summer. Nothing like that here. Everywhere I look it resembles something closer to a jungle. Soon we hear the brook and are walking down alongside it. Dr. Bailey points to an area where he says moose have browsed. Sure enough, the thick green bushes are all mowed down to a uniform height. He moves his stick to reveal a large pile of brown droppings. "Yup, been right here. They love this hobblebush."

I'm used to seeing deer poop in the woods, but these droppings are huge, the size of baseballs. After making a comeback, moose are on the decline again in the East. The trend of increasingly warmer winters has given ticks the opportunity to survive winter in such numbers that come spring they attack the moose in droves, draining them of their blood to the point that the moose, especially the young, are too weak to survive.

Dr. Bailey, who has been busy putting a pin on the GPS map on his phone to mark the moose browse spot, looks up and watches me poking at the enormous dung with my stick. "If you want some," he jokes, "you can buy shellacked moose poop pendants in Conway."

We continue hiking down, following the side of Zig Zag Brook, when Dr. Burchsted stops and points ahead to where a few trees have tipped and have either fallen over into the brook or are about to. Each is a mature tree, with a girth the size of a basketball.

"Are these logs examples of river discontinuum?" I ask.

We look at the stream where the water splits and then veers to the right. Dr. Burchsted nods, adding, "This is normal river behavior here. It is just a little bit of a traffic jam, just baby stuff." She walks forward and points out the blue tag on the fallen tree; it is one of the logs she and her students had tagged pre-Covid to monitor its rate of decay, function, and longevity. Dr. Burchsted is curious to see if any of those have since fallen.

"I like these logs," she says, giving one of them a satisfied thump as she walks by, "but we should keep hiking so you can see real discontinuity."

I quickly begin to understand what Dr. Burchsted meant when she said a woodland river system is dynamic. Where she is now standing, the brook widens into a wide bank of rock, at least fifteen feet across. This was clearly once the path of a wide, fast-moving current, but now in July, the brook has shrunk down to a slow-moving tongue of water narrow enough for me to jump across.

"These side channels are so interesting in terms of the ecology," she explains, pointing to the now dry channel threads. "In a big river these threads could be half a mile apart and you'll find insects living in both channels that are part of the same community even though they are now living far apart." An amazing number of aquatic insects live in the sediment of a river—black flies, mayflies, stone flies, damselflies, caddisflies, gnats, and mosquitoes. And that wasn't even considering the tiny invertebrates that scraped and shredded and grazed on the organic matter, or filtered the muddy water for the tiniest bits of food.

I point to some orange tags by the bank.

"No, not mine," Dr. Burchsted says. "I think that's a salamander study."

Dr. Bailey leaves off marking the location of plants on his phone and walks up. "Yes, that's the salamander group. If you see it out here, somebody is studying it. This place is crawling with scientists." He examines some of the tags and adds, "If you want to find a scientist's habitat, come here—look under rotten logs, turn over rocks—I guarantee you will find a scientist."

Just ahead is an impressive sight; a huge tree is leaning across the brook. Dr. Bailey walks under it and fingers the peeling grey bark. "Yellow birch," he says simply.

"How old?" I'm looking at the tree and wondering if I could even reach my arms around half of it.

"Two hundred years," he answers, matter-of-fact.

I am awestruck. "A mother tree."

"More like a grandmother tree," says Dr. Burchsted, now standing beside me staring at the trunk.

For much of our drive up the New Hampshire interstate, Dr. Burchsted and I discussed the research of Dr. Suzanne Simard, a forester who has spent the last twenty years researching the way trees communicate. Using radio isotopes, Dr. Simard has tracked the ways that trees in a forest not only trade nutrients through the mycorrhizae, the fungal network, but also send chemical signals that constitute a complex form of communication. Research conducted by Dr. Simard and teams of researchers in Switzerland has proven without a doubt that the forest is organized in ways that resemble kinship groups, with the oldest trees playing key roles. Simard calls these the "mother trees." A mother tree can send nutrients to kin over non-kin even among the same species, and if there is a plant intruder, can send warning signals to her kin, or poison to the intruder. When you learn of this research, it starts to make sense to think of trees as the "tree people" of the Algonquian Great Beaver stories.

The forest, spliced with sun. The powerful but now quiet brook. The toppled birch. We stand for a moment taking in this bewitching spot and listen to the brook while we stare at the tree; its great limbs, still full of green leaves, seem to hang suspended in midair. How long will it take for it to fall?

Dr. Bailey pats the tree as if in farewell and Dr. Burchsted sighs, then heads on down the watershed, explaining as she goes, "This is what I mean that the idea of free-flowing river is a myth, it just isn't a thing...Gravity is the law. Gravity only pulls things down, and what is at the bottom is the river valley. When a tree falls, gravity does its job, and usually it ends up in the river."

Soon we have followed the many zigs and zags that the brook is named after and have reached the junction where it feeds into Hubbard Brook. The "mouth" of a brook (or river) is where it ends, gasping out its waters, while the "head" is where it begins. We are at the mouth of Zig Zag. When it meets Hubbard Brook, it spills around several angular boulders to fill a large pool. Dr. Burchsted bends down and looks at the pool, then feels a few rocks.

"Slimy," she says. "This water is being fed by nutrients. Look up ahead, you'll see the beaver meadow." She points ahead to where the trees open out. Then she looks back at the reddish tinge of the bottom of the pool approvingly.

"Got some iron slop going on here. That's a good sign of organic matter. Diatoms and algae being fed by the water still in the meadow. That will feed insects, and this is what fish eat."

As we continue, I keep looking down so I don't slip on the rocks, but when I glance up, I see Dr. Bailey through the trees. He is standing on what looks like a dam a good five feet up above the brook, grinning.

"What do you think of this?" he asks. "Do you remember a lodge here?"

"Totally," answers Dr. Burchsted cheerfully, clearly pleased to see this beaver site again. "I'll eat my hat if there isn't a lodge farther up."

We climb up and soon we are pushing through spires of goldenrod and spirea and sawgrass. Dr. Burchsted explains meadow succession—as usual, the health of the forest goes back to what is going on underneath the ground.

"Grass can outcompete trees because there is no mycorrhizae after the water goes down," she explains, referring to the fungal networks. "That takes a while to build up, it is actually the movement of mammals back into the meadow that spread spores and bring fungus. In this way, trees follow small mammals."

She walks on, but not before cutting her hand on a particularly sharp blade of sawgrass. She laughs. "Ouch, that's sharp. My theory is that sawgrass evolved to be so obnoxious in order to keep mammals out, and thus keep trees from coming in."

Dr. Bailey points to a group of seedlings. "Yellow birch," he says happily. "They need disruption like this to get a start. The forest floor is too thick with duff and leaf matter for the seeds to get a start, but in a mud flat like this the roots can penetrate and they can grow."

The recent drought has left only a thin skim of water that deepens occasionally into pools skirted by mud. When we step around one pool, I see the tracks of large dark hoof. Thick, cloven toes. Moose. The tracks look freshly made and are as wide as my hand. I feel myself stiffen and glance toward the tree line. The undergrowth is so thick that we can't see anything past the first line of trees, but a moose, if it were there, could see and hear us. If they feel threatened, or if they just feel like it, moose can charge and have been known to seriously injure people who come too close to them. But Dr. Bailey and Dr. Burchsted seem unconcerned. They are now head down, looking at a place where the once deep water has scoured a part of the bank, revealing layers of sediment in varying shades of grey and brown.

"Are we looking at glacial fluvial deposit?" asks Dr. Bailey.

Dr. Burchsted runs her hand through it. "It's fine sand and silt," she answers. "This pond was here for a long time to have collected this much sediment." She points to the different layers as Dr. Bailey becomes animated.

"We could be looking at deposits made over hundreds of years—or thousands. This soil could have been deposited ten to fourteen thousand years ago during deglaciation."

Dr. Burchsted pulls out a white turnip from her backpack, the only food I'll see her eat until we get back down to her car. "Sorry, I missed lunch." She crunches the raw turnip and keeps looking at the soil layers. "My theory is that this was the result of glaciation, not beavers. The beaver influence is maybe the layers of soil on top of these layers of sand and silt."

I listen, but by now talk of glaciers and sediment layers dating back to the early Holocene is no longer surprising. I pull out my own lunch, an egg salad sandwich, which is now so flat and compressed it resembles my notepad, and eat it quickly. While I sit there, a dragonfly lands on a rock, its black geometric wings resembling a tiny, futuristic drone.

We walk back down to rejoin Hubbard Brook and press on. I see Dr. Burchsted lean her head down toward the brook, now running fast, and when I bend down I hear the low rumbling sound of rocks being pummeled beneath the current. "Okay, we're getting somewhere," she says, unable to keep the excitement from her voice. Dr. Bailey has already forged ahead. When we make the next turn, we see him standing on what could easily be mistaken for a water feature.

Before us rises one of the most beautiful beaver constructions I have ever seen, too complex to even take in at once. On one side, a stack of thick logs, wedged between boulders, holds back the water, which brims over the top and presses through many cracks and crannies in the center. But the other half of the brook—it takes me a second to register what I am seeing, but this is still Hubbard Brook—is being held back by a basket weave of sticks; the current swirls in gentle eddies as if it had been caught in a huge bird's nest. In many places the brook trickles through the weave of sticks, while in other spots it spills over and cascades down as a series of mini waterfalls that descend into rock pools. The sounds of the water as it rushes and spills and splashes down are as varied and beautiful as the interplay of wood and water and stone. Along the top of the narrow dam I see a green frill of branches with telltale chewed white points. Then spreading back beyond and far into the woods on either side is a large pool, the surface taut as a drum; that too is brook, only spread out a good forty feet so that the water surrounds nearby trees. I have seen pictures of much larger beaver dams in the Lake Superior region. One dam in northern Wisconsin measured twelve feet high and nine feet across; it was holding back over fifty acres of water. But when I look at this site, I feel like laughing—the whole thing is so playful and goofy it looks like some kind of beaver water park.

Who says beavers have no sense of humor?

Dr. Burchsted grins. This is one of the sites she had most wanted me to see. "The beavers had no business damming the brook here." She has to raise her voice to be heard over the water. "This brook is just way too strong, it's too big!"

"It's a conspiracy." Dr. Bailey laughs. "You have a debris pile there where two or three dead fir came together and lodged along this other dead tree on top of the boulder, then the beavers got to work...It's a big conspiracy."

We all want to take pictures of ourselves with this wonder of a beaver construction with logjam. But as soon as that is done Dr. Burchsted and Dr. Bailey are off like hounds, following the tracks left by the brook, the dry current where it had once raced through the forest on either side, leaving a blueprint of its spring runoff, or pre-drought, shape. They study the ground, pointing out areas of pressed-down fern, or places where the duff has been worn away, a bank of gravel. At one point Dr. Bailey hollers, "Look at this elbow. Look at this oxbow here."

I watch them pointing out scour marks and places where branches and leaf litter, carried down on the current, have been left in piles where the brook took a turn and the leaves became snagged on rocks or brush. They are more interested in this dry river channel than the water rushing serenely on behind us. I turn back to the beaver pond created right in the middle of the brook. On the far side I can see a bank lodge. Several maple trees have been half bitten through. The beavers must still be here somewhere.

When I catch up to Dr. Burchsted and Dr. Bailey they are studying places twenty and thirty feet from the brook where beaver have been harvesting.

"They were working on that red maple over there."

"Yes, and more recent scars here."

"So, are they still around?"

"Not sure," says Dr. Burchsted. "They could be up at the farther pond, we'll see."

Beaver were rare in New Hampshire at the end of the eighteenth century, although an exact date of extirpation was never noted. Neither was the exact year of their return. Henry David Thoreau was greatly concerned when some sixty years later he could no longer find any sign of beaver (or wolves) at Walden Pond in nearby Massachusetts. He famously wrote in his journal on March 23, 1856: "When I consider that the nobler animals have been exterminated here—the cougar, the panther, lynx, wolverine, wolf, bear, moose, deer, the beaver... I cannot but feel as if I live in a tamed, and, as it were, emasculated country."

Beaver were never restocked to New Hampshire as they were in Connecticut, New York, and many other states, although some found their way here from Maine and Canada. The first official sightings occurred in 1912 in the White Mountains, and by 1915 an estimated 240 beaver were thought to be living in the state. In 1926 a conservation officer trapped four beaver in Pittsburgh, New Hampshire, and released them near Concord. In 1930 a pair of beaver were live-trapped for display during the Rochester Fair, then liberated at Middleton. By 1940 the beaver had adapted and begun to thrive so much that an estimated 7,000 beaver now filled the state. The Fish and Game Department opened a limited trapping season in just one area that year and 369 beavers were taken by fifty-seven trappers. The entire state was opened for beaver trapping in 1943. But trapping and hunting are not allowed in the Hubbard Brook research center, so the beavers have had sixty years to reestablish themselves in the watershed. No one has counted the number of beavers living here, but clearly it is still far from the density that once existed. Statewide, the trapping season starts in October and ends in April; there is no limit on the number of beaver an individual can trap.

Finally, we have located Torpedo Trout Pond, named this by Dr. Burchsted because it was here that years ago, her son, who as a grade school kid often accompanied her in her research, caught his first trout. Back then, the pond was large and full of beavers, and apparently trout as well. The pond is just a glimmer and an open spot through the trees, and we all stop to catch our breath. We've been bushwhacking for over an hour with

Dr. Burchsted in the lead and Dr. Bailey following. I bring up the rear, close on Dr. Bailey's heels. I am grateful for his big stride, which presses down the grasses, and his walking stick, which beats back the undergrowth to open a way forward. Every step is monotony: lush undergrowth, towering trees, blast of hot sun, mosquitoes. But before us is a change in the pattern, a uniform forest of conifers. Dr. Bailey looks at my puzzled expression and explains, "From 1880 to 1910 this area would have been bottomland spruce, then once it was cut out, the fir that you see here came in."

"What was the spruce used for?"

"The wood is lightweight and strong," says Dr. Bailey. "They built Boston with it."

We are looking at an area that European colonists had deforested by the late 1800s, the second wave of environmental devastation that followed the removal of the beaver. By the time Europeans arrived to build homesteads in New Hampshire and other parts of interior New England, the fur trade—and thus the beaver extinction—was well under way. Suddenly my feet begin sinking. We've hit forest wetland, which means we are getting close. Then we turn a corner and we all stop to take in the beauty of what is now before us. Spreading out in a wave of green is a rippling meadow that looks more like Colorado than New England with its ring of dark conifers. In the distance are the looming humps of mountains.

"This end was always meadow," says Dr. Burchsted, "but at the far end was a lodge and an active pond. This is I think the source population for the beavers we saw working farther down. Shall we try to find it?"

No one wants to stop now. As we continue on we pass a series of small dams in the brooks leading to the pond.

Dr. Burchsted looks down at one and jokes, "I have the feeling that beavers kick the juveniles out for the day the way farm families used to kick teenagers out to go build stone walls—they go out and build stuff like this, you see a lot of small dams around beaver ponds with not much function." Dr. Bailey interjects, "Boomerang kids, I have some of those."

"Me too," adds Dr. Burchsted. And we talk for a minute of how the pandemic landscape has changed life for college-age kids. Then Dr. Burchsted adds, "Beavers can come back and live in the same pond, they just have to build a new apartment. You take some lodges apart and there are different areas where the young beavers have returned."

As they talk I think of the graph illustrating the growth of beaver population on the Connecticut Department of Energy and Environment Protection website. In the graph, beavers reproduce at Rodentia speed: Two beavers bear four kits a year, which quickly becomes sixteen, then the numbers explode. The fur trappers I knew cited this information in trapping education classes and clinics to support the general assumption that culling 30–35 percent of the beaver every year helped keep the population stable. The problem was these numbers were hypothetical. Two-year-old beavers did leave the lodge to find mates, but for reasons no one knows, some return to their family, content to stay on as babysitters for the next season of kits. And when food is scarce, beaver reproduction declines. Or the kits do not survive. The dams and lodges and canals that beavers construct are well studied, but as I kept discovering, relatively little research has been conducted on the animal itself.

We keep walking, but soon we are climbing over a mound of earth that we all realize is an overgrown dam. And there, just beyond a huge exposed boulder that sticks up like a rounded bone, is a beaver lodge. But there is no sign of live beavers.

Dr. Burchsted studies the edges and comes back. She shrugs.

"Maybe this is why the beavers were working so hard farther down," Dr. Bailey offers.

"Maybe," she replies. They discuss the possible reasons why the beavers have left while Dr. Bailey puts a pin in his phone and makes a note to check on the site in the fall.

By the time we have hiked back up to the car, dropped Dr. Bailey at the research station, and headed down, the sun is low on the horizon. We follow the road in silence for a bit, then Dr. Burchsted says brightly, "Up ahead is the Pemigewasett. Want to see it?"

"You bet."

She turns onto a bridge and we look down at the river, now a rather narrow body of water flanked by a wide cobble beach. As we stand there, enjoying the waves of now cool air, the gleam of sun on the water, Dr. Burchsted adds, "We have this perception that is really at the root of a lot of our modern environmental problems—that nature is a place where there are no humans—and this is false for starters. Secondly, it is actually racist, since it erases the presence of Indigenous people who stewarded that land for literally millennia."

Her comment underscores emerging (albeit overdue) conversations about race and American history that are now underscoring contemporary writing about North American environments. The ideal of the great North American wilderness as an antipode to civilization (in the spirit of some of our most impassioned voices for environmental preservation, such as Ralph Waldo Emerson, Henry David Thoreau, John Muir, and Aldo Leopold) can only exist if you have removed the humans who lived and are still living in these lands.

The name Pemigewasett comes from the Algonquian word meaning "where the side current is," and the river runs south to join the Merrimack and eventually pour out into the Atlantic Ocean. By the end of the seventeenth century, it would become yet another site of Native American genocide. In the aftermath of the short but bloody King Philip's War, when many Nipmuc and Pequot from Connecticut and Massachusetts, who had sided with Metacom against the English, sought to flee, they followed the watershed north by canoe. Their destination was the headwaters of the Connecticut River, the mythic homeland of Great Beaver—two lakes far up north where they believed they would be safe. But along the way were bounty hunters, like Lt. Thomas Baker, whose company of scouts received scalp bounties for destroying a Pemigewasett Village. On our way out, Dr. Burchsted and I will try to find the marker, built by the Asquamchumauke chapter of the Daughters of the American Revolution to commemorate Baker, who was made a captain after the raid.

"Time to go?"

"Time to go."

We drive for a while in silence, watching sunlight bounce along the cobble banks of the Pemigewasett. It seems only right to feel and see the horror of this history. Colonization had exacted a high price on humans as well as the environment.

Before long, we enter a cute New Hampshire summer town that still bears the almost jarring register of summer tourism. Awnings are out, flags and neon lights blare "Open," tables fill the sidewalks in front of cafés and bakeries, and people wander, relaxed and sandaled, or booted up for a hike. Lines of cars fill both sides of the road, barely visible under loads of kayaks and bicycles. After hours of silence in the woods, it feels strange to suddenly be surrounded by so much interaction. We jump out and quickly get some food to munch during the next leg of our drive south.

When we are on the road again, I ask Dr. Burchsted what could be done to return a river like the Pemigewasett to its natural state. I am thinking of the road that runs alongside it and the town we have just passed through. "You have to go back a step," she answers, "and ask, what is our right relationship with rivers? We are only learning that now. The Hubbard Brook site is one of the only ones I know where the river has the most freedom to respond. Beavers there have a wide valley and food opportunity. The bottom line is, if you want to see a river act like a river, you have to go far from a road. The problem with roads is that they depend on stability, but the only thing in nature we can count on is change."

I push away our snacks to take notes. Back in 1948, when he wrote *A Sand County Almanac*, Aldo Leopold was already worried about the environmental impact of building so many roads to, ironically, give Americans access to wilderness. Dr. Burchsted adds gravely, "I think we are headed for a reckoning, because we are on a shockingly unsustainable path and we've known it for a long time."

By the time I get home, the moon is bright and cicadas are whipping the night into a frenzy of sound. I stand outside in the yard for a moment, my toes, released from hot and cramped hiking boots, spread out into the sharp, cool grass.

What I saw today was sobering. But more than that, it was hopeful. The Hubbard Brook watershed was a forest healing from at least three successive waves of human-accelerated environmental change, or, to put it more bluntly, environmental devastation. The first was the overtrapping of the beavers, resulting in the "great drying" of wetlands and degradation of the river system; the second was the deforestation and further drying of the forest when European colonists arrived, beginning the massive waves of timber harvesting that resulted in deforestation and further impact on the river system through the intensive implementation of sawmills and mill dams; the third was the damage from industrial pollution, in the massive destruction of trees due to acid rain. And this wasn't even considering the ongoing impact of climate change. Smart policies enacted just in time, such as the Clean Air and Clean Water acts signed into legislation by a Republican administration back when the Republican Party was still interested in protecting the environment, were critical.

But what was clear in that lush New England forest was the incredible power of the natural world to adapt and, if given a chance, to heal. And in this regeneration, beavers played a significant role. I thought back to the moment we had all stepped out of the forest and back onto the dirt road. Just before the car, Dr. Bailey had pushed aside the ferns with his walking stick and pointed. "Thought I saw a flash of wings," he said simply. Near his boot, tucked into the grass, was a twist of nest, in which lay three bright blue eggs. A hermit thrush. Each delicate egg was no bigger than the nail of my thumb.

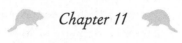

Chapter 11

The Beaverhood

I couldn't stop thinking about something Dr. Burchsted had said: Beavers can make streams switch watersheds. "Beavers will send water wherever they want it to go. They even send water where it should not go. They break all the rules." She went on to add, "I could take satellite imagery of a mountainous area with clearly defined ridges separating one watershed from another, and it would only take me fifteen minutes to show you a beaver pond that is actually sending water back toward the mountain—even opposite the slope."

As soon as I could I pulled up the satellite imagery I had collected about the beaver pond by my house on Taylor Brook that was now a beaver meadow. There the spot was in 2009, a long green patch between the trees, meaning no trees but some form of marshy meadow, then in 2010 you can see that light green patch beginning to fill with water, and dark water spreads out like an ink stain from the spot where the brook runs under the culvert of the bridge. By late 2010, that dark stain of water covers half the area, and by 2012 it is a full pond, .42 miles long and .49 miles wide.

It is when I pull up the lidar image of the area, a form of infrared photography that shows only the landforms minus any vegetation, that I suddenly see the obvious. In the grey-and-white image, in which landforms look as if they have been carefully sculpted from clay, our beaver pond lies in just one of what is a field of interconnected valleys. On either side of the pond, the drumlins rise up six hundred feet above sea level. No wonder that with the brook running through its center and the accumulation of rain and snowmelt that would have been shed by the drumlins, there was enough water here to attract beaver. All they had to do was build a simple dam, and presto, water filled the valley.

Geologists salivate over pictures of Woodstock, calling it the most famous "drumlin field" in the Northeast. That is because pretty much the entire sixty-four square miles of the town rises up and down as a series of glacier-carved hills, now mostly wooded. Between the drumlins run brooks and streams, which comprise the watershed for the Quinebaug River, which in turn is part of the Thames River basin.

In the lidar map I see how Taylor Brook runs south from our beaver pond to connect to similarly small valleys nestled between drumlins, the brook large enough to see clearly as it heads south. It crosses under a road, then it is joined by another brook, which I see is actually the brook at the end of our road, less than half a mile from the beaver pond. A bit farther south, both brooks flow into the valley formed by a huge drumlin, the largest in this part of the map.

Dr. Burchsted had pointed out that in a drumlin field, water passes through one valley, then, because the glacier scoured hills in random patterns, it tends to hit the edge of the next drumlin, where it has to turn right or left to follow the downward slope of the land. As she explained this, I'd imagined a vast pinball machine, with water moving down lever to lever, going right or left. Ping, ping. But then she'd pointed out how beavers will pop the water where they want it, complicating the path of the water, which might have just followed gravity, inertia, and slope, but now was being directed by a furry engineer. And if beavers could pop water around, then who could tell where streams would go, or which streams would be full and which would have dried up? More to the point, what if some of those valleys I was looking at on the lidar image were now filled with water? If they had water, they could also have beavers.

I grabbed the map and headed out by car to follow the stream south. I knew the landowner of one of the largest drumlins and had permission to walk the three hundred acres of meadow and field that comprised his land, so I started there. Sure enough, just off the road, I saw how the stream ran along for a bit then opened out into a pond. This pond was clearly man-made, a beautiful oval complete with a few carefully placed boulders around the edges, and stands of purple Joe Pye weed, and I didn't see any beavers. But I had skated on the pond with neighbors more than a few times and I did remember them saying that they sometimes saw otters there, playing and chirping. Otters, like mink, followed beaver because the beaver's pond and wetlands became home to healthy populations of amphibians and fish, things they would eat.

At the edge of the drumlin, I stood for a minute taking in the thick, sweet scent of wild asters and Queen Anne's lace; the meadow was filled with wildflowers, as if someone had thrown handfuls of colored confetti, yellow, purple, white. When I saw that the stream continued south from that pond, I began walking along it. The ground underfoot was rocky, muddy, and overgrown with shrubs where the stream entered the woods. I plunged in but was soon stopped by razor-sharp brambles. After carefully dislodging the sharp points twisted into my pants and the one strand that had drawn blood on one arm, I backed up slowly and veered up to continue along the ridge of the drumlin. Eventually the trees gave way and opened out into a marshy area. I plunged back down and this time was able to wade through the tall grasses. The stream now spread out into what looked like a forested wetland; large trees, still alive, but completely surrounded by water. Sun slid along the surface of the water in sly lines, parting the tree shadows, confusing my sense of distance and space, but even so, I found it. There, by the far edge, almost hidden by a towering maple, rose that telltale pile of greying sticks and mud, a beaver lodge. I couldn't believe it.

The lodge was not particularly large and had a lopsided look, and I didn't see a feed pile, but there it was; proof that beavers were there, or had been.

I circled the edge of the water, which spread out deeper until the tree line ended and suddenly curved out into a round pond banked with meadow. Wind was brushing the water, causing riffles, and it was dark, implying depth. I wondered if originally this pond, like the previous one, had been man-made and the beavers had moved in, extending it, or if it had been created by them entirely and the water had filled this low spot in the land.

At the far end, the pond was bordered by a bank upon which ran a farm road. The stream ran over the road, but as a wide sheet of water so vehicles could easily manage it. When I looked down I saw the marks where tractors had driven through. The beavers had cleverly dammed the stream here just enough to keep the pond full, but they had not tried to stop the water entirely—a constant flow was trickling and spilling through. I still didn't see a feed pile or a beaver slide where they might be coming and going, but the dam was in good repair, topped up with an even line of carefully patted mud. Beavers were here. Somewhere. I sped forward, practically tripping over the uneven ground in my excitement.

There was the stream continuing through woods, still heading south, following the downward slope of the land, and then, as if on cue, it spread out again into a wide marshy area filled with tufts of grass. This long marshy pond was shallow and it took me ten minutes to walk to the end of it, but there, where it ended, the water was filled with water lilies and I saw another dam. This time the beavers had dammed the water when it took a left turn at the edge of the drumlin and began running down the slope.

It was incredible—the beavers had actually turned the water east so that it was pouring down the steep side of the drumlin, becoming a fast-moving woodland stream, not unlike the first- and second-order streams I had hiked along in the White Mountains with Dr. Burchsted. Of course, I scrambled through the ferns, down the bank, and followed it. The drumlin, named Rocky Hill, is one of the largest in this part of town, measuring nine hundred feet above sea level at the top. This stream was rushing down its far side into another surprise. Through the trees far below, I could see a silver glimmer. The stream was cascading into what looked like a very long, large pond.

Heading back to my car, I drove back along the road to find it. A sharp right on the next road over and I was there standing at the side of an impressive pond with an equally impressive beaver lodge tucked up against the bank on the far side. I heard rushing water and looked down to see a large culvert that ran under the road, enabling the stream to continue flowing down farther east to join the woods on the other side. How had I missed this? Later I would measure the pond at a half mile long and just under a quarter mile wide. And I recognized the pond now by the cutoff on the road. Some winters ago, weather conspired to make perfect black ice, and for a time it was our favorite skating spot.

We were literally just over a mile from my house now, closer as the crow flies. This was plenty near enough for beavers to have traveled from the

Taylor Brook site. Beavers have been recorded traversing mountains, traveling as much as a hundred miles to reach water. Our beavers might have come from here. Or—and I hung on to this thought because I so wanted it to be true—perhaps the beavers now living there on the Rocky Hill drumlin or in the pond here along New Sweden Road were from our pond. They had been hunted, but some had survived. Or the younger generation of yearlings had moved on, found this beaver paradise, and stayed.

Driving back, I felt as if a great weight had lifted. It wasn't that our beavers were completely gone; I simply had to look harder and smarter. As usual, the beavers were leading me deeper and deeper into an understanding of things I had previously misunderstood or missed completely. I needed to think about the brook system the way the beavers did—as an interconnected highway that led them, if there was low-lying land, woody material, and water, to more and more beaver pasture. What I was looking at was not just one isolated beaver spot, but a population of beavers living in the same brook, stream, river system.

Ironically, in some ways this was connected to the way fur trappers I knew here talked about beavers: not as individuals living in particular sites, but as part of a larger population. This was their rationale for trapping a certain percentage of beavers in a given area. Their concern was to maintain what they called the "carrying capacity," a wildlife management term meaning the correct number of animals that a specific area can provide enough food and habitat to sustain. And they did not want to see those wooded areas developed and the habitat destroyed. When they lobbied for town and state lands to be kept open and maintained, they were doing so to preserve beavers in the state.

I wasn't interested in doing any fur trapping. I was angry just to think that a poacher might have killed some of our beavers. But I was also aware of things being a lot more complicated than they seemed. Even Mike Callahan, who promoted beaver education and conservation, and was a fervent beaver believer, had commented in more than one public venue that here on the East Coast, there were times when beaver could not remain in a particular location and had to be removed, code for "trapped out."

In this corner of Woodstock, beavers had space and food and their waterways were not bothering humans. They were quietly doing all the things beavers do to slow water down, to store it, to clean it, and thus help recharge the aquifer, all the while raising the biodiversity of their neighborhood. Most of all, what I had discovered was that my state of mourning for my lost beavers could finally end. Our beavers were not completely gone; human meddling had not erased them from the landscape. I had found proof that beavers were still here, maybe not by my house where I wished I could still see them, but not far; their new lodge and dam constructed as part of what could be called a beaver network. My mother would have laughed to hear I had found my beavers, and it was moments like this— when I had seen or witnessed something wonderful and wanted to share it with her—that I missed her the most.

Beavers did not conduct fabulous migrations from the depths of the Sargasso Sea like Atlantic eels, or fly hundreds of miles on wings as delicate as paper like monarch butterflies, but their journeys were no less remarkable, because if you followed them, that familiar place you thought you knew became a country you had never seen. Beavers were changing how I saw everything. That swamp by the side of the road was no longer just a messy patch of water. Now I saw a beaver pond, rich with biodiversity, a wetland, connected to the larger river system working like a vast kidney to cleanse the water; what remained, or was in the process of becoming once again, a glimmer of Beaverland.

Chapter 12

Stone Walls

Beavers were leading me astray. Of course they would; beavers are hard-wired to complicate and obstruct. They divert streams and brooks, even rivers, until they overflow their banks, swelling out into shallow ponds or the channel splits, dividing into threads of water that press into the land. When we imagine streams in North America, chances are we envision water rippling over stones as it follows a groove. But as I had learned while following Dr. Burchsted, that is a stream without beavers. Seen from above, a riverine system with a healthy population of beaver resembles a great spiderweb, the intricate lines of water thickening at regular intervals. Here in southern New England, to follow a beaver-worked stream through the woods requires fortitude and bushwhacking. At times the only sign that you are following a beaver stream is the way your feet sink into mud with each step.

My idea had been straightforward enough: Now that I had discovered beavers living one drumlin over, part of the larger beaver neighborhood, I wanted to return to the beaver pond down the road from my house and construct a timeline of the environmental impacts of human interaction. I'd start with colonization and European settlement. But Algonquian people had been living here for almost ten thousand years before the first Europeans arrived, so I would not ignore the ways they had managed the land through controlled burning of meadows, methods of hunting, their agricultural practices, and the general monitoring of game. It now seemed likely that beavers had lived in the valley between those drumlins throughout the earliest years of the Holocene. But I had noticed something curious about the beaver pond: It was ringed by stone walls. The beavers had actually used three large stones that had been placed over the brook as a kind of keystone from which they built their dam. I began to study those stone walls for evidence as if I were a forensic archeologist, breaking the walls down into the stones themselves, the manner of construction, the wall's size and shape. Only later would I understand how relevant it was to think of the stone walls here as a crime scene.

Woodstock had been founded in 1686 when this corner of modern-day Connecticut still belonged to the Massachusetts Bay Colony. A detailed town history had been published in 1926, and much of the history of early founding and land transactions had been recorded there in what was popularly called "Bowen's History of Woodstock," named for Clarence Bowen, who assembled it. I was able to locate colonial records about the founding of the town along with two curiously detailed maps from the eighteenth and nineteenth centuries. The later map, drawn by John S. Lester in 1883, turned out to be a fantastic resource, for it referenced Native American sites, homesteads, roads and brooks, sawmills, and businesses. By that time, the town population had grown to 3,610, with two distilleries, three taverns, a trading post, a pottery, a brickyard, and many small establishments including a wheelwright, a saddlery, and a tannery. Three grist mills and too many sawmills to count. Lester had drawn the topography, marking out what appeared to be every drumlin, carefully indicating the slopes with fine lines so that the map looked as if it were a mass of dark polka dots. Within the 59.5 squares miles of town documented then, he carefully drew with fine-tipped pen, over one hundred glacial hills. Each meadow, road, and drumlin on the map was named. The usual list of place names you might expect—"Fox hill," "Horse hill," "Forest hill," "Chestnut hill"—then names that held a story, even if no one remembered anymore exactly what the story was about. There was the "Wash on toh Minunk" drumlin, an Algonquian word or name derived from an English interpretation of the Native language; then there was the drumlin by the town's distillery with the cryptic name of "Nobody's Hill," a compromise after a country feud over ownership of a place that for dark reasons no one wanted to claim. The map was riddled with brooks, some named, others just wavering lines.

Interestingly, most of the swamps were identified, with names like the "great swamp," "the dark swamp," "the great dire swamp," or "witch woods"; no doubt each name also told a story. We lived on the drumlin that rose up along the west side of the beaver pond. It was named "Weavers Hill," while the drumlin across the other side of the pond was "Fisher Hill." I couldn't find any people named Weaver or Fisher listed in early town directories or in Bowen's encyclopedic early history of the town, which like all early American histories recorded the names and achievements of the big men in town (along with their marriages and children), but there were families named Weaver and Fisher in neighboring towns, so perhaps they had only lived here for a time.

Then in 1886, the Lester map was annotated by George Clinton Williams, a medical doctor and amateur historian. He had drawn in red pen words like "Indian Burial site," "Indian graves," and the word "INDIAN" in large red capital letters over the drumlin just up from the beaver pond. This was an elevated meadow named "Fort Hill" and described in Bowen's history and through town lore as the site where Native people had once gathered. Why and when was not explained, just that years later, during King Philip's War, and after when tensions between Native Americans and colonists ran high, early Woodstock residents had built a wooden fort there at the top of the hill to which they retreated when there was word of a possible raid.

From the start, the conversion of Native people to Christianity was integral to the mission of the Massachusetts Bay Colony. The colony's seal told it all—it featured a Native man holding a bow and arrow, leaves modestly covering the crotch of his otherwise naked body; from his mouth floated the words "Come over and Help us." The English pastor John Eliot took up this mission with passion and worked to Christianize Native Americans by setting up so-called praying towns of early converts. Eliot was the first Englishman to make a serious effort to learn Massachusett, the Algonquian language spoken by the Native people of eastern New England. By 1663, Eliot had not only translated the Bible into an Algonquian language, he'd published several copies of it, along with numerous pamphlets for distribution.

When John Eliot traveled here in 1674 with Daniel Gookin, the magistrate for the Commonwealth, Eliot was the founder of thirteen thriving praying towns in Massachusetts. Within ten years, he would end up railing against the mistreatment of the Native people by the English, famously stating "what they are experiencing is worse than death," but his initial efforts to Christianize Indigenous people were funded by the Massachusetts Bay Colony with the obvious goal of eradicating Native cultural practices. Native people living in "Christian Indian" towns were called "red puritans," and it was expected that they not only convert but in doing so become anglicized. They were given English-style clothing and Christian names. Significantly, they were encouraged to transition away from their traditional practices of planting the "three sisters" of maize, squash, and beans together in hills (which was an efficient agricultural practice for the beans grew up along the stalks of corn, while the large leaves of the squash plants helped shade the soil, keeping it cooler during times of heat and drought). Traditionally, Native people had set up their wigwams in spring and summer at sites that were good for planting. Then in fall and winter they moved closer to places where hunting was good. To discourage this seasonal mobility, the Native people were given seed and domestic animals so that they could practice English-style agriculture.

The more I learned about this history, uncovering the story of John Eliot, the "Apostle to the Indians," and his work to establish a missionizing community here, the more I saw connections to the beavers. The beaver pond in the woods by my house was located along a town road that had been named to memorialize this history; it was called Pulpit Rock Road. According to the town lore, documented in every history from Bowen's onward, this name referred to a large glacial erratic that sat by the side of the road. As the story goes, in 1674 John Eliot leapt on this boulder and began to preach to the Indigenous people, his new converts. This was the story of a man so impassioned and inventive that he would even spontaneously use a large, flat glacial erratic for his pulpit. And it is the story of a man so charismatic and eloquent that he could draw people to him even deep in the woods. But letters between Eliot and Gookin reveal another tale.

The Wabbaquasett band of Algonquian people who lived here would not gather in Eliot's church. They would worship the Christian God, but only in ways that made sense to them, which meant they met outside for worship in places they valued, reflecting the Indigenous tradition of experiencing the land as inhabited by presences we would call the divine. That the Wabbaquasett met here by the pond meant that they valued this spot. Was it because of the beavers? As with many Indigenous people, the Algonquian cultures had many rituals and specific practices regarding the hunting of beaver that served as effective brakes on overhunting. Additionally, they knew that the ponds of *amiskw* brought game. Then there was the story of Great Beaver, whose mischief formed the Connecticut River valley.

While the story of Pulpit Rock Road implies that the preacher John Eliot was so effective that he could draw Native people to hear him, even from atop a remote boulder in the woods, in reality it was most likely the other way around and he was preaching there in order to get the attention of the local people. The 1674 census of Christian Towns records 150 Wabbaquasett converts living here when John Eliot visited, meaning that when he arrived this area was a thriving Native American settlement. This makes sense given the proximity of rivers with their fertile floodplains and what would have been beaver-filled woods. If Eliot leapt upon the boulder here, he did so because in order to preach to the Indigenous people, he had to go to them and at a stop they considered important, like a beaver pond.

A glacial boulder, a beaver pond, and the Wabbaquasett who lived here were connected in ways I would only begin to understand fully when I looked again at that nineteenth-century Lester map on which someone had glaringly written the word "INDIAN." Why write the word in all caps right there on the drumlin that rose up just a few hundred yards to the east of the beaver pond? None of the town histories included much information about its Indigenous inhabitants, and most of what I found concerned the various transactions that transferred ownership of the land to colonists.

The Native people of what became New England are all Algonquian people and many share a common language: Massachusett. But within this population, different bands existed—the Pequot, the Mohegan, the Wabbaquasett, to name a few. The names of each band were usually connected in some way to the environment in which they lived. The Nipmuc inhabited the inland areas of Massachusetts, Connecticut, and Rhode Island; their name literally means "fresh water people," or "fresh water cousins." Here in Woodstock, the Nipmuc called themselves the Wabbaquasett, a name meaning "place of mats"; they lived in an area where rushes were plentiful (thanks to beavers and their work making wetlands). Rushes were a valuable resource that the Wabbaquasett wove into baskets and used to make the walls of their wigwams.

In 2005, while researching her master's thesis in anthropology at the University of Connecticut, Native scholar Dr. Rae Gould, who is now the executive director of the Native American and Indigenous Studies Initiative at Brown, set out to see if she could find the location of John Eliot's seventeenth-century congregation in Woodstock. She identified the location of several Nipmuc settlements in Woodstock, one of which in all likelihood became identified as the "praying village." But the main takeaway of her study was that the area around Woodstock had been so densely populated with Nipmuc clans and their settlements in the late seventeenth century that the narrative of Eliot bringing Native people together to found a settlement was false to begin with; the Nipmuc had already been living here, spread out over a large area.

But Dr. Gould outlined an area of Native settlement that most likely would have been part of Eliot's praying town, and I was thrilled to see that this area included the infamous boulder, a stretch of what would become Pulpit Rock Road, and the wetlands that began at the beaver pond.

The history of the road supported Dr. Gould's findings. On the Lester map, Pulpit Rock Road was identified as "Somer's Turnpike," and Bowen's town history describes it as having been built by a group of proprietors who managed it as a toll road for many years until the town finally took it over. But before it had been improved as a nineteenth-century turnpike, it had been part of the legendary "Connecticut Path" that helped connect the colony seats of Boston, Hartford, New Haven, and New York. And as with most colonial roads, the Connecticut Path followed existing Native American pathways, a network of woodland trails that explorers and fur traders knew as the "Great Trail of New England."

The beaver pond was most likely in the area of the praying village—part of a Native American settlement before John Eliot's arrival. But who had lived on that land since, and how had the beavers shaped it? If you followed Taylor Brook south, it merged with other brooks until it spread out into a long narrow pond, which Lester had marked on his map. In Lester's map, several sawmills had been drawn along those brooks. It was not uncommon for colonists to make use of existing beaver dams to power sawmills and, later, to establish larger grist mills. If the gradient was right and the stream large enough, beaver dams often impounded enough water for them to get a grist mill started while they worked on building a larger, more permanent dam. Later, in the 1950s, a developer built a concrete dam on that spot, creating present-day Quassett Lake.

The state of Connecticut had aerial photographs going back to 1934, and land deeds dating back to the seventeenth century. The photographs chronicled over eighty years of beaver activity. In some of the photographs, the brook was just a thin line through the valley, but other years, water had swelled out, completely filling the area. The photographs connected with what my neighbor and the town trapper had told me; beavers had been in that site longer than anyone could remember. Some of the paper trail had gone up in smoke; many courthouse records had been obliterated by a fire more than a hundred years ago. But the agricultural census of 1850 revealed that the farm on which the beaver pond was located was valued at $9,000. It included ninety-five acres of improved land that raised fifty bushels of corn, forty bushels of oats, two hundred bushels of potatoes, twenty bushels of barley, and eight bushels of wheat. The farm had swine and milk cows and working oxen and sheep. That year they sold 640 pounds of wool.

The census confirmed that the woods around the beaver pond had not been left for timber but had been cleared. I walked back down to the beaver pond, to see if I could find any clues as to whether the slopes had been used for crops or for pasture. That is when I noticed something curious. The beavers I had been observing had built their dam by incorporating a stone wall that ran from one side of the valley, and at the center of the dam, where it crossed the brook, were three enormous flat stones that the beavers had made use of in building their dam as a kind of keystone. At some point, people had placed the large flat boulders over the brook; they were way too heavy for beavers to have moved. And while glacial erratics filled the woods around here, these had been carefully placed so that they overlapped, allowing the stream to pass underneath. I stared at the crude stone bridge and began to wonder, who had built this bridge here and when? And why had humans constructed a stone wall around the beaver pond? Had the wall and the bridge been built at the same time? If not, which had come first?

The Native Americans who lived and traveled through here would not have needed a stone bridge to cross the stream. In fact, they probably used the surface of the original beaver dam.

Once European colonists arrived, however, they brought with them oxen and horses and carts and would have needed some kind of a surface to keep their wheels from getting stuck. But the stone walls that circled the pond made no sense. Why fence in the shallow valley of a beaver pond or a beaver meadow that had a brook running through it, meaning that even when beavers were not actively living there, the low-lying marsh regularly flooded?

Agricultural census records like the 1850 census revealed the nineteenth-century heyday of agriculture here, then the shift from agriculture to industrialization, and with that, the slow decline of New England farms. By 1870, most of southern New England was growing back into forest. This was a remarkable change, since the most dramatic impact of seventeenth-century colonization was rapid deforestation. The first European inhabitants here cut down trees to build the houses, barns, bridges, meetinghouses, and a church, which they were required to erect and maintain as part of the terms of their agreement with the Massachusetts Bay Colony. And they cut down trees to create fields for English-style agriculture. Then within decades, trees became fuel to power the early iron furnaces of the early Industrial Revolution. It wasn't long before 80 percent of the woods we now think of as the representative landscape of southern New England were gone.

As the trees were removed, soil temperatures warmed, drying the earth. In this region where most of the soil is shallow upland till that barely covers solid layers of bedrock, erosion soon followed. Soils thinned and streams and river systems filled with sediment. The beavers would have had to work harder to collect water and keep their ponds and canals from filling in. They would have also had to work hard to evade hunters and trappers. From 1652 to 1658, William Pynchon, who controlled the fur trading post of Springfield, recorded that his son John managed to obtain nine thousand beaver pelts from Native people in the Connecticut River valley, although from the eighteenth century on, the fur trade here dwindled. Bowen's history of Woodstock documents a trading post called Corben's, just a mile from the beaver pond where furs were bought from Native people, but he does not specifically mention the types of fur traded. By 1790, the fur trade had moved west as fur buyers shifted their focus inland toward central New York and Pennsylvania and beyond, or north to Canada. Even so, until they were officially eradicated from the state in 1890, beaver pelts brought what farmers called "egg money" and were sold to local fur buyers for cash on the spot. In other words, beavers might have survived here, although it is more likely that they were trapped out until twentieth-century conservation efforts brought them back.

Beavers are remarkably resilient. With climate change warming large areas of the Arctic tundra, beavers have recently been photographed at night climbing the north ridge in Alaska, practically scaling cliffs to get to the marshy areas on the other side. But here in southern New England during colonization, in addition to the problems of deforestation, beavers faced the additional challenge of drier, hotter soils resulting from the introduction of English-style agriculture. The foundation of European agriculture for centuries had been to combine the raising of crops with the rearing of domestic animals. Raising animals for food is a land-intensive practice, for in addition to pastures, fields are needed to grow corn and hay to feed the animals. Unless measures are taken to rotate crops and plant for soil regeneration, the vast world of microorganisms in the soil begin to die off, resulting in an avalanche of problems.

The English were certainly not the first humans to impact this woodland environment. To create better hunting grounds, the Algonquian people burned woodlands to create meadows and thin out the underbrush. In other places they coppiced and pruned trees. Starting in 1000 BC they began raising maize, squash, and beans and burning fields in order to plant. But there was a key difference—Native people continued to rely on hunting and fishing for meat. When the English arrived in the late 1600s, in addition to oxen and horses to help them clear the land, they brought chickens, cattle, goats, sheep, and swine. Fences were needed to separate the two as well as to keep animals from wandering. And more land was needed for hay and pasture, which meant more woods had to come down. Swine were often let loose in the forest, trampling woodland flora. After 1812, when bans on British goods led to a shortage of wool, sheep raising began in earnest and the intense grazing of pastures further dried out the soil. The cumulative effect on the beaver meadow (for it is safe to assume the beavers were gone during that time) was greater sedimentation in the brook that ran the length of the shallow valley. Soil erosion was so extreme in southern

New England, GPS studies have shown that in some cases, streambeds rose as much as six feet in height.

Imported plants and animals added to the problem. In addition to domestic animals, Europeans brought animal stowaways that soon invaded the landscape. Rats are probably the best-known, but even tiny creatures had an impact. In addition to rats, Europeans brought the adorable, now ubiquitous house mouse to the New World, but also earthworms, which quickly invaded forest soils, disrupting the vast ecosystem of micoorganisms that lie hidden beneath the soil and further changing the soil chemistry.

Ironically, by the time I came to be looking at them, the stone walls here had begun to play an important role in countering these years of environmental degradation; the walls were now habitat for any number of animal species, and had created new microclimates for woodland plants. Once the Clean Air Act of 1972 began to reduce the corrosive damage caused by acid rain, lichen—that weird algae-fungal partnership so critical for forest heath—began to bloom on the tumbled lines of stone. The parallel lines of stone walls that ran north to south on the slopes of the drumlins on either side of the beaver meadow held back erosion and helped keep the beaver meadow from filling with sedimentation. My town valued its stone walls so highly that strict zoning regulations prohibited removing them or taking away the stones, particularly on roads like the one I lived on, which was registered with the state as "scenic."

The more I pondered the fact of the stone walls that ringed the beaver pond, the more closely human and beaver histories became entangled; which had come first, the stone walls or the beaver pond? That beavers had lived here for thousands of years now seemed likely. But beavers might have been temporarily gone when the first colonists arrived. Or the area had been a swamp and, seeing the opportunity for pasture or tillage, the colonists had drained it by digging a canal. Or the stream had been harnessed for waterpower. Sawmills were so in demand that if a stream had enough water running through it to power a portable sawmill, it was usually put to use. There was no direct evidence of colonists having built a canal to drain the swamp, but in three hundred years the canal could have filled back in, reverting to its form as a wide, shallow stream.

An astounding number of miles of stone walls ran through nineteenth-century New England. In 1871, the U.S. Department of Agriculture conducted a yearlong survey that recorded 240,000 miles of stone walls here. Connecticut alone had 20,500 miles of stone walls, while the tiny state of Rhode Island was covered with almost seven times that number. Most of the walls here, as with the rest of New England, were "tossed" walls made from a single line of stones, but there were also double walls and walls that were dumped, laid, chinked, or built in a mosaic pattern. Some were topped with copestone. Most of the stone used was gneiss, but all of it was ancient mud that just before the continents separated had been buried, squeezed, and sheared, then heated, then eventually cooled until it became New England's famously hard bedrock. The geology was fantastic, as were the sheer number of miles of stone walls right here in my rural town; the average nineteenth-century Connecticut farm was surrounded by five miles of stone.

Then I noticed the date when most of the stone walls had been built—between 1775 and 1825. That was at least eighty years after English colonists first arrived here. I had always imagined that the walls had been built by those first Yankee farmers, heroic in their way as they cleared fields and planted homesteads. I had thought each stone wall was distinct to that farmer and that farm and the local source of stone and made by hand and in this way was also kind of folk art.

But of course, those first farmers, the thirty "goers" who left the mother colony of New Roxbury near Boston to build a town in what was then the hinterlands here, would have been too busy clearing land, erecting shelter, and planting first crops to do the intensive labor of building stone walls. The Commonwealth had promised to fund them, relieving them of taxes and paying them £100 a year for five years. But they needed these start-up funds to buy equipment, horses, oxen, chickens, cows, and seed. They had an obligation to set up farms but also to build a church and a meetinghouse within the first year, and they had memories of staving off hunger. Especially after the second wave of migration brought colonists in 1630, food was scarce in the colonies, often desperately so. A massive hurricane in 1635, followed by a harsh winter, typical of the Little Ice Age, destroyed crops for both English settlers and Native Americans alike.

The first English farmers needed fences to contain their cattle and horses, oxen, goats, and sheep, but they made them from wood. Called "worm fences" after their zigzag pattern, these barriers could be quickly made by forming panels of wooden poles that were set at an angle to one another so that the fence held itself up without the need for digging post holes. The stones they removed from fields in order to plow and plant were tossed into huge piles. English colonists had stone walls in their DNA—for hundreds of years the people of the British Isles had been living among farms ringed with hedges and stone walls—but it would be years until Yankee farmers here had the resources to bound their own farms.

If that was the case, who had built these stone walls? The answer was becoming as obvious as it was terrible; these beautiful stone walls were connected to one of America's cardinal sins, slavery.

And it would all connect back to beavers, or rather beaver fur, in ways that were as disturbing as they were perfectly obvious. In the spring of 1636, in nearby Mystic, the neighboring Pequot were brutally massacred by the English, who needed control of the Pequot people and of the Pequot's wampum production in order to expand their reach in the fur trade. By the end of this short war, the taking of Native captives became paramount. Hundreds of Pequot were enslaved and sent to work in colonial households here in New England. Many more were loaded onto vessels and shipped to the Caribbean where they were sold as human chattel.

I had known that Native people had faced invasion and displacement, had suffered as beloved lands became the property of others, but I had not known the chilling truth that so many of them had been enslaved in the process.

In her 2015 work on slavery in colonial America, *Brethren by Nature*, Margaret Newell outlines ways that the enslavement of Native Americans, then imported Africans, underpinned the economies of many New England towns. In 1641, Massachusetts Bay passed the first slave law in the English Atlantic world, in large part to define the legal status of the hundreds of enslaved Pequot people who had been incorporated into households after the end of the Pequot war. Before 1700, Native Americans represented the dominant form of nonwhite labor. Once the New England–Caribbean slave trade began, Connecticut took the lead. By 1774, in the larger cities of Hartford, Norwich, and New Haven, half of the ministers, lawyers, and public officials in the area owned slaves, as well as a third of all the doctors. The public records of the colony of Connecticut show 42 enslaved people listed for my town. On the eve of the American Revolution, Connecticut had 6,464 enslaved people, the largest enslaved population of all the colonies in New England. Meanwhile, in 1771 in neighboring Rhode Island, John Sainsbury estimated that 35.5 percent of Native Americans were residing among non-Native families, where they worked as indentured servants.

And those first enslaved Pequot played another historic role—their transport and sale had facilitated the beginning of the African slave trade in New England. In 1638, the slave ship *Desire* arrived in Boston, bringing the first African prisoners to the Commonwealth and starting the terrible legacy of the New England–Caribbean slave trade. What is less well known is that she was actually on her return trip from an outgoing trip to deliver human chattel. In her cargo were seventeen Pequot who had been captured in Connecticut and shipped to the Caribbean for the slave trade there.

History became a kaleidoscope; new information had shifted the lens and I was watching as the pattern broke apart and reassembled—the same colors, the same shapes, but it was all coming back together radically changed. Beavers were one of the first trade items of North America, generating astronomical profits, but colonizing these lands required more than capital. It required massive amounts of labor.

Alan Taylor and other historians have documented how the colonial need for labor complicated from the start our narratives of American identity. But I had never considered the direct connection between the enslavement of Native Americans and the fur trade and the stone walls in my town. The only mention of Native Americans in the town histories was in the context of the "Indian problem," or dealing with Native resistance to colonization.

Many of the Wabbaquasett who lived in this area had initially been protected from English aggression as they were members of a praying town, but during the next attempt by Native Americans to resist English domination, King Philip's War of 1675–76, the Nipmuc sided with Metacom (whom the English called King Philip). When Metacom was defeated, the Nipmuc returned from the war to discover that their praying town had been disbanded and they had lost even more of their land. As in the earlier Pequot war, many were enslaved for local labor or shipped to the Caribbean. Of those who remained, many were arrested for any number of "crimes"—for drunkenness, disorderliness, theft, or vagrancy (which was not uncommon since their lands and culture and means of livelihood had been taken). Those were often given the option of working off their sentence. What historians call judicial slavery—punishing crimes with enslavement—funneled many more Native Americans into the forced labor pool of early America.

While slavery was abolished in Connecticut in 1784 by an act of gradual abolition, then fully abolished in 1848, Native Americans did not gain citizenship in the United States until Congress passed the "Indian Citizenship Act" in 1924. Until then, they were considered minors at law and "non compos mentis," wards of the state who could not buy a house, borrow money, or own land without permission. For this reason, more than one Native American chose to identify themselves in other ways—including, as I discovered, as "negroes."

One afternoon, while trying to decipher colonial census data on enslaved Africans and Native people in the digital archives of the Connecticut State Library, I found a faded yellow broadsheet—an ad from 1805 taken out by a prominent lawyer whose family could be traced back to the original founders of the town. The large black font read "Ten Dollars Reward!" The sheet went on to describe how he was looking for his runaway slave, an eighteen-year-old with the given name of Caesar. I knew the descendants of this nineteenth-century lawyer; they were neighbors. I had often walked the bounds of their historic farm just down the road. How I had loved watching my retriever, Coda, leap up and run along the top of the tall stone walls that bounded every length of their orchards and fields. Suddenly, I was no longer a bystander to the horrific history of the place where I lived. It was a sickening realization, but a necessary one.

As I write this it is early March, and the owls are calling. Yesterday a bobcat ran across the field, head high as if following a scent, the large paws bounding. I missed seeing beavers by our house so much that I drove to the beaver pond I had found on the drumlin just to the south. With me was the new pup we had finally decided we were ready to take in after having lost Coda. We waited there, the pup and I, just as Coda and I had done years before at the beaver pond by the house. Evening began to settle and the peepers lit up the woods with sound. Then I saw it, a ripple in the water, a brown head, and, as always, the sight filled me with awe. A beaver began swimming in circles in the pond before us, not one bit afraid, clearly reveling in the freedom of swimming in a pond no longer bound with ice. The pup barked, but he is an English shepherd, bred to work cattle and sheep, and while he can run like the wind, he will not swim. The beaver did not flinch at the sudden loud sound, but kept on circling.

Here in New England, early spring is when the stones are most restless; frost has heaved them again and again, up from the soil, while the days of warming have had the opposite effect so that they sink into the first inches of spring mud. The early colonists cleared the fields of stone, only to discover that each spring so many more were pushed up from below by the warming and freezing that they had to clear them again. They called the stones "Satan's potatoes" and piled them at the edges of fields.

Every place has its stories to tell. Walking around the beaver pond, all these years, the stone walls had seemed to run through the woods like ancient poetry, beautiful relics of that time before and of our agricultural past. I had loved the mystery of those tumbled stones, each a missive from deep time when the earth was forming. Now the sight of those same walls chilled me. The stones themselves, glacial scoured and ancient, might still hold mysteries, and each wall was still a form of folk art, built by skilled hands. But now I knew their terrible secrets—invasion, displacement, murder, the radical transformation of the environment, cultural erasure, servitude, enslavement. Whatever else they were, the stone walls are also a monument to the cultural and environmental annihilation of North America's Indigenous peoples, and the kidnapping and enslavement of African people.

Why was the beaver meadow near my house ringed with stone walls? The farmers or landowners might have overseen the work, but the actual labor of lifting and placing those initial stones was more than likely done by indentured servants, or enslaved people. Later generations would then have tended them, making repairs. Like so many other, more famous

American landmarks, the walls were beautiful, but their history was complicated in ways that fundamentally changed the way I saw them. For this awareness I was sad, I was angry, I was shocked, and I was horrified, but I was also humbled—grateful.

Work on this book would continue in this way, as if even at my desk I was still following a beaver stream. One step forward and my foot met solid ground, but on the next step my boots were sinking. The only way forward was to follow the water, which was being shaped, of course, by beavers, that unassuming animal at the center of it all.

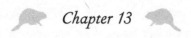

Chapter 13

Thinking Like a Watershed

PART I

"Are you ready to open the closet and enter Narnia?"

Scott McGill stands at the edge of Long Green Creek in the Chesapeake watershed. I can hear rustling and chirping, then the loud, regal cry of a hawk.

"I'm ready."

McGill is the founder of a visionary environmental restoration company called Ecotone, based in Forest Park, Maryland. A slim man dressed in jeans and a green T-shirt, he exudes enthusiasm and confidence. McGill gives a quick nod then disappears into a thicket of willows. I am only a few steps behind, but the underbrush swallows him so completely that for a moment I can follow only by listening for the sloshing sounds of his boots plunging forward through water. His wife, Moira, relaxed and cheerful, brings up the rear.

Narnia is what McGill calls the wetland area that beavers have created here by damming the creek that runs through Long Green Farm, fifteen miles north of Baltimore. As soon as I step into the wetland, the landscape changes so dramatically, it feels as if I might just have slipped through the enchanted wardrobe in C. S. Lewis's famous series. While just a moment ago we were standing on a farm road, flanked on either side by wide fields of soybeans and hay, we are now moving through an iconic forest wetland. The air has cooled and before us the ground is silvered with water. Somewhere near the center and down deep in this swampy expanse, Long Green Creek is running through, but you wouldn't know it unless you hiked to the far end and saw the dam that the beavers have built there. Spires of dead trees punctuate the scene, which is teeming with birds. Meanwhile, everywhere I look I see an extraordinary variety of grasses, sedge, and aquatic vegetation. McGill turns around and grins. I am glad I wore my waders, because the water is way above my knees. Once they entered the wardrobe, that famous portal to Narnia, the kids met Mr. and Mrs. Beaver, who stood on two legs and spoke to the children, becoming their guides. The beavers we are looking for here moved in six years ago.

McGill looks admiringly across the water. "When I walk in here it's another world."

McGill is proud to be known in the environmental restoration industry as the "beaver whisperer." He's evangelical in his belief that beavers can help solve environmental problems. He thinks it is a tragedy that they are part of our history, but not part of our culture. Here in the Chesapeake watershed, in Maryland, Pennsylvania, and New Jersey where he does most of his work, he has been striving since 2016 to help shift the culture around beavers and stream restoration by showcasing what he calls the "ecosystem services" of beavers. *Let the rodents do the work* is one of his mottos. I loved this idea that beavers, these wonderfully weird animals that in so many ways had made America a country, could now play a role in helping to save the land itself. And I wanted it to be true. Beavers had certainly shaped and maintained the river system of North America's past, but could they play a significant role in helping save our troubled rivers now? How many beavers would it take? Was there enough available open land here in the East for them to let rivers slow and spread? What would it cost to create the conditions necessary for beavers to become established and thrive?

I was here in Hydes, Maryland, on this sunny October morning because I wanted answers to those questions. All up and down the Atlantic seaboard, if you looked, you could find beavers at work. And when they were left alone for long enough, within decades they could reshape the ways water moved through the land, bringing back the rich biodiversity of paleo-rivers. But those areas were for the most part open land, or tracts of forest set aside for scientific study and conservation. Could beavers be used successfully for large-scale stream restoration and floodwater control in places full of people?

As I had driven south along the interstates connecting New York, New Jersey, Delaware, and Maryland, it was hard to imagine how the river systems I was crossing over, much less the native beavers that for eons had been those rivers' keepers, could be fully restored; our comfortable American lifestyles were dependent on those miles of roadway, factories, power plants, ports, and urban sprawl. And we are well into our new era of climate instability, having directly transformed more than half of the ice-free land on earth.

In her darkly funny but thought-provoking book *Under a White Sky: The Nature of the Future,* Elizabeth Kolbert points out that even the term "control of nature" seems quaint in the twenty-first century; our survival now depends upon our ability to control our attempts to control nature. But as I was about to discover, McGill believes it is possible to "reseed" the East Coast landscape with beaver, and he has done enough restoration work with beavers now to prove that these efforts work and can make a difference, saving his clients, which include individual landowners, farmers, towns, and municipalities, a great deal of money. Environmental restoration is now a multibillion-dollar business throughout the United States, but especially in Maryland where in part due to the incredible rate of development, every county is now under pressure from the Environmental Protection Agency to help clean the water running into the Chesapeake Bay.

Spanning sixty-four thousand square miles, the Chesapeake is the largest watershed on the Atlantic seaboard, intersected by over a hundred rivers and thousands of creeks. And every drop of rain that falls in the watershed—an area that covers almost one-sixth of the East Coast—finds its way into the Chesapeake Bay. Because this area extends over six states, all of which have been transformed by intensive development—the area is now home to some eighteen million people—the Chesapeake Bay is more affected by land use than almost any comparable body of water on earth. This stunning fact is particularly concerning because where the freshwater rivers feed into the Atlantic Ocean, they form a vast estuary of brackish water that is critical for the survival and reproduction of the 350 species of fish that live in the bay, not to mention the valuable bottom dwellers—oysters, clams, and the famous blue crabs of Maryland crab cakes. The Chesapeake estuary, which extends two hundred miles, contains some eighteen trillion gallons of water, which is now threatened by pollution and sediment. The larger waters of the bay are also at risk, for they are now experiencing extensive "dead zones" where there is so little oxygen that aquatic life suffocates. Five years ago, the EPA issued warnings that counties that lay within the watershed had to act.

McGill suggested I start my visit here on Long Green Creek because he considers it a "poster child" for how beavers have been put to work. But I am most excited to observe the Ecotone site on Beaver Creek because along twenty acres of the creek there, his company is in the process of installing sixty-seven beaver dam analogs (BDAs). Once these human versions of beaver dams are in place, they will plant the banks of the creek with fast-growing willows and other tasty beaver foods. Their goal is for beavers to move into the area and begin making their own series of dams and ponds; the operative principle is *If you build it they will come.*

Sun had been glancing off the grapevines when I drove through the manicured entrance of Long Green Farm and followed the farm road along until I saw a white truck parked by the side. We had scheduled to meet at 8 a.m. and I was early, but McGill and Moira were already there, ready to go. We quickly walked along the farm road to the low spot where the creek ran over it in a thin sheet of water.

Now we are lost in the spell of this beaver world, our boots rhythmically sloshing, conversation having given way to the hush and promise of the gleaming water before us, to the poignant islands of trees. The only visible difference between a marsh and a swamp is that swamps include trees while marshes are wetlands mostly full of grass. At the next bend, McGill points to a group of dead trees. "The ecosystem services of a dead tree can sometimes be more than what a live tree can be," he says, which surprises me. We stand for a minute and stare at the trees, jutting up like grey bones. Dead trees are of immense value to the invisible universe of the forest—the fungal networks that run throughout the soil, some of them spanning six thousand feet. It has been estimated that every step we take everywhere on the globe we are walking on three hundred miles of hidden fungi. Those fungal networks rely on decomposing wood, from which they absorb carbon that they store in the soil along with the carbon they receive from plant leaves that pull carbon dioxide from the atmosphere through photosynthesis. As Western science is now rapidly documenting with increasing precision, the fungal networks, called mycorrhizae, not only sequester huge amounts of carbon, they also ensure the health of the larger forest. Fungi, which become known to most of us mostly when they "fruit" as mushrooms, rely on nutrients and minerals that enter the soil from decomposing wood.

We all stand for some time staring at the dead trees, because today they are alive with birds of all kinds, rummaging and pecking for bugs. Although McGill is no longer being paid to oversee this site, he and Moira visit regularly to check on the beaver. He also has an agreement with the landowners that he can harvest willow stakes for planting in other locations. Ecotone has its own nursery of native plants that it uses for replanting stream banks. When McGill spies a tuft of grass he does not recognize, he bends down, snaps a picture of it on his phone, and looks it up using the iNaturalist app.

"Yup, calyx," he says, "thought so," and begins to explain that this is a particular variety of wetland sedge. When I ask about the depth, for the pond seems relatively shallow, McGill answers, "Beavers down here only need two feet of water to get through winter, not like New England where they need a good three feet. We don't have ice to contend with."

He bends over another clump of willows and is clearly happy with what he sees. "You plant one willow," he says, "then come back in five years and you'll have fifty."

Soon we come to a gap in the undergrowth, and McGill pauses before taking an extra-wide step. "Be careful, there's a beaver canal in here that is pretty deep," he says as he gives a small jump to the other side. "I've gone right in, and it has gotten a few visiting photographers."

I look at the water but see no discernible canal. When he is standing on the far side, McGill motions for me to follow. I throw my notepad over to him, then jump across. We slosh on. Soon we are close to the beaver lodge, which is a large and surprisingly unruly affair, as if the beavers couldn't be bothered with the iconic teepee shape, but had fun slinging mud and sticks about. Moira laughs gaily and shares an anecdote from her work as a preschool teacher. One time she brought a group of young students here and one boy solemnly asked if they had arrived at the ocean; he had never been in a forest wetland or to the ocean. Moira is retired now, but both she and McGill spend a considerable amount of time on educational outreach to show people the importance of restoring biodiversity.

"Part of what I am doing is bringing myths to the surface and challenging those myths," McGill will tell me later. "I tell people all the time, 'Don't believe everything you think.'"

One of the myths about beavers is that they negatively impact trout. Trout fishing is big business, with historically strong support, and the removal of beaver dams and the trapping of beavers to protect trout streams has been standard policy for most wildlife departments ever since beavers returned in the early twentieth century. Even though there are no longer native brook trout in Maryland, brown trout, which were introduced via fisheries, are protected as a cold-water species. Like salmon, trout need cold water to thrive and gravel banks to spawn; beavers are believed to warm the water to unacceptable levels and fill gravel banks with sediment, although as researchers in the last twenty years have begun to show, those deeply entrenched ideas were based mostly on anecdote rather than scientific study.

As he walks forward, McGill turns his head back regularly to make sure we are both okay, then continues talking. "Fishery folks at the state level have this idea that if it is a beaver pond it has to increase water temperature and so beaver and trout can't possibly coexist." He continues, "But they coevolved over millions of years, so that is very absurd if you think about it."

McGill stops just ahead and Moira and I join him. The water is now too deep for us to walk any closer, but we can look at the lodge and wait. We know that beavers are crepuscular, usually coming out at twilight, but there is a theory that this is a learned behavior that began with the onset of the fur trade; early explorers recount seeing beaver out in daylight, sitting on their lodges or swimming near the entrance.

"I've come here in broad daylight and seen them swimming around," says McGill. "They slap their tails, but they didn't seem afraid."

We all scan the water eagerly. You just never know when beavers might decide to appear, a brown head breaking through the water, the sudden surprise of it, then the square nose, the tiny, bearlike ears swimming hard, eye level with the water like an alligator. Was it the surprise, the way you could never predict when beavers might surface, that was part of their allure? I thought of some of the strange beaver facts I knew: beavers never walked backward; they ate their food twice; they could not doggy paddle; they had ever-growing orange teeth; the kits made such plaintive, human-like noises that it was reportedly a Native American practice to give beaver kits to mothers who had lost babies to help them with their grief; early European explorers had been perplexed by the sight of beavers sometimes trundling around an encampment. And I wondered if it was this element of weirdness and otherworldly surprise that prompted C. S. Lewis to make beavers the spirit guides that led the children into Narnia. Lewis was living in Oxford when he wrote the Narnia trilogy, but in those years from 1949 to 1954 beavers had not yet been "re-wilded" throughout Great Britain and had been gone from the English countryside since the 1500s when Europe's craze for beaver felt hats began. Lewis probably came upon mention of beavers in Pliny, and may well have been intrigued enough to look up the gorgeous illustrations of medieval beavers in the famous Bodleian illuminated bestiary. But he knew little about living beavers, for in Narnia he has Mr. and Mrs. Beaver eat fish; beavers are herbivores.

"Shall we head back?" McGill's words bring me back to the present. No beavers are coming out today. Moira and I nod and we follow him back toward the road. As we walk out, McGill recounts how one summer he installed temperature monitoring devices here, which gave readings every half an hour all summer, and they found no differences in water temperature upstream and downstream from the beaver dam.

"What we actually found," McGill explains, "is that the beaver pond created cold-water refugia in the center. If I am a trout maybe I don't like the beaver canals and shallow areas in July and August, but in spring and fall the food availability is of a different magnitude here than in a single-channel stream. And in a beaver pond you can go deep and not get eaten by a blue heron."

Like many people my age, I think of great blue heron as rare, because they were when I was growing up in the late 1970s. Now they are everywhere and feast on juvenile trout. I touch the surface of the water with my fingertips, enjoying the refreshing chill.

McGill's observations that trout benefit from beaver ponds are supported by research on a similar anadromous fish, Pacific salmon. In his environmental history of salmon, *King of Fish*, David Montgomery observed how trappers and explorers found many of the watercourses of the northwest jammed with enormous old-growth trees. All that woody debris slowing down the water created prime fish habitat. And beaver dams did the same.

Ironically, McGill's interest in Long Green Creek began with his passion for trout fishing. Like Lewis Henry Morgan, who became America's first beaver expert, McGill was also a "trout man" who discovered beavers because he loved to fly fish. In 1994, when McGill was serving as vice president of resources for the Maryland chapter of Trout Unlimited, he heard about this stretch of the Long Green, which by all accounts was in pretty bad shape. The stream ran through a cow pasture, and because there were no trees to shade and cool the water or native plants along the banks to keep the banks from eroding, the stream had warmed and become so deeply channeled it resembled a narrow but meandering canal. McGill approached the landowners to see if they would fence out the cows and allow streambank fencing to be erected along several thousand feet. The owners of Long Green Farm agreed to this proposal, and funded by a small grant and a troop of volunteers, Trout Unlimited fenced out the cows and planted the banks with fast-growing willows. The change to the stream was not dramatic, but it was a start.

Then in 2000, McGill had a client at Ecotone, his newly formed environmental restoration company, that needed to perform some wetland restoration somewhere in the county. McGill thought of this section of Long Green Creek and proposed that the client fund stream restoration here. In that initial restoration, McGill's company followed the industry standard of an engineered approach: They used heavy equipment to grade the banks of the creek down so that the water could rise up over the banks during times of high water, then they installed wooden barriers at strategic points to force the stream to bend and meander, slowing the water down. Ecotone then built two shallow-water containment ponds on one side of the creek to create landing spots for migrating ducks and geese. When this was done, they planted riparian vegetation along the banks—willows, birch, sycamore, and red maple.

Just before we step out through the willows and back onto the road, McGill turns and grins. "We didn't know it at the time, but we were planting beaver food. It all started to grow in and the beaver moved in quickly. We had inadvertently created fantastic beaver habitat!"

As McGill speaks I take one last look around me at this hidden wetland; sunlight is bouncing through the leaves and branches, pouring everywhere, connecting one thing to another, erasing boundaries. Underneath the interweaving threads of birdsong, a great rustling seems to swell the trees, the rustling and rummaging of hidden claws and feet. Farms are always those places of tension between ecology and evolutionary need—where the wildness of the natural world meets our human desires to harness that wildness. But standing here, surrounded by this pocket wetland, I would never have known that only a hundred yards away I can walk out into groomed fields, vineyards, then a barn complex that routinely transforms into a busy wine-tasting venue filled with people and cars. Or that just a half mile downstream, the creek reverts back into a deeply channelized degraded canal that serves as a conduit to wash sediment and pollutants down into the bay. The natural world's ability to regenerate (in this case, because of the work of the beavers) was a kind of magic. For the first time I think I understand McGill's allusion to this place as Narnia.

Soon we are back at the truck. I pull off my waders and slip into sneakers. Moira heads across the road to walk along the creek as it continues downstream. McGill leans back against the truck, uncharacteristically relaxed as he begins to tell me the story of the site.

At first the landowners were worried about the trees, and as McGill will be the first to admit, beavers make change quickly. When the beavers began eating the newly planted trees, the landowners hired a trapper and began to trap them out, but every year beavers returned.

Then in 2015, the family's younger generation came forward and asked the family if they could stop trapping the beavers. They were water fowlers and had discovered that the duck hunting where the beavers had made their pond was amazing. Duck hunters are as serious about their sport as are trout fishermen, and the sale of duck hunting leases in the mid-Atlantic (the right to exclusively hunt a particular place for three or four weekends a year) can bring up to $10,000 a season. So the family moved the walking paths a bit farther up from the water and let the beavers stay. Within three years the beavers had built a second lodge and a bigger dam and the pocket wetland had grown into an eight-acre pond, a resource that served the duck hunters and the river system by storing and cleaning water.

The initial goal of the stream restoration back in 1994 was to create shade to cool the water for trout, then later through the grading and embankment work, the stream's current was slowed along that area to prevent the kinds of flooding that was washing soil down along the creek and into Long Green Run, then into the Big Gunpowder, which runs into the bay. But once the beaver pond was established, it began to serve another, more valuable service: It began to cleanse the water of nitrogen and phosphorus.

Increased use of nitrogen and phosphorus fertilizers after World War II led to the "green revolution" of agricultural production, but within fifty years their use grew so astronomically that it led to water contamination. Almost half of the pollution damaging the Chesapeake comes from agricultural runoff; it has been calculated that 40 percent of the nitrogen and 50 percent of the phosphorus entering the bay in Maryland come directly from the beautiful pastoral landscape of its farms. One of McGill's goals is to increase beaver restoration work on farmlands.

But when beavers live on agricultural sites, they often bring conflicts because beavers are farmers too and often are in competition with humans for low-lying land. Humans want this land along creeks and rivers to raise crops, and beavers want it to build their water pasture. The Long Green Farm beavers were no exception, and by 2018, water was creeping up into the hay fields and flooding the road too deeply for the tractors to navigate at certain times of the year. The family called McGill and McGill called Mike Callahan, of Beaver Solutions in Massachusetts, and asked him to help design a pond leveler for the site that could keep the water down to an acceptable level. So far, the leveler has worked: The landowners are happy, the beavers are thriving, water draining from these fields is being cleansed of sediment and pollutants by the wetland, and by all accounts the trout are thriving too.

McGill pauses and looks at me as if to say, *That's the story*, then suggests we look at the other side of the farm road from the wetland, downstream where his company restored the stream but beavers have not been allowed to colonize. We walk down along the creek to see the wooden structures he built along the banks to force the stream to meander and to stabilize the banks. This restoration is the engineered solution that McGill now believes is often misguided. When we look at the structures, he points out that while it is working to some degree, the emphasis upon locking a creek into place with reinforced embankments is ultimately counterproductive, because creeks and streams and rivers want to move.

"Stream restoration in the regulatory environment is measured in feet," explains McGill, pointing to the bank, "but once you start working with beavers, you need to think in terms of acres."

We both look back across the road where back behind the willows the beavers have built an impoundment holding eight acres of water.

McGill admits that it is challenging for people to see all the water that beavers bring into a location and not grow nervous; will they be able to control the flooding? McGill reminds clients that the key to river stability is increasing the ecological connectivity—the interaction between the vegetation on its banks and floodplains and water moving through it.

"The thing is, a beaver pond is super stable."

To make his point, McGill points to the creek downstream from the beaver pond, which now spans about four feet across but is still a single-channel current. Then he points back to the beaver pond.

"In that pond over there," he explains, "the water is spread out and it's low-energy"—meaning it catches sediment instead of carrying it downstream—"and we've created a lot of fish habitat."

Ecotone has grown so quickly that McGill now employs a staff of engineers, geomorphologists, environmental consultants, researchers, and construction specialists. He bought his first skid steer in 2000 and now has dozens of front-loaders, along with a fleet of excavators. Ecotone recently partnered with a major bank and now offers consultation, design, implementation, construction, and funding, and is set up to help clients seek and apply for grants. Ecotone has ten projects under construction the day I visit, with two in the development phase. McGill can no longer oversee all of the on-site construction and leaves this part of the business to his project manager, Greg Gibbons, whom I'll be meeting in the afternoon. Four of the current projects actively make use of beavers as part of the restoration plan. "We are currently working on six miles of restoration where we are not using a bulldozer or an excavator," explains McGill. "We call it 'low-diesel.'" Not all of Ecotone's work involves solving environmental problems with beavers, but if it were up to McGill, most of them would.

I ask McGill how many beavers he thinks it would take to make an impact on water quality in Maryland. His answer surprises me. "The Department of Resources estimates that trappers take out three thousand beaver a year, and it would take about three thousand more beaver in the landscape than we have now. So, if we just changed policy and improved those numbers slightly, the improvement of water going into the bay would be immense."

McGill has a vision for Maryland in which farmers would not just be paid for leaving land in conservation, but for letting beavers stay on their land doing their ecological restoration work.

"Is there enough space here?" I ask, looking across the fields to the road. Driving in I'd passed plenty of strip malls and residential areas pocketed between farmland. McGill answers immediately, and it's clear he's been giving this some thought. He points out that the government currently pays farmers all kinds of incentives for how they use their land and goes on to say, "Why shouldn't we pay farmers to leave beavers on land and incentivize it?" He continues, "What if we said, 'Let beaver stay and have impoundments and we will give you a lease for ten thousand dollars'? You are never going to get that from growing those same acres as corn or hay. If we paid farmers and landowners to have beaver on their land, everyone would start saying, 'Hey, I want beavers.'"

What McGill is proposing sounds reasonable—why not subsidize farmers for the ecological benefits beavers can bring? But then I think about our American cultural history of hunting and trapping; the right to hunt is even written into many state constitutions.

"And fur trapping," I ask. "How would that fit in?"

"The thing is," he says emphatically, "our current path of policies shows that we are only thinking of beavers as a commodity. We need to start thinking about beavers and strategies for coexisting. Ducks Unlimited, other duck hunting groups, they should all be supporting beaver restoration."

McGill was right in observing that fur trappers and wildlife advocates had more in common than either side seemed to think; for one thing, they both wanted beavers to thrive. Ecotone has grown to become a major environmental restoration company because McGill is clearly that rare combination of pragmatic businessman and idealist. The difference is that while twenty years ago his first response to a flooding problem involving beavers was to call a trapper, he now studies alternatives first. "The fear is that beaver are going to inhabit places where we want to be," continues McGill, as if he has been following my thinking, "and sometimes they have to be moved or trapped, but trapping is still the number one go-to and we should make it third on the list."

The problem, of course, is that beavers don't follow rules or guidelines or property lines; they build dams where it makes sense to them. Good luck getting beavers to leave an area where they wish to live but might be flooding a septic system, a railroad line, or a section of pasture someone plans to use for crops. But paying a trapper to remove beaver from a particular habitat tends to be an expensive fool's errand because beavers, as in the case of Long Green Farm, will move back in. McGill encourages people bothered by beavers to consider the possibility of installing a pond leveler or other adjustments before removing beavers from a site.

Looking to the future, beaver believers like McGill and many others I have met, particularly out west, where beaver have proven to both stave off drought and create critical refugia even during massive wildfires, would like to see policies in place to prevent trapping beavers in restoration areas. If someone dug up all the trees that had been planted to stabilize a riverbank, it would be considered vandalism; why not protect the beavers that are working to benefit the environment? As McGill speaks I imagine signs like the ones we used to see with Smokey the Bear, teaching us not to light forest fires, only featuring graphics of smiling beavers teaching us to let them get on with their work.

We walk back up along the creek to the road and at the truck meet Moira. McGill looks at his watch and says they probably should go, but the warm sun has us all in slow motion. After days of rain it is great to be warmed by the hot, shimmering light. I take a deep breath, enjoying the sweet vanilla smells of Queen Anne's lace and wild asters.

We all lean back against the truck, enjoying the Maryland sun, which still feels like summer. I ask McGill again about how he discovered the ecological importance of beavers. His answer does and doesn't surprise me; it involves wolves. His reply explains the company motto, *Think Like a Mountain*, which is printed on all of Ecotone's glossy brochures. "Thinking Like a Mountain" is the title of a famous essay by Aldo Leopold, who is considered the father of wildlife ecology studies. In that essay, first published as a chapter in his famous work *A Sand County Almanac*, Leopold describes how the removal of wolves from North America resulted in such an overpopulation of elk and deer that it caused a devastating ecological collapse and starvation for ungulates. This phenomenon has been well studied and documented in one of our most beloved national parks, Yellowstone. In wildlife management terms, what happened in Yellowstone Park is called a *trophic cascade*, where the removal of one species, usually an apex predator like the wolf, causes a series of negative outcomes.

McGill's face becomes animated when he recounts this now well-documented interdependence of wolf and elk and beaver—research now being extended by an ambitious wolf study being conducted in Voyageurs National Park in Minnesota.

"It cost maybe one to two million dollars to reintroduce wolves to Yellowstone," explains McGill, "and it saved billions."

For McGill, the connection to his work here in Maryland was the trophic cascade effect of one species and the economic value of restoring the larger river ecosystem. There were no apex predators left in Maryland, unless you counted *Homo sapiens*, but there was a growing population of beavers.

McGill began to realize that in his work on environmental restoration work here in the Chesapeake, he needed to start with a consideration of the larger ecosystem when seeking solutions to issues of water retention, flood control, and river restoration. That was 2016, a time when for his own health McGill was forced to consider new approaches to medicine. He became dramatically sick with Lyme disease and did not respond to the standard treatment of antibiotics; his Lyme disease became chronic and debilitating. One day he saw a flyer about Reiki healing and, thinking he had nothing to lose, tried it. He believes that undergoing Reiki treatment and other nontraditional treatments cured him of chronic Lyme, and to this day he wears Reiki beads around his left wrist. As to why Reiki healing works for some but not for others, McGill has a simple answer: "You have to be open to alternative ways of thinking."

To enlarge his perspective on trout stream restoration, McGill decided to attend a conference on a related cold-water fish, Pacific salmon. At the conference, he learned about the groundbreaking studies in Central Oregon that were demonstrating the connection between salmon health and beavers. He learned about the work of Joe Wheaton in Utah, who had developed the Beaver Restoration Assessment Tool (BRAT), which was a formula for calculating the number of beaver a river system could support, and the use of something called the beaver dam analog as a stream restoration tool. By using BDAs, researchers in Oregon were making human dams that stored enough water to create habitats that could support beaver in drought-parched areas of Central Oregon. In places like Bridge Creek, beaver were being helped to return and propagate with remarkable success, restoring water to arid areas.

When McGill is done talking, he looks toward the fields then pulls out his phone to check the list of appointments his assistant back at the office has scheduled for him. Suddenly we hear the noise of a motor and a white golf cart comes bouncing over the hill. "That's the landowner," says McGill and waves. A jovial-looking man jumps out, and his yellow Lab follows.

"Hello, Moonbeam," says Moira and reaches to pat the Lab.

"That's Moonshine," says the landowner, laughing. "Moonbeam is getting too old to ride along. She's back at the house." Moira is unfazed—apparently the two yellow Labs look a great deal alike—and continues stroking the dog's head. McGill introduces me, then they start going over the schedule for filling the wildlife pond and discuss the farm. Before the landowner drives away, I ask him what he thinks of the beavers.

"At first, we thought of them as enemies, because they eat the trees we planted...but now, well..." He looks at me and smiles and says without a tinge of irony or sarcasm, "They are really interesting creatures."

As the golf cart bumps over the hill, the yellow Lab now leaping along beside it, I ask McGill what he meant about filling the pond. McGill motions for me to follow him across the field to the side of the creek, and soon we are standing beside two square-shaped shallow ponds. One of them is completely dry. When he did the stream restoration in 2000, McGill had used the soil from grading the banks to build a berm, and then he dug out the two ponds and compacted the soil to keep water from infiltrating out. They serve as wildlife areas for migrating ducks and geese to land. The cost to design, then use heavy machinery to dig out, compact, then reinforce the ponds was about $100,000.

McGill glances at the empty pond the landowner will soon be filling with water pumped from the creek, then gestures back to the area behind the trees where the beaver have an eight-acre impoundment of water, and his point is simple. While the two wildfowl landing ponds serve a function, they don't attract as many ducks or geese or bring the biodiversity and water cleansing benefits of the beavers' pond, and they dry up over the summer and have to be filled each fall. By this time, Moira, who had walked off to inspect some wildflowers, has rejoined us. Again, McGill points back to where the beavers are living.

"To build a storm water management pond with that kind of water retention would cost one to two million dollars," he says matter-of-factly.

I am visibly stunned at the price. "One to two million?"

"Yes," answers McGill. "You have to build the embankment, the core, an outlet structure, you have to design and plan the whole thing. We've built those; we have contracts with counties throughout Maryland where it is one after the other. But beavers did all this…" He swings his arm in a wide gesture for emphasis. Moira, who has been listening, interjects with a grin, "For zero dollars!" She laughs, and so does McGill, both of them energized and delighted by this thought.

If he is worried about losing business because beavers can create stormwater retention ponds for about a million dollars cheaper than his company can, McGill does not show it.

"We do stormwater management, construction, renovation, fire retention areas, we do a lot of stream wetland restoration," he continues, "but the thing is the water quality benefits of a beaver pond are very much similar to what we want to see in an engineered storm management pond."

Once he is on the subject of the economic savings of utilizing beavers, McGill has no limit of case studies to share. He begins to describe some restoration work Ecotone did on a tidal creek twenty years ago. "The county and state were spending millions dredging it every ten years," he explains. When the town called up to ask McGill to do something about some beavers that had moved in, McGill convinced them to put in a flow device instead of removing them. The flow device cost about $8,000 to install and monitor, but McGill figures that the ecosystem services that the beavers there provide is probably worth millions.

"We try to take the approach where we coexist," he continues. "We say, 'Let's let the beaver stay and get the ecosystem benefits they provide.' The creation of water storage and sediment storage—the cost-benefit ratio of using beavers is astronomical."

When I ask why the idea of using beavers hasn't taken hold more generally, his face becomes pensive; he's half proud or half sheepish about what he is about to say. "In my industry I'm still a bit of a unicorn...I'm still..." He pauses now, choosing his words, slowing down. "Well, I've got a few more unicorns in the tribe, but most folks are stuck in an engineering approach."

As usual my notebook is out and I am making notes as fast as I can. McGill is perhaps choosing what he does or doesn't want to go into print, then continues slowly, "There is an ecological industrial complex that has been built." Again, he pauses. "And there are some big companies that view beavers as a threat to their existence."

PART II

Within an hour I've arrived in western Maryland where Greg Gibbons, the Ecotone project manager, is overseeing restoration work on Beaver Creek. As soon as I step out of my car, I hear the sounds of heavy machinery echoing through the trees. The door of a truck parked nearby opens. A large man steps out. He has a calm manner and wears a safety glow vest and hard hat.

"You found it," Gibbons says, his voice full of cheer, and hands me a similar vest and hard hat. He nods as I pull the vest on and position the hat. "We'll keep our distance, but the guys need to see us. It is dangerous in there."

While I am getting out my notebook, two men walk up and Greg introduces me to Elmer Weibley and his assistant, Mark, who are here from the

Washington County Soil Conservation District to inspect and make sure that the project is moving along as intended and that the water leaving the site is clean.

They head off and Gibbons and I start walking across the meadow toward the creek. Immediately I notice the impact of the recent flood, which has pushed the long grasses down into a thick mat. Last week the entire site was underwater. They were worried because that was the second time they had to stop work due to heavy rains since the start of the project almost a month ago and they only had one-third of the planned sixty-seven beaver dam analogs installed at that point. This was the recent storm event McGill had been so excited about earlier; the site had completely flooded, but already the BDAs were working like beaver dams to slow the water down and spread it evenly through the area.

As we walk onto a freshly made road that winds through trees, Gibbons points to a spot along a barbed-wire fence. That is the property line, where the creek leaves the neighboring cow pasture and enters this twenty-acre conservation area. I should be used to the site of a degraded creek by now, but I am shocked to see the narrow canal snaking through the grasses; the banks of the creek have been so deeply incised I can't even see the water.

"That's the creek," says Gibbons solemnly. We turn to follow it down through a stand of trees. This area had been designated a conservation spot ten years ago and had been planted with willows, sycamore, and red maple.

At the next bend, Gibbons stops and points to the ground. And then I see it—first the creek, then the beaver dam analog structure. Logs have been placed lengthwise across the creek and held in place with a series of posts through which branches have been interwoven. I bend over to look more closely. I have only seen pictures of BDAs in books and slide presentations, and I'm curious to see a site under construction. Beavers always place some branches parallel to the stream's current, sticking out downstream so that the force of the water further braces them in place, but this human beaver dam doesn't need that kind of reinforcement because posts have been tamped down to hold the logs and branches in place. I see water trickling over the top and also through the sides.

"We want the creek to pool over here," explains Gibbons, "not to scour." He explains that they have found the BDAs work best when placed in pairs.

"What you want to do here during a high flow event like we had this past week," he says, bending down to show me how the water is pooling up behind the logs, although a significant flow is still running through, "is to shoot water over here."

He points to where the creek now pushes out in an elbow shape. "The force of the water will gouge out some sediment and send water down to the next structure." He points about twelve feet farther down where I see the next BDA, of similar size and shape; replicating what beavers do is surprisingly complex.

"Here, we want the water to come over here and kick out some of the soil on this side then carry it down. That sediment will get caught by the next BDA. When we started this was just a very thin stream, maybe two feet across, but now it is widening out."

I look downstream to where the creek spreads and then at the next juncture splits. Sure enough, when we walk up I see a series of BDA structures, then something slightly different, a barrier that is a stack of logs held in place with thick cedar posts. Greg explains that it is what they call a PALS, a post-assisted log structure. "We are trying to get the stream to meander through this area. The more time it spends working its way through, the more opportunity for it to clean the water."

Gibbons looks back toward the road and points to where I can make out the roof of a barn. "This site could act like a giant filter for those farms," he says, and I can hear the growing excitement in his voice. We are on the northwestern side of the state here just thirty miles from Pennsylvania. Here the creek runs through a wide valley, flanked by ridges of low mountains on either side. Within the long valley, farmland stretches for miles along the roadways. Farther down, the creek is known as a favorite trout stream, running cold and deep, but here it has begun to dry out during the summer, so it is now considered a "sinking stream," meaning it dries up in summer. He is careful to explain that the creek is still there, it is just that the groundwater is no longer visible. As he explains this I remember my lessons in river morphology 101 with Dr. Burchsted—river systems are extremely diverse, dynamic, and flexible.

Once the barriers are installed, Ecotone will quickly plant the area with willow and a variety of fast-growing trees so they can get a start this fall.

Their goal is to create ideal beaver habitat, meaning enough food and water. We listen to the creek gurgling over the new set of dams. When I ask Gibbons if he thinks beaver will come to the site, given its history of drying over the summer, he answers calmly, "If this does end up being a dry system, maybe beavers will come up and say, 'Not yet, I'll come back and check it out in a couple of years from now.'"

Later, when I scroll through the Ecotone website where projects are listed I see that in 2018 they restored 3,675 linear feet of stream along Bear Cabin Branch in Forest Hill, Maryland. The Bear Cabin Branch creek had been badly degraded, the water running through deeply incised banks that for the most part were completely isolated from the creek's floodplain; instead of escaping the channel to disperse during high flow events, the water raced through, gaining velocity and scouring banks, which washed down large amounts of legacy sediment. The design and build costs were $1,169,126.73, and that hefty price tag brought results. Nitrogen was reduced by 216.75 pounds per year and phosphorus by 31.96 pounds. That section of the creek now captured 10.5 tons of sediment yearly.

We walk on, insects chirr and birds rustle then flit through the trees, but the sounds of heavy machinery are growing closer. As we walk, Gibbons explains that one of the main goals of this particular project is detaining sediment from washing downstream. "Essentially, we've got three streams running parallel to one another. The idea is to get the whole area saturated as much as possible."

Beaver Creek eventually crosses out of Maryland to run into the Potomac, which feeds into the Chesapeake Bay. Sediment runoff has a long history here, dating back to the arrival of the first colonists. Massive clearcutting for timber, along with European farming practices, destabilized the rivers so that pretty quickly they began to wash soil downstream, and this thick layer of soil, in some cases two and three feet deep, filled wetlands and streams and the mouths of rivers to the extent that as early as the eighteenth century, ports and river mouths were getting clogged. Modern-day Baltimore was founded in part due to environmental devastation caused by runoff sediment. The British colonial town of Joppa had been founded on the Gunpowder River in 1707. Named after the biblical town of Jaffa in the Holy Land, the town prospered, becoming such an important port city that it was designated the third county seat of Baltimore by 1717. But within fifty years, clear-cutting and farming practices in the watershed upriver from the port washed so much sediment down into the creeks and rivers and into the harbor that it became too clogged for ships to maneuver. Without a shipping trade, business in the city declined, and not long after, in 1768, the county seat was moved to the deeper port of Baltimore.

Sediment is a pressing issue in the Chesapeake Bay, because sediment not only clogs ports and rivers, impacting the shipping and tourism industry (particularly boating), but it also directly affects the fishing industry and the overall ecological health of the bay. Bottom dwellers like oysters, clams, and blue crabs suffocate when sediment covers them. Fish spawn are similarly unable to thrive under layers of silt. While pollutants like excess nitrogen and phosphorus provide the main fuel for algae blooms in the bay, sediment contributes.

The problem is largely the rate at which water now moves through the watershed. From the Pleistocene until three hundred years ago it took months for a drop of water to get down to the Chesapeake Bay; water had to get through hundreds of beaver ponds and wetlands, trickling down, which meant there was basically no sediment getting into the Chesapeake. In other words, throughout thousands of years of Beaverland because beavers were slowing the water that flowed into the bay from every creek and stream like this one, the whole watershed was a lush mosaic of wetlands.

Paleoecologist Grace Brush, a researcher at Johns Hopkins, was one of the first to prove the dramatic drying out of the watershed by analyzing sediment cores drilled deep into the bottom of the Chesapeake Bay. During the 1970s, she began studying these muddy cylinders for clues as to the types of plants and trees that had flourished in the watershed over time. Her research unlocked a record dating back thousands of years, and she documented a dramatic shift in the early nineteenth century. The core samples revealed that while for thousands of years the mud was filled with the pollen from swamp plants, that pollen suddenly disappeared and was replaced by pollen from dryland plants in the mid-1800s. This was proof of a dramatic loss of wetlands (and water) throughout the watershed. It was also proof that it had happened fast—after only three hundred years of European colonization. Grace Brush's work supported what researchers in

other states and in Canada were discovering—the removal of the beavers
during the fur trade, then the decades of deforestation, coupled with massive draining of wetlands to harness waterpower and for agriculture—had
greatly contributed to many of the environmental problems we were now
struggling to address. Without beavers there was more flooding and topsoil
loss, and in the Chesapeake Bay devastating amounts of runoff sediment
were now clogging the whole river system.

Soon our feet echo on the wooden planks of a bridge. We clomp to the
other side and turn left. We have arrived at the next site under construction. I see a skid steer carrying a load of cedar posts parked by the bank.
Meanwhile two men are standing on the next post-assisted log structure,
bending down over the water. Then they jump back to the bank and one of
the men raises his hand. The excavator roars to life as the operator mobi-
lizes the enormous bucket. He eases it over a dead ash tree and the giant
bucket opens, pinches the log, then lifts it over the creek to place it on the
other two logs already wedged there, creating the start of the dam. The
man on the bank jumps back to the side and, not more than ten feet from
the moving log, which could easily crush him, signals to the operator where
he should lower it. The log is gently placed on the structure. "Good!" shouts
the man on the ground and raises his fist up, the signal to stop. Now he
and the second worker, who had been waiting nearby, walk quickly over to
the skid steer. They each grab one of the thick cedar posts. The posts are
almost twice as long as the men, but they hoist the heavy posts up on their
shoulders and walk easily back to the structure.

The two men position the posts on the downstream side and again
the man signals to the man operating the excavator. Again, the giant
bucket rises up, but this time it gently moves over until the giant metal
bucket hangs over a post. The man gestures it to be lowered and the bucket
descends. We witness this carefully orchestrated conversation between the
men and the machine and do not speak. A small mistake, a jerk of the lever
that could send the bucket too quickly to one side, or too far, and the man
signaling would be crushed. The coordination and trust among the team
is impressive, as is their speed. Within what seems like minutes, they repeat
the process. While we watch, they install six posts downstream and five on

the upstream side. The machines are shut off. Break time. The foreman looks up.

"Another one done!" he shouts.

"Great," Gibbons shouts back. He is smiling.

"Seventeen more to go!"

I check my watch—the construction team is so efficient, the entire procedure of placing the final log then placing and tamping down the eleven posts took twenty minutes. Gibbons and I head out. We are only a few steps along the way, heading back to the highway, when I hear the motors roar to life again. They are back at work building the next human version of a beaver dam.

In his 1995 book *Hope, Human and Wild*, Bill McKibben describes the beaver dam near his house as a "post-utopia" model of realism and hope. After what I'd observed in Maryland, and up in the White Mountains, and even in the creeks and streams of the Yale-Myers Forest near my own home, I could understand what he meant. All up and down the broken landscapes of the eastern seaboard you could find environmental restoration being aided by beavers.

McKibben joined a larger canon of American writers and thinkers from Thoreau on who had noticed beavers in our landscapes. Some, like Enos A. Mills and Archie Belaney (a.k.a. Grey Owl) and Dorothy Richards, had become passionate beaver advocates, but again and again their insights about beavers were ignored or forgotten. Was it just too hard to accept that a mammal with a brain so much smaller than ours was so important to the larger environment?

McGill was right in noting that we had a long history with beavers, but still hadn't figured out a contemporary culture of living with them. It wasn't just that we had ecological amnesia about beavers because we lived in landscapes so transformed by colonization, then successive waves of development; somehow, we still couldn't take beavers seriously.

The first images of beavers in North America that reached Europe were made by Arnoldus Montanus in 1671. Montanus was a Dutch scholar who had never set foot in North America, and his beavers have the bodies of sheep, only their legs end in claws and their small heads resemble bemused gargoyles. In his engraving, which he titled *Wonders of the New World*, a stag with antlers as large as its body and a majestic unicorn stand near the two beavers. But even those fantasy beavers from mythic seventeenth-century America looked almost comic. Beavers don't have dramatic antlers or horns like stags and unicorns, or scary fangs like wolves and bears; they just have goofy faces with winsome bearlike ears, their furry lips curving up as if in a perpetual grin.

Beavers could help restore our landscapes, but could we restore enough land for the beavers to thrive? More to the point, could we learn to live with the consequences of having beavers create their wetlands nearby? We didn't like change, especially when it happened in our own backyards, and transforming where they lived was hardwired into a beaver's DNA. They were the Shiva of the animal world, destroying what was in order to make way for something new.

WONDERS OF THE NEW WORLD.

This 1671 engraving by Arnoldus Montanus features the first image of North American beavers published in Europe.

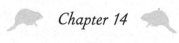

Chapter 14

Teale's Beavers

As soon as she heard that the beaver dam was breached, Sarah Heminway, the director of the Connecticut Audubon Society's Northeast Region, suspected she had a problem. Then the phone started ringing and Heminway learned just how big that problem was. During the night, nine million gallons of water had rushed out of the beaver pond, turning Hampton Brook into a mini tsunami; the flood tore through the woods, scouring the brook and washing out the Trail Wood Sanctuary's driveway, then the driveway next door, then the local road, then the larger state road, half a mile downstream. Luckily, no one was hurt. Traffic was diverted and loads of riprap were brought in to repair the damage. But people began calling Heminway, demanding that she kill the beavers.

"I realized it was a public safety issue," said Heminway. "People were saying you have to do something about *your* beavers, but I told them first of all, they aren't *our* beavers, they are wild animals. And trapping solves the problem for what, two-three years, then they will be back, this is perfect habitat for them."

And these were special beavers. Their pond was located at Trail Wood: the Edwin Way Teale Memorial Sanctuary, the former home of the naturalist Edwin Way Teale, who had gifted the 150-acre sanctuary to the Audubon Society when he died in 1980. Visitors to Trail Wood came specially to hike through the meadows and down through the woods to the beaver pond that Teale had written about.

Heminway called Mike Callahan of Beaver Solutions and arranged for him to do a site visit. Callahan had a reputation for being able to solve flooding problems by installing pond levelers or, in the cases of blocked culverts, by installing diversion dams. The goal of a pond leveler is to create a permanent leak in the beaver dam, lowering the water level so that it prevents the pond from growing and makes the dam more resilient to flooding. Callahan proposed installing two pond levelers, one in the main dam of the pond and one in the secondary dam just downstream.

Beavers tend to build a series of dams in close proximity along a stream gradient in order to prevent the kind of major washout that had just occurred; if the upstream dam is breached, the second dam is there to catch the overflow until the beavers can repair it. In sixty years, the Teale Center dam had breached before, but never so dramatically; climate change was now intensifying the duration and severity of rainstorms in the Northeast, increasing the frequency of flood events. At the end of the summer, two back-to-back storms caused flooding, and then Hurricane Ida arrived. So much water rushed into the pond so fast that the dam gave way. The caretaker, who heard the dam burst, described hearing a loud crash then what sounded like a freight train rushing through the woods.

Installing and maintaining the two leveling devices was going to cost almost $4,000, and the center ran on a tight budget, but Heminway did not hesitate. Callahan was waiting on fifteen-inch black plastic culvert pipe, which was back-ordered due to the pandemic, but as soon as the materials arrived, he promised to do the installation.

The wait was tense; if the rest of the dam gave way, even more of the pond's water could escape, causing more damage. "People kept calling to say, kill the beavers and be done with it," said Heminway. "But we want the beavers here. We want the biodiversity they bring and we need the water. Earlier in the summer, during the drought, I was grateful the beavers were there—they held in so much needed water."

The Teale Center beavers also had a special legacy. Hampton is just ten miles south of Union, where the first beavers to Connecticut had been reintroduced in 1914. As the colony grew, those beavers traveled the river system, which included Hampton Brook. Teale's beavers were probably the fourth-generation descendants of the original pair of beavers brought from Oregon as part of the wildlife reintroduction program; they were the stars of one of the biggest environmental success stories of the twentieth century—the reintroduction of beavers to North America. The beavers here also had another legacy; Teale had met Dorothy Richards, the "beaver lady."

By the time Edwin Way Teale bought the 150-acre farm on Hampton Brook in 1959, he was already a well-known naturalist, writer, and photographer. Readers knew of his writing for *Popular Science* and for the books that followed. In 1943, Teale had traveled up to the southern Adirondacks to meet Dorothy Richards and visited Beaversprite. He was so impressed by her work and the beavers that he wrote an article about his visit for *Natural History* magazine. When years later he discovered that beavers were moving into his farm, he was thrilled.

"How much wilder our wild acres seemed: beavers had come to Trail Wood!" he recounted in his book *A Naturalist Buys an Old Farm*.

Like Richards, Teale began making evening visits to check on the beavers and he named favorite viewing spots around the pond: Beaver Rock, Azalea Shore, Mosquito Cove. When locals advised him to trap the beavers, he refused. The pond grew. Teale's beavers built their dam where the brook ran through a low-lying flat area of the woods. The upstream side was flanked by a steep drumlin, so that once water filled the area, it resembled an amphitheater. Successive generations of beavers lived in the pond, extending the dam until it stretched 150 feet along the downstream side and the pond spread out over ten acres: a woodland gem.

On this cold September morning, I stand in the rain at the edge of Teale's beaver pond next to Sarah Heminway, who is still fielding calls. Heminway is tense because while the rain is not heavy now, high winds are predicted, which means she might have to close the nature center, shutting down the installation. Mike Callahan's nephew, John, who now works with Callahan full-time, is in the pond by the dam. He is checking for the deepest spot where the channel runs through; this is where they want to place the pond leveler. John takes a step forward and the water comes up to his neck. "I think I found it," he calls, "deeper than I thought it would be!" On the bank, Callahan nods. "Okay, let's get it in." Callahan is busy attaching wires to the pond leveler. A volunteer, dressed in waders and a raincoat, is on the dam peering over. Sarah and I are huddled in raincoats, but Callahan, who resembles a commercial fisherman with his ruddy good looks and salt-and-pepper beard, is used to getting wet; his orange T-shirt with the Beaver Solutions logo is soaked, as are his pants, but he doesn't seem to notice.

We are standing by a pond that has lost 30 percent of its water. The sides are slopes of mud and the brook pours over a wide gap in the dam. I look at two mature trees lying beside the pond, their trunks chewed to enormous points, one still yellow with fresh sap. When I come back at the end of the week to check on the pond, I will measure each trunk at fifty-nine inches, almost five feet around. While the main limbs of the trees are intact, the smaller branches have been stripped clean. Contrary to popular thinking, beavers do not need to constantly chew trees to keep their teeth from growing too long; they spend idle moments grinding their teeth to both sharpen them and keep them at the right length. It is curious that the beavers took out the two mature trees, because the pond is loaded with one of their favorite foods—water lilies. No doubt, much of the tree has been pulled underwater and added to the large winter feed pile I see sticking up from the water near the lodge. But a large piece of tree lies across the top of the dam; possibly the beavers took down that tree in an attempt to bolster the dam after the first storms hit. Most of the large trees that ring the pond are untouched.

A pond leveler, also called a flow device, is essentially a long section of heavy-duty black corrugated plastic pipe that connects to a wire cage. After years of trial and error, Callahan and others have found that forty feet is the optimum length for the pipe, and fifteen inches a good diameter to move water through a dam on bigger ponds. The round wire cage is made from galvanized fencing wire with four-inch squares; once constructed and attached to the end of the pipe it resembles a giant hamster wheel. One end of the culvert pipe will be inserted into the dam, while the other end, which serves as a water inlet, lies on the bottom of the pond, protected by the wire cage. The height at which they insert the culvert pipe through the dam determines the height of the pond. Callahan discovered that if they put the water inlet to the pipe forty feet back from the dam, beavers tend to leave it alone. Similarly, a five-foot-wide cage discourages them from blocking the pipe even if they come across the sound of running water. The cage also prevents beavers and other animals from crawling into the pipe.

John marks the place on the dam where the pipe will go through and wades back to shore. The volunteer jumps down from the dam to help. "Okay, let's get it in," says Callahan cheerfully. The three men gently ease the pipe and the wire cage into the water. The cage floats because it has been attached to PVC pontoons, and John pulls it out slowly toward the dam, the enormous black plastic pipe trailing behind. Soon he has the leveler in the right location, and after signaling to Callahan that he is going to drop it, he begins pulling off the pontoons. The cage tilts then slips under the water with a loud whoosh. The volunteer hoots. Everyone grins.

While John keeps hold of the pipe where it goes through the dam, Callahan wades out with cement bricks and ties them to the black plastic pipe so that soon it too sinks beneath the water. Satisfied that the cage and pipe are on the bottom of the pond, they get to work securing the pipe through the dam by covering it with sticks and mud. Water immediately begins pouring through the pipe, lowering the pond. They cover the end with wire mesh to prevent animals from crawling into it, then Callahan breaks a few small holes in the dam. He calls it a diversion tactic; the beavers will think those small holes are the reason their pond level is going down and get busy patching the holes and ignore the actual leak, which is the pipe. He doesn't want the beavers to get spooked. He has learned that they will tolerate the water going down about a foot; any lower and there is risk that they will fear the pond has become too dangerous and abandon it, or start building a new dam farther down. In cases where the water has to be lowered twenty-four inches or more, Callahan knows that the beavers will not accept the new water level and he does not recommend a pond leveler. In those instances, the beavers have to go.

Within an hour, the installation is complete. Heminway gives a visible sigh of relief and turns to go. Callahan lets John clean up and begins to hike quickly back to his truck because he has another site to visit in the next town over where beavers are flooding. He and John have completed over one hundred installations this summer, but they still have a list of people who have asked for a site visit. They can work until the first of December; after that, the ice is too thick. Callahan will check on the site in a week to make sure the water level of the pond is where it should be, then the leveler will only need to be checked once a year to make sure that over the winter the pond has remained at the desired level and ice has not damaged the intake fence, or that the pipe has become exposed or chewed upon. The galvanized wire lasts five to ten years depending upon the water conditions, so the cage will need to be replaced, but the black plastic pipe lasts indefinitely.

Known generically as a flow device, the first pipe system used to prevent beavers from detecting the flow of water was developed in the mid-1980s at the Clemson University Cooperative Extension Service. Constructed out of PVC pipe, it was named the Clemson Pond Leveler. While working for the Penobscot Nation in the 1990s, a wildlife manager named Skip Lisle improved on the Clemson Pond Leveler to produce what is considered the first efficient pond leveling device. He called his design the Castor Master.

Under Lisle's management, the Penobscot Nation, which covers 150,000 acres in Maine, became the first large landowner in the world to solve all of its beaver flooding problems without using lethal force. Lisle also developed the first effective fence system to protect road culverts from beaver damming, a trapezoidal system he named the Beaver Deceiver. Lisle, who is based in Vermont, has since installed hundreds of pond levelers and culvert fencing systems throughout the country and in Canada. His work is also referenced in Europe and the UK, where beaver reintroduction programs have been on the rise since the 1990s. In Canada, several people invented versions of pond levelers, including Michel LeClair, who has installed over a hundred flow devices in Gatineau Park, where he manages a five-hundred-acre ecotourism nature park he calls an "aquatic labyrinth."

Mike Callahan first learned about nonlethal methods of managing beavers when he and his wife (who is a nuisance wildlife trapper) attended a workshop offered by Skip Lisle. Callahan and his wife became involved in volunteer efforts to help keep beavers in the landscape using pond levelers. Then, in 1998, Callahan gradually left his career as a physician's assistant to do more volunteer work for beavers, and in 2000 he formed his company, Beaver Solutions. Seventeen years later, he founded the Beaver Institute, a nonprofit organization dedicated to helping educate the public about beavers and their benefit to the larger environment. His website is full of information about nonlethal methods for managing beaver problems.

Callahan's business has grown, in large part due to the tremendous energy he puts into educating not just the general public but also highway departments and town officials about how to manage beavers when they cause trouble. Town officials are interested because pond levelers and culvert dam diversions save money. In the town of Billerica, Massachusetts, beavers had become a significant problem by 1999. Three years earlier, a statewide referendum had banned foothold traps and most fur trappers quit. Not surprisingly, the beaver population shot up, having been said to go from twenty-four thousand to seventy thousand in just a few years, although those numbers were never substantiated. But beaver flooding was beginning to damage roads and railway lines, farmland, private property, and public utilities. The town of Billerica chose to install pond levelers and culvert fencing in forty-three of its trouble locations. From 2000 to 2019, this saved the taxpayers $7,740 each year. To hire a trapper cost $409 annually per site, but installing pond levelers and dam diversions cost only $229. Across the Northeast, highway departments and towns are finding that unless they had a volunteer fur trapper like Herb Sobanski willing to come in and work for free, nonlethal methods save money.

Beavers in all the wrong places have become headline news. Following global warming trends, beavers have moved into the tundra of northwestern Alaska, and their ponds are helping warm the permafrost, which releases trapped methane, hastening global warming. Beavers recently chewed through optical cables in Tumbler, British Columbia, cutting off internet for hundreds of people before the chewed lengths of wire and tubing were found lying on top of a beaver dam and the problem was identified. Glynnis Hood, one of the top beaver researchers (and advocates) in Canada, acknowledges that in Alberta alone, beavers do about $3 million worth of damage annually. Here on the crowded East Coast, accounts vary, but we have mostly built our cities and towns around rivers, which is where beavers are going to go, if they haven't arrived already. As Hood aptly stated, beavers are "water superheroes," but can we find ways to live with them?

Beavers may have a new role in twenty-first-century North America; they are fast becoming the stars of what is now called "wildlife recreation" because they are fun to watch. And they will not run off with your cat like a coyote, or eat your chickens like bobcats and raccoons, and they won't devour your garden like deer, rabbits, and woodchucks. The beavers of Martinez, California, have been in the news. In 2007, residents mobilized to save the beavers that were living in the creek that runs through the center of town. They voted to put in pond levelers to control flooding; then, to make sure the town leaders didn't go back in and remove them, organized a yearly beaver festival, which is a well-attended community event that now brings hundreds of tourists. Today you can sit in Starbucks and watch the Martinez beavers in Alhambra Creek as you sip your latte.

"Wildlife creates community cohesion," said Heidi Perryman, one of the original beaver activists and founder of the beaver education website Worth a Dam. Perryman is a retired therapist who has thrown herself into beaver advocacy and education, not just in her hometown but across the country. She loves the irony that Martinez was the last home of one of America's most important environmentalists, John Muir, but also the home of one of California's most famous fur trappers, John R. Walker. In Martinez, beavers, fur trappers, and conservationists are braided into the local history.

Martinez is a model for how communities can find new ways of making use of beavers. "Beavers do so much for the environment, we should be protecting them as a valuable environmental asset," said Perryman. "And they are good for a community. Studies have shown that where there is wildlife in a community, crime rates go down."

The beavers of Martinez might be some of the most famous in the country, but especially during the months of restricted travel during the pandemic, many people discovered wildlife in their own backyards. One summer evening I stopped with Mike Callahan to check on a dam diversion he had installed not far from the Sturbridge exit on the Mass Pike. Beavers had moved into the large wetland there and had dammed up the culvert going under the road. From a beaver's perspective, a road running alongside their pond is simply a man-made dam and the culvert a pesky hole; they will never stop trying to block it. In this case, the road the beavers had flooded by jamming sticks into the culvert was an important access road for the highway and the local town.

By the time we arrived, the hot summer sun was beginning to sink through the trees. We came upon a group of residents already lounging back in lawn chairs as they chatted and handed around bags of popcorn and soft drinks. Kids were throwing bread to the ducks and a group of bird watchers was standing ready with binoculars and cameras. Then someone shouted, "Here he comes!" We watched an enormous beaver swim steadily over to the pond's edge, peer up at the people, then crawl up onto the large black corrugated pipe and begin packing mud around it. The beaver was moving with the calm of a seasoned performer; he slipped under the water, came back up with his paws full of mud, packed some around the pipe, then looked back at the people.

I asked Callahan if he thought the beaver was hamming it up.

"Could be," he answered. "You never quite know what a beaver will do."

Cameras clicked. Some people clapped. Others shouted greetings to the beaver. The beaver slipped back down and repeated the show. It was social hour at the beaver pond.

Chapter 15

Kintsugi

It is late October. *Ping of acorn. Rustle of leaves,* and she stops for a moment, just a pause, her top incisors still deep in the wood. She feels the heavy air, vibrations of sound; a crow calls, that sudden tear in the silence, and she whips her head around. Things she cannot see are moving; she hears the rustling and scampering in the brush, pad of feet, scratch of claws. She sniffs, taking in the sweet aroma of mushroom rot and dying leaves, the sharp bite of pine. She can smell the seasons changing. Her need to chew is stronger than her fear. She turns back to the branch and sinks her teeth into the sweet bark. Bite, rip, spit. The wood chip falls and she bites again, pulling the bark from the soft wood, faster. All the world is hurry now and she can feel it. No more days of slowly swimming through the heat, floating, eyes and nose on the surface, front paws tucked, letting her strong back legs kick and glide, kick and glide. Her body buzzes with an even stronger urge to chew and rip and carry all the branches she can to the water's edge, then grab them in her mouth and swim, quick as she can, back to the lodge. Her tail is still thick with fat, but by spring it will be thin and weak, the fat depleted to keep her alive. All winter she will nibble the underwater bark she and the other beavers have dragged to the feed pile, her body pulling nutrients from the thin layer of cambium under the bark. She needs enough food to survive until the first underwater shoots emerge on the bottom of the pond in spring.

As soon as I reach the beaver pond, I see the winter feed pile; branches stick out above the water in a great unruly heap. I was so happy to discover the beavers here in July when I returned from the White Mountains with Dr. Burchsted. I'd been coming here almost every day since, but I don't need to see the beavers swimming; the sight of the lodge shining with freshly packed mud is enough. Fall is the busiest season for beavers; they must gather enough food for the lodge to survive the winter, winterproof and strengthen the lodge with sticks and mud, then do their best to reinforce and raise the height of the dam. When water freezes it expands, both ripping things apart and sealing the pond over. Beavers can get oxygen from the thin layer of air caught between the ice and the water when a pond freezes, but if they miscalculate the depth of the water, it can be fatal. Should the water not be deep enough and the underwater exit and entry passages to the lodge freeze over, they will be imprisoned in the lodge and starve. Inside the lodge, beavers surface onto a platform where they feed.

All winter the beavers will swim to the feed pile, bite off some branches, then bring them back into the lodge to eat. Curiously, in the center section, where the brook runs through, they have stuck holly branches, still filled with red berries along the top, giving it a festive, Christmasy look. Was the choice to place a red frill of berries along the top of the dam deliberate? We know that the neural capacity of black-capped chickadees increases in the fall. The part of the brain that stores spatial information gets larger and more complex, allowing the chickadees to remember the locations of seeds and insects. But we know very little about beaver brain chemistry and how it might change with the seasons.

As I had crossed the meadow to get here, my feet had crunched through a white haze: the first frost. Then I looked up, stopped by what sounded like bells ringing in the trees. The half-bare treetops seemed to be waving with leaves, only they weren't leaves, they were wings, hundreds of them, maybe thousands, then the noise swelled into a great din. While I stood there, the entire mass of starlings suddenly lifted up from the trees, a great cacophony of beating wings and such a loud frenzy of urgent calling that it was as if great metal pans were clanging in the trees. So many birds swooped up they formed a black veil against the sky. Then, in response to another invisible cue, the veil dropped down and melted into the trees at the far end of the meadow. The birds stayed there shouting; I felt stunned by the power of this evolutionary urge, their fall migration. Another sign that all of New England was now readying for winter.

All September I'd watched the trees make that critical calculation of when to give up and shut down photosynthesis, letting their leaves turn gold and umber, orange, or red. Every day it seemed another tree let loose until finally the oaks were sending down their leaves in a great clatter and the understory bushes flamed scarlet against the grey trunks. Chevrons of geese were now a constant sight and the ground underfoot was rolling with acorns. The forest floor had been popping up with mushrooms, which came and went, and the path was littered with scat: coyote, fox, fisher, and mink. Everyone was on the move.

I take one last look at the lodge rising up at the far end of the pond, a black mound, and turn to head downstream. I want to look farther along where the beavers swelled the water into a foraging pond, then turned the water so it cascaded down the far side of the drumlin. As I walk, my legs swish through thick stands of dead meadow grasses, each a silvery brown. In sixteenth-century Japan, where the serving of tea became a revered art form, one of the most treasured objects was an imported Chinese jar used for storing the tea leaves and named by one of its owners *Chigusa*, "thousand grasses." The name *Chigusa* was full of meaning. The phrase, also translated as "myriad things," was from medieval poetry, in which an image of dying autumn grasses reflects a zenith of aesthetic, religious, and philosophical understandings; the ideals of *wabi*, an appreciation for the beauty of imperfection in all things; and *sabi*, a sudden and keen awareness of the evanescence of nature.

When I reach the section of stream where the beavers have swelled the water into an oblong, slightly heart-shaped pond, I see that they have also bolstered this dam with fresh mud. And just as curiously as on the main pond, they have decorated the top with a jolly line of holly branches, berries still attached. But even more eye-catching is the water, now full of bright yellow leaves. So many leaves have fallen on the water and been carried downstream that they fill the sides of the banks and cover much of the pond with a skin of gold.

In medieval Japan, a daimyo's attendant once dropped his favorite tea bowl and it shattered. The daimyo was furious, but an artisan repaired it with seams of lacquer and polished gold powder, and the bowl, with its patterns of irregular shimmering lines, became so beautiful it started a trend. From then on, treasured tea bowls that had been broken and repaired with lacquer and gold, a technique called *kintsugi*, became even more valuable.

I look down at the quiet stream, shimmering yellow with fallen leaves. We can't stop climate change. We could slow the rate of our planet's warming if we acted fast enough to start reducing the global emission of carbon, but we could only prevent more damage. We are facing a future in which we will witness loss and change in the places we love, and it was foolish to ignore this, but it was just as foolish to relinquish hope. As a species, we humans had our flaws, and beavers weren't going to solve our environmental problems, but when it came to water—the lack or overabundance of which, that was certainly going to define our future—beavers could make a difference.

Wherever we lived, whether it was in a city or a town, the suburbs or a rural location, chances were beavers were already at work somewhere—managing, cleansing, and restoring the water and biodiversity of that place. For thousands of years the Indigenous people of North America had looked to the "tree biter" as a source of environmental wisdom and teaching. When beavers have a problem, like a leaking dam, anything to hand—sticks, rocks, mud, grass, chunks of log, a hubcap, strands of telephone wire—becomes part of the solution and gets stuffed into that hole in the dam. And when the dam is breached yet again, they swim right back out to fix it. Maybe I admired beavers so much because in ways they reminded me of my mother; even in the last weeks of her life she was determined to walk to the kitchen so she could look out the window over the orchards and plan what trees to prune first.

These brooks and streams and creeks, shifted and lengthened and bulged, like the one before me, were our seams of gold; they were beavers at work, repairing our broken landscapes.

Epilogue

The Story of the Book

Prologue: Ktsi Amiskw, *the Story of Great Beaver*

When oral literature is written down and recorded, as the story of Great Beaver has been time and again, much of the cultural context is lost as each version is communicated across particular regional and tribal values. Oral literature is a sonic experience, voice embodying and connecting history and culture and place through time. The Great Beaver story has survived for thousands of years because as a narrative it is both subversive and brilliant. As the plot unfolds we gradually take in the story's wisdom, and the critical instruction it provides: You cannot ignore your obligations to other living things and expect to survive.

In many versions of the northern Algonquian stories of Great Beaver, it is not the shaper-creator who vanquishes *Ktsi Amiskw* but, rather, Gluskap, called the man from nothing, who had the ability to make such changes. Gluskap is featured in Algonquian storytelling because he struggles like humans to live a good life. Through his mistakes and adventures, listeners empathize and absorb a moral code. Gluskap is central to Great Beaver stories up and down the maritime East, particularly in Canada.

In *Braiding Sweetgrass*, Robin Wall Kimmerer, an ethnobotanist, elegantly makes the case that while there are important differences between Western science and Indigenous science, they are not mutually exclusive. Inspired by the work of Kimmerer and other Native writers, scientists, and scholars, I was determined to track down as many versions of the Great Beaver story as I could find (along with any other Indigenous stories involving beavers). This became quite a journey. I began with Charles Leland's

1884 collection of "Algonquian legends," then located William Jones's 1919 collection of "Ojibwe tales." I then turned to Frank G. Speck's extensive research and writing about Penobscot shamanism, religion, and story-telling published during the 1930s. But my enquiry continued, for it also seemed relevant to find out more about these early anthropologists and their working methods. Because, of course, it was important to pose the question: To what extent were the stories they collected faithful to the origi-nal understandings of the Indigenous community from which they were collected?

Recent scholarship has revealed the complex relationships between early American anthropologists like Frank Gouldsmith Speck (1881–1950) and their informants. Speck, who had been trained by Franz Boas and went on to chair the anthropology department at the University of Pennsylvania, had students the likes of Loren Eisley, who went on to become famous. But he also taught and mentored a Mohegan woman named Gladys Iola Tanta-quidgeon (1899–2005) who became his research assistant. Tantaquidgeon provided Speck with critical access as his translator. Speck was of particu-lar interest to me in researching this book because he spent summers not far from where I live in northeastern Connecticut and, as a teenager, met members of the Mohegan tribe (which was how he would come to learn about Gladys and help her enroll in the University of Pennsylvania). It was fascinating to learn how deeply both stories of Great Beaver and early schol-arship on Algonquian culture were rooted in this place. It is a sad fact that Native peoples are still widely portrayed as inhabitants of the past rather than as contemporary members of society. I am indebted to my colleague, the historian Thomas Doughton at the College of the Holy Cross, for many conversations on this topic, which helped illuminate me and, I hope, left me more sensitive to the ways in which this marginalization continues. Pro-fessor Doughton is himself of Nipmuc ancestry, with family roots back to the Woodstock area.

Finally, I did my best to locate information about beaver stories in the work of contemporary Native scholars and writers such as Lisa Brooks, Mar-garet Bruchac, Rosalyn LaPier, Cheryl Savageau, and Leanne Betasamosake Simpson. Bruchac recorded a powerful telling of the story for the *Raid on Deerfield: The Many Stories of 1704* website for the Pocumtuck Valley Memorial

Association's Memorial Hall Museum in 2020. The linguist Ives Goddard, considered the world's leading authority on the Algonquian language, helped clarify certain Algonquian words. Linguist Steven Bird, who works with Indigenous communities in Darwin, Australia, provided additional insights. If I missed any important contributions, I offer my sincere apologies.

Chapter 1. At the Beaver Pond

The first time I encountered the term "Beaverland" I was on the trapline with Herb Sobanski in 2016. He pointed across the magnificent woodland swamp we were traversing and half-shouted, "Beaverland!" This name seemed such a perfect description for how beavers shape the environment that I wrote it down. The second time was in Jacques Cousteau's "Beavers of the North Country," a 1975 episode of his classic TV series. As he is flying over the Saskatchewan wilderness in a small airplane, Cousteau describes with awe (in his beautiful accent) the extensive beaver damming complexes he is seeing and calls them "beaverland." In 1923, concerned about the disappearance of wild beaver, Russia established the Voronezh Nature Reserve—one of the first beaver sanctuaries in the world. This beaver research and breeding center is part of a larger biosphere reserve recognized as a United Nations Educational, Scientific and Cultural Organization (UNESCO). The Voronezh website describes the 310 km² sanctuary as "beaver land." The first author to write this down here in North America might be Frances Backhouse, who used the term in her beautifully researched book on beavers in Canada, *Once They Were Hats*.

"Those who do not know the animals well may think I have humanized them, but those who have lived so near them as to know somewhat of their ways and their minds will not think so." Ernest Thompson Seton wrote those lines in the opening of "Raggylug," his tale about a rabbit in *Lobo, Rag, and Vixen*, a slim volume of animal stories published in 1900. I spent a good deal of my childhood reading books about animals, many written by authors like Seton, who unabashedly bring animals to life as characters on the page. No doubt these writers came back to me when I was working on this book, and one day I decided to myself unabashedly dive into a beaver pond while pondering the facts of a particular beaver. In terms of style, I was further inspired by Jo Ann Beard's wonderful essay, "Coyote."

It is worth noting that new research by animal behaviorists such as Frans de Waal and others is quickly and radically enlarging our understanding of the emotional lives of animals and our own ability as humans to understand animals through emotional empathy. And with this new understanding has come a reevaluation of the term "anthropomorphism," which is defined as "attributing human characteristics to animals." Increasingly, the identification of a strict line between what is purely human and purely animal seems dated. New research on "mirror neurons"—the name given to the part of the brain that enables us to understand another's behavior—for example, suggests that there is a neurological basis for the ways we can have "cognitive empathy" for the emotional and mental states of others. And if there is a neurobiological underpinning to empathy, why would it not exist in some form in animals?

The term "keystone species" was coined by R. T. Paine and introduced to the world in his "Note on Trophic Complexity and Community Stability" (*American Naturalist*, 1969). Since then it has been widely discussed in scientific literature. Beavers were first identified as *ecosystem engineers* twenty-three years later, in the paper "Organisms as Ecosystem Engineers" by Clive G. Jones, John H. Lawton, and Moshe Shachak (*Oikos*, 1994).

When did Giant Beavers trundle throughout North America and when did they die out?

Castoridae, the beaver family, originated in North America at the end of the Eocene—about 37 million years ago—and spread to Europe and Asia by way of the Beringia land bridge. Since then, the fossil record shows that over millions of years, upwards of thirty genera of beavers have evolved and vanished. The beavers we see today in North America are *Castor canadensis*, and at one point twenty-five separate species lived throughout the continent. The beavers found in Europe today, called *Castor fiber*, are considered cousins of North American beavers because they are similar in appearance and habit but have slight chromosomal differences.

The earliest and perhaps the weirdest of the beavers was *Paleocastor*, which dug strange corkscrew-shaped burrows. These proto-beavers did not (as far as we can tell) gnaw down trees, but they did excavate their burrows with their teeth. One of the next to come along was *Dipoides*, an early beaver that lived in water some 24 million years ago and definitely chewed wood.

But the beaver that most captures the imagination is *Castoriodes ohioensis*, the giant beaver that lived during the Pleistocene and was the size of a bear. The first known fossil remains of a giant beaver were found in the first half of the nineteenth century in a peat bog near Nashport, Ohio—hence the species name, *Ohioensis*. Giant beavers loved ponds, lakes, and swamps, and remains have been found throughout the eastern half of the United States, the Great Lakes region up through the southern margin of the Canadian shield, and in Alaska. Along with the other megafauna, *Castoriodes* died out during the late Wisconsinan glaciation, about 10,000 years ago.

Chapter 2. On the Trap Line

I conducted many interviews with the late Herb Sobanski Jr. between 2016 and 2019. Some were conducted as sit-down interviews, many more were conversations documented during the course of reporting. Sadly, Herb Sobanski suffered a fatal heart attack in the fall of 2019. I am grateful to his widow, Sherri Sobanski, for her strong commitment to this book, as I drew upon those interviews and notes to write Herb's extended profile. My understanding of fur trapping and the contemporary culture of fur trapping in the East was supplemented by reporting on and off trap lines. In addition, I attended trapper gatherings and fur auctions large and small. In 2017, I attended the North American Fur Auction (NAFA) in Toronto. The following year I spent three days at the National Trappers Association annual conference, held that year in Escanaba, Michigan. I also visited the Trap History Museum in Galloway, Ohio. I had many hours of conversation with many individuals who do not appear in this book, but whose comments and observations I relied upon to further my understanding of fur trapping, the history of the steel trap in America, the dynamics of the global fur trade, and the contemporary culture of fur trappers. Some individuals involved in the fur trade allowed me to use their names, others asked to remain anonymous. I am grateful to them all.

Tips to Trappers was published by Sears, Roebuck from 1925 to 1958.

How many beavers inhabited North America before colonization? The fact is, we don't know. The figure of 60–400 million that is routinely cited in the scientific literature is derived from Ernest Thompson Seton's 1929 classic, *The Lives of Game Animals*. In that book, Seton estimated that there were 60 to 400 million beavers living in North America prior to European contact, but he doesn't explain how he came up with this range. Theoretically, this census is possible.

How many beavers live in North America now? Scientific literature in the United States and Canada routinely cites the beaver population to be anywhere from 6 to 20 million, but there have been no comprehensive studies of population in either country. In the United States, estimates of beaver population tend to be extrapolated from the number of beaver pelts tagged by individual states, or by the number of beaver complaints. According to the United States Environmental Protection Agency, 3.5 million miles of rivers and streams run through the United States. In theory you could estimate that beavers populate a river system at a rate of about one colony each half mile and come up with the following figure: 7 million beaver colonies each housing 6 beaver would mean that 42 million beaver live along those 3.5 million miles of river system. But this figure does not consider wetlands and intermittent streams, or the fact that humans tend to want to live in the same places that beavers do—low-lying land along rivers—and have taken over much of that habitat. The land mass of the United States is roughly 3.8 million square miles. The population as of 2022 was close to 333 million people.

In *The Romance of the Beaver*, published in 1892, A. Radclyffe Dugmore observed a beaver-cut stump in Montana that was forty-two inches—over three feet—wide. Similarly impressive beaver tree fellings and constructions had been previously documented by Lewis Henry Morgan in his 1868 classic *The American Beaver*. Enos Mills would also recount beavers felling trees and making dams with impressive speed in his book, *In Beaver World*, which he published forty-five years later.

The longest beaver dam in the world was found with Google Earth by Jean Thie, the director of EcoInformatics International (October 2, 2007). Thie found the dam, quite by accident when he was studying the rate of melting of permafrost wetlands. The dam has been measured at 2,790 feet and has existed at this spot in Northern Alberta for more than twenty-five years. It can be observed on the 1990 Landsat 7 Pseudo Color Imagery provided by NASA World Wind. Jean Thie's satellite-assisted research is documented on his EcoInformatics website: https://www.geostrategis .com/p_beavers-longestdam.htm.

Flying beavers: The 1948 Idaho beaver drop—when seventy-some beavers were airlifted in crates and dropped by parachute into the almost impenetrable and inaccessible high mountain meadows in the rugged Chamberlain basin—is too fun to ignore. I am indebted to the Idaho Fish and Game department for digging up old archival photographs and articles about the project. To learn more see: "Beaver Dropped from Sky to New Homes" in the *Idaho Wildlife Review*, October 1948; and "Transplanting Beavers by Airplane and Parachute," told by Elmo W. Heter, *Journal of Wildlife Management*, 1950.

Chapter 3. Looking for Astor in Astoria

In 2019 I visited Astoria, Oregon. In addition to historical information drawn from books, information for this chapter was gleaned from visiting several sites there worth visiting. These include: the Heritage Museum, the Maritime Museum, and the Lewis and Clark Discovery Center, and the magnificent overlook where the mouth of the Columbia river pours into the Pacific.

My understanding of fur trade history was greatly supplemented by a summer that I spent at the American Antiquarian Society in Worcester in 2017 as an Artist's and Writer's Baron Fellow. Of particular use were the following collections: America's Historical Newspapers 1690–1922; American Historical Periodicals pre-1876 / post-1876; New England Diaries 17th, 18th, 19th century; and their extensive collections of manufacturing catalogues. These materials enabled me to get a sense of how fur trappers and the fur trade was depicted during the late 1800s. I found wonderful resources like the American Dime Store series, *Old Ruff the Trapper*, published in 1873. I also made use of the Astor Family Papers, 1792–1916, located in the Manuscripts and Archives Division of the New York Public Library.

The two beaver restoration projects I briefly mention in this chapter are as follows: The Methow Beaver Restoration Project in North-Central Washington, and the Bridge Creek Beaver Restoration Project in Central Oregon. The initial focus of the Methow Beaver Restoration Project, which began in 2008, was to relocate nuisance beavers from private lands into the public lands of the Methow forest to create resiliency and watershed health in the face of crippling wildfires. The considerable extent to which beaver-created wetlands serve as critical refugia during wildfires has been well documented by Dr. Emily Fairfax, of the California State University Channel Islands, and others. More recently—studying wildfires in California, Oregon, Washington, and Colorado—Dr. Fairfax has documented the valuable role beaver wetlands play when a fire is over, by cleansing the water. Since 2008, the Methow Project has shifted its focus from relocating nuisance beavers to trying to educate the public on ways to keep beavers in the landscape. They still do beaver relocation to public lands, but their emphasis is now upon supporting the beavers in the Methow watershed by restoring degraded river systems so that the beavers already living there can further propagate.

The Bridge Creek Restoration Project, which began in 2009, was the brainchild of Michael Pollock, a fisheries biologist at NOAA, who came up with the idea of building human-made dams, or beaver dam analogs (BDAs) to restore Bridge Creek, a degraded tributary of the John Day river in Central Oregon. The goal was to restore the river in order to improve salmonid habitat. Within three years, Michael Pollock, joined by fish biologist Chris Jordan and others, had installed 121 beaver dam analogs. They then spent the next four years monitoring the fate of juvenile steelhead, publishing their game-changing findings in *Scientific Reports*. Their 2016 study proved without a doubt that beaver dams are beneficial to salmon. Juvenile steelhead on Bridge Creek, where beaver dam analogs and beaver dams were present, were three times more abundant than in a control stream that had been left in its degraded state. Previously, fish biologists had believed that beaver dams caused an overall increase in water temperature, which is detrimental to steelhead salmon who thrive in cold water. What they found, however, was that while a beaver-worked stream system does warm the water in some areas, it creates deep pockets of cold water in others. The beaver dams and beaver dam analogs also served to actually cool the water further downstream by forcing water underground, a process called hyporheic exchange.

Chapter 4. Man's Land

This chapter is based on extensive interviews with the late Herb Sobanski Jr. I also interviewed the wildlife biologist Tom Decker, who works for Region 5 (the Northeast Region) of the United States Fish & Wildlife Service.

In addition, I spent several days at the Trap History Museum in Galloway, Ohio, where the founder and director, Tom Parr, generously gave me access to his extensive collection of fur trapping literature and ephemera. For more information, the following websites provide useful information:

National Trappers Association: https://www.nationaltrappers.com/
North American Trap Collectors Association: https://northamerican traps.com/
North American Trap History Museum http://www.traphistorymu seum.com/

Who can forget images of the so-called QAnon shaman as he stood on the steps of our nation's Capitol as part of the January 6 insurrection, wearing his self-fashioned headdress of bison horns and raccoon and coyote fur? His bizarre regalia combined elements of Indigenous culture with the trope of the fur-trapping Mountain Man, fused together to seemingly represent the freedom of the wild west. In her provocative article for the *Washington Post* ("QAnon's Unexpected Roots in New Age Spirituality: Masculinity, Faith and the Strange Convergence of Counterculture and Hate," March 29, 2021), Marisa Meltzer outlines the idea that western culture (and white men) have lost their way and can be easily exploited and turned toward extremist venues. She points out how some members of QAnon groups trace the origin of their ideas back to *Iron John*. Bly's attempt to tie masculinity back to the sacred and the mythological (and, ironically, an essential vulnerability) has been converted by certain counterculture movements toward an embrace of toxic masculinity.

Herb Sobanski Jr. would not live to see the January 6 insurrection, which saw hundreds of Americans attempt to overturn the results of the 2020 presidential election by storming the capitol. But when he was alive he spoke at length and on more than one occasion about how important he felt Bly's book had been to him because reading Bly had helped him turn away from an addiction to anger, and in doing so had transformed his life.

Chapter 5. Wild Fur

This chapter is based on interviews conducted with many of the individuals who appear in the scene of the fur auction at Herkimer, including Paul Johnson, who runs the sale, and Bob Hughes, the fur auctioneer. Some of these interviews were formal sit-down occasions, tape recorder in hand, and others were conducted on site as part of reportage. I visited the Herkimer fur sale three consecutive springs starting in 2017, but the scene is based on one particular day in 2019. A few individuals featured in this chapter wished to remain anonymous. Some wanted a pseudonym used because they feared reprisal if they were identified with the fur trade. To respect the concerns of these individuals, who spoke to me candidly, I have changed their names. This is the only chapter where I have changed the names of individuals who appear in this book.

In 2019 I traveled to Toronto to spend two days at the North American Fur Auction (NAFA), which traces its heritage back to the historic Hudson's Bay Company, the HBC. At the fur auction, the fur trader Harlen Lien took me under his wing, showing me how to study the fur before the sale, use the extensive catalog, and make bids. He also introduced me to many buyers and fur traders from around the world with whom I had numerous conversations. Usually press is not allowed into the auction.

"It's on its last legs…it's just about over!" was a common refrain among trappers and fur traders, but 2019 was a turning point. That spring, San Francisco and Los Angeles, then the whole state of California, moved to ban the sale of fur coats and other clothing made from fur. New York City took up consideration of a similar bill. Then on October 31, 2019, NAFA, which had been financially struggling for some years, declared bankruptcy. Trappers and fur traders who still had fur on consignment with the auction house never received payment for their furs. Some lost a bit of money, but speculators and investors lost a lot. When the historic auction closed, it marked the end of the historic Hudson's Bay Company, which had received an original charter from King Charles in 1670 for a good part of what would become modern-day Canada.

The only remaining international auction in North America for wild fur is now the Fur Harvesters auction in Winnipeg. But fur trappers have not stopped trapping, and local country buyers like Harlen Lien, whom I describe at the Herkimer fur sale, are still buying and selling fur.

In April 2022, the Herkimer fur sale was the biggest in years. Paul Johnson recorded the sale of five thousand pelts that brought in more than $40,000— almost twice the value of the sale I had witnessed three years earlier in 2019.

Harlen Lien explained that he bought so much fur he had to rent a U-Haul van and make three trips to pick up the furs and beaver castor that he had bought. As usual, when I asked him where he was going to sell all that fur, he grinned, then shouted, "Put that pen down and I'll tell you." I put the pen down (my book was written, after all), but, sly as ever, he never did.

Chapter 6. Beaversprite

I visited Little Falls, Sharon and Owen Brown's beaver sanctuary, and *Beaversprite* in 2019 and 2020. In addition to reportage from those visits, I conducted several follow-up interviews with Sharon Brown, who is working on a biography of Dorothy Richards. She generously helped me track down photographs and information about Dorothy Richards's early life.

To try to understand the complicated paradox of Grey Owl, I read as much as I could about imposter theory and the dynamics of ethnic appropriation. I relied on Archibald Belaney's own writings, in particular, on his international best-seller *Pilgrims of the Wild*. And I learned a great deal from the two excellent biographies listed in the Sources. Readers who are still interested might turn to another memoir, *Devil in Deerskins: My Life with Grey Owl* (New Press, 1972), written by his third wife, Anahareo. I barely had time in this book to do justice to the serious topic of ethnic and racial appropriation and its lasting violence.

Who first named the movement of beaver enthusiasts "Beaver Believers"?

The sports team booster chant for Oregon State University is "beaver believer" (Oregon State's first mascot was Jimmy the Coyote, but Benny the Beaver replaced Jimmy in 1952), so chances are the phrase migrated from Oregon and probably was first used at the annual State of the Beaver Conferences held in southwestern Oregon since 2011. I called many people now associated with the beaver believer movement, but no one could identify exactly when the term came into use and who coined it. Without a doubt, the name of the movement gained a boost from the evocative 2019 documentary *The Beaver Believers* by Sarah Koenigsberg and from the fine book by Ben Goldfarb, *Eager*, which came out the previous year.

In 2020, I attended the Maryland conference, BeaverCon, which brought together beaver believers from across the country and from Europe. I spent a fascinating three days listening to talks and presentations and meeting many of the researchers, scientists, and environmental consultants whose work I draw upon in this book. It was simply not possible to mention all the environmental restoration efforts now under way to utilize beavers. In particular, I wished I had been able to devote more space to the visionary work of Bob Boucher, who, in addition to his work in the Milwaukee Watershed, is one of the founders of the Superior Bio-Conservancy. This project, which has been called a "health plan for this region of the earth," is a remarkable collaboration between individuals in governmental and tribal agencies, research centers, and private foundations; their goal is to create wildlife corridors in the greater Lake Superior Region, in many places by using the tribal usufructuary rights of the Native peoples who live in those areas. The Western Great Lakes bioregion encompasses parts of Wisconsin, Minnesota, and Michigan plus southwestern Ontario. On the U.S. side, it covers 56 million acres of land. The Superior Bio-Conservancy plan would enable more than 100 million Tg of carbon to be sequestered in that region over ten years (one Tg, or teragram, is the equivalent of one *million metric tons of carbon dioxide*). Yes, with the help of beavers.

See https://superiorbioconservancy.weebly.com.

To learn more about the beaver believer movement and beaver restoration projects and research, see archived talks and presentations for the following conferences:

State of the Beaver Conference, Oregon, 2011—present (https://native fishsociety.org/events/2017-state-of-the-beaver-conference-1)

The New Mexico Beaver Summit, New Mexico, 2020 (https://nmbea versummit.org/)

California Beaver Summit, California, 2021: (https://cabeaversummit .org/)

BeaverCon, Maryland, 2020, 2022 (https://www.beavercon.org/)

And the following organizations in the United States:

The Beaver Institute (https://www.beaverinstitute.org/)
The Beaver Coalition (https://www.beavercoalition.org/)

Worth a Dam (https://www.martinezbeavers.org/wordpress/tag/heidi
-perryman/)

Beavers: Wetlands & Wildlife (https://www.beaversww.org/)

See also the following organizations in Europe:

BACE—Beaver Advisory Committee for England (https://beaversin
england.com)

Rewilding Britain (https://www.rewildingbritain.org.uk/blog/saving
-scotlands-wild-beavers)

Scottish Wildlife Trust (https://scottishwildlifetrust.org.uk/our-work
/our-projects/scottish-beavers/)

Scottish Wild Beaver Group (https://www.scottishwildbeavers.org.uk
/about-us/)

Norwegian Institute for Nature Research (NINA), Trondheim, Norway
(https://www.nina.no/english/hom)

University of South-Eastern Norway (https://www.usn.no/english/search
/?q=frank+rosell)

Bund Naturschutz Bavaria (German-language website) (https://www
.bund-naturschutz.de)

What I describe as the "canonical list" of sources—that continuum
of books about beavers written by self-taught nineteenth- and twentieth-
century American naturalists—deserves further attention. The first writing
about beavers in North America appears in the accounts of explorers, and
fur traders and trappers, but the first book on the subject was Lewis Henry
Morgan's 1868 classic *The American Beaver and His Works*. For the next fifty-
four years, *The American Beaver*, with its beautiful engravings of dams and
ponds, would remain the authoritative account of beavers in North America. In 1892, it would be joined by a similarly expansive work titled *Castorologia, Or the History and Traditions of the Canadian Beaver*, which was published
in Canada by Horace Tassie Martin. Martin's book offered a range of information about beavers and included a small image that he claimed was the
earliest known engraving of a North American beaver, printed in 1685; it
is a small creature with a tail shaped like a large pine cone and a strangely

humanlike face. In a way, his book could be subtitled *The Natural History of our Most Endearing Extractable Resource*, for it chronicled the way the Hudson's Bay Company, chartered by King Charles, had controlled the territory that would become Canada for almost two hundred years through the beaver fur trade. In broad terms, both of these books reflect a nineteenth-century approach to beavers; both writers admire the beaver as an animal endowed with some qualities of reason and admire the beaver's ability to construct dams, canals, and ponds, but they do not connect beavers to the larger ecology of the boreal and northern hardwood forests they described, nor do they consider the formative role beavers had played in the history of water on the continent. Morgan, in particular, is neutral on the subject of trapping and completely mum on the topic of beaver conservation.

That would be it for books on American beavers in North America, until twenty or so years later, when Enos Abijah Mills and A. Radclyffe Dugmore published works that demonstrate a significant shift in thinking about beavers—they make the case for beaver conservation. In appealing to readers for wildlife conservation, they were both reflecting their era. In 1893, at the American Historical Association, Frederick Jackson Turner delivered his famous paper "The Significance of the Frontier in American History," in which he made the dramatic announcement that, on the basis of the 1890 census, the American frontier was closed. The 1890 census had shown that the frontier line—a point beyond which the population density was less than 2 persons per square mile—no longer existed.

By the beginning of the twentieth century, the impact of three hundred years of intensive resource extraction without regard for replenishing these resources was evident in North American environments. In the United States, the vanishing American wilderness was a topic of national concern.

By the time he published *In Beaver World* in 1913, Mills had spent twenty-seven years observing beavers in the Rockies and was already known in the Denver area as the "Snow Man." For some years he had been entertaining readers with colorful accounts, published in the popular press, about hiking out in subzero weather to measure the amount of snow that had fallen in the watershed. With the publication of *In Beaver World*, however, which was generally well received, Mills become America's first beaver spokesman.

In literary terms, he also introduced a quirky style, anthropomorphizing beavers without apology. His message is clear and sometimes strident: Americans need to stop thinking of beavers only as a commercial resource and start valuing their role in wilderness preservation.

The following year, A. Radclyffe Dugmore, a Canadian writer, published a handsome volume titled *The Romance of the Beaver*, in which he also championed the animals. Like Mills, he observed that the presence of beavers in a river system helps reduce flooding and prevents periods of extreme drought. Neither book seems to have been very widely read, and they are rarely cited in contemporary writing about beavers. More significant, the concept of utilizing beavers to help restore and maintain river systems was not picked up in the early twentieth century by the recently formed Federal Wildlife Bureau or state wildlife departments. Across the country, many states had begun beaver reintroduction programs by this time, but the goal was to restore beavers to the land as "furbearers," a resource for hunting and trapping.

Dorothy Richards, who had Mills's book on her shelf, must have loved the way he wrote about beavers, brazenly anthropomorphizing them. At times he describes beavers as "folk" or "people," or as "fur-clad pioneers," and he has no qualms about attributing a moral code to beavers. At times he even imagines beavers speaking, as when a beaver he has named Flat-top recounts the history of his beaver pond and lodge. When I reread his book, after learning of Dorothy's interest in it, I was struck by something more notable even than his whimsical approach; back in 1914 he understood the role beavers play in maintaining river systems, and he understood the role they could play in repairing damaged environments. In one chapter he describes in detail the ways beavers can maintain American rivers, making them "more manageable." He even goes on to predict that beavers "can make America beautiful."

Mills's observations are impressive, as he was writing more than a hundred years before human-induced climate change would thrust water into the news. Every environmental challenge we are facing now—whether it is too much rain leading to flooding, rising sea levels that are erasing coastlines, or periods of drought so intense they are making it impossible to farm and are fueling wildfires—is connected to water and how it moves through the land (or not). And how water moves through the North American continent is directly connected to the presence (or lack thereof) of beavers and the wetland systems they build and maintain. Mills was writing ninety years before "Anthropocene" was coined in 2002 by the geologist Paul Crutzen. Yet there in his concluding chapter, titled "The Original Conservationist," Mills describes how beavers both manage and maintain stream resources. He concludes that "a live beaver is more valuable to mankind than a dead one." Mills was not a trained fluvial geomorphologist, nor did he have degrees in either engineering, ecology, or wildlife biology, yet by observing beavers he had come to understand the impact they have on the environment. And he was restating knowledge that had helped shape the attitudes of the Indigenous peoples of North America toward beavers until the disruption of the fur trade. He observed what we are just now in twenty-first-century North America beginning to understand: that beavers are critical to the health of our watersheds and river systems. In the water cycle, water lands on the earth as rain, but unless it is slowed down along the way (with the help of wetlands created by beavers) this water rushes over the surface of the earth and back out into the sea, taking a good deal of the topsoil with it.

I began to wonder why *In Beaver World* had fallen into such relative obscurity. Mills had picked some fights during his lifetime, including with the president of the United States, Theodore Roosevelt. From 1907 to 1909 Mills served as the spokesman for the newly created U.S. Forest Service. He traveled the country, speaking at schools and churches and community centers about the need to save and preserve America's endangered forests. The dwindling American wilderness was a huge national concern. By 1907, the use of the automobile was changing American life, as was the recent introduction of electricity into rural areas. Roosevelt had only recently created the first National Bird Reserve, and the National Audubon Society had only recently formed. The term "smog" had been coined in London to describe its air pollution. But Mills felt that Roosevelt had come under the influence of the head of the Forest Service, Gifford Pinchot, who emphasized resource extraction, and had begun to abandon a commitment to American wildlife. By 1911, Mills was openly critical of Roosevelt's new Forest Service.

And Roosevelt had no time for writers who imagined the inner lives of animals; he believed that since the closing of the frontier, American culture had been going soft. He hoped that a return to the outdoor life, and to hunting in particular, could restore the vitality of the white American male. The "wild life" that Archie Belaney (a.k.a. Grey Owl) had pursued and wrote passionately about as part of his conservation ethos was connected to Roosevelt's belief in the outdoors as a testing ground for manhood. And this was a trope that had been carried forward by most of the fur trappers I knew, men like Herb Sobanski, who felt that through this ancient connection to the natural world as a hunter, something vitally important was being preserved.

Mills was quiet on the subject of hunting and above all wanted readers to think of the beavers he had been observing for twenty-seven years as beings with particular personalities and an abiding intelligence. He included affectionate anecdotes of his pet beaver, Diver, which he had acquired from a fur trapper. He describes Diver accompanying him on his travels, perched on top of a pack saddle. Whenever the young beaver saw Mills saddling his horse, he would fling his arms up like a toddler and cry piteously until Mills reached for those beaver arms and picked him up to place him in the saddle. Mills went on to name some of the beavers he observed in the wild. Mills described one particular beaver (Flat-top), whom he observed for eighteen years, as a "pioneer" and a "colony founder." When Flat-top died he eulogized the beaver's life as "long, stirring and adventurous."

What must have engaged Dorothy (and no doubt would have irritated Theodore Roosevelt) was the way in which Mills imagined what beavers are thinking and, at times, even put words into their mouths so that it seemed they were speaking. When I read these sections, I was fascinated; Mills must have been aware that he was going overboard, but he was also trying to make a point: He wanted readers to throw off embedded ideas about humans having dominion over the animals and understand that beavers were capable of reason.

Mills even went on to insist that beavers had a sense of history—they built beaver dams on the installment plan, after all, with each generation building on what was there, enlarging an existing dam. In several places he describes beavers responding to situations in ways that required them to make particular decisions. In one such example, Mills watched a beaver at work cutting down a tree, a behavior that is usually discussed as "instinctual" and thus not influenced by reason. When a hard wind began to blow, however, Mills described the beaver moving to the other side of the tree so that he was no longer facing the wind as he chewed the tree. By moving so that the wind was at his back, the beaver not only kept himself from being crushed by the tree, but actually harnessed the wind power that was now pushing the tree in the direction he wanted it to fall. "I have so often seen him change his plans," wrote Mills, "so wisely and meet emergencies so promptly and well that I can think of him only as a reasoner."

No wonder Dorothy kept *In Beaver World* close by on her shelf. His observations about beavers reflected her beliefs: Beavers were rational creatures full of personality and affection. Her goal in writing *Beaversprite* was similar to the concerns of Enos Mills; she wanted to convince Americans to stop hunting and trapping beavers and find ways to coexist with them in the landscape.

Chapter 7. Lewis Henry Morgan and the Great Beaver Dam

To research this chapter, I took two separate trips to Marquette, Michigan, in 2018 and 2019. I am grateful to the Superior Watershed Partnership and Land Trust and to the Cedar Tree Institute for helping me with research during these visits. In addition to the excellent books on Lewis Henry Morgan listed in the sources, I made use of the Lewis Henry Morgan Papers, 1826–2000, located in the Rare Books, Special Collections, and Preservation at the University of Rochester.

Morgan's passion was beaver-damming complexes, but he also took the time to admire the iconic teepee-shaped construction of beaver lodges. In the stories of many Indigenous communities, a human descent into the beaver lodge is a central feature. The original Blackfeet Beaver Bundle is thought to reflect the many teachings brought back to the human world from the world of the beavers by a man who spent a winter in a beaver lodge. In many other Indigenous teaching stories, women marry beavers and live in the beaver lodge, eventually bringing critical wisdoms and prosperity back from the world of the beavers.

The beaver lodge has also been a source of mystery and awe within

Western literary imagination. When Henry Longfellow wrote "The Song of Hiawatha" in 1855, he imagined the mythic hero, Hiawatha, explaining that the source of his peoples' legends and traditions may be found "[i]n the bird's-nest of the forest, in the lodges of the beaver."

When the evil Pau-Pak-Keewis is being chased by Hiawatha, he pleads with the King of the Ahmeek to let him hide with them underwater in their lodge. The chief of the beavers is sly and agrees. He changes Pau-Pak-Keewis into a very large beaver, so large that when Hiawatha arrives, Pau-Pak Keewis, "swollen like a bladder," becomes stuck in the exit of the beaver lodge when he tries to flee. Hiawatha soon smites him dead. Just over a century later, when Howard Frank Mosher wrote his classic of life in the Northeastern Kingdom of Vermont, *Where the Rivers Flow North*, he imagines the character Coville, an iconic woodsman-Vermonter, climbing into a beaver lodge to die when the old logger realizes he is too sick to carry on.

Chapter 8. Kitaiksisskstaki *and the Story of the Beaver Bundle*

When did beavers first use their teeth to cut down a tree?

In 2007, Natalia Rybczynski, a renowned paleontologist at the University of Canada who has a particular interest in the fossil record of beavers, put forth two theories. According to Dr. Rybczynski, the first ur-cutter may have evolved in the early Miocene when the High Arctic underwent dramatic cooling and the lakes and ponds where beavers were living began to freeze. Wood-cutting may have evolved then as a strategy for survival, as beavers began to construct piles of edible sticks—the origin of food caches—to help them survive the winters when there was no vegetation. Alternatively, cutting sticks may have enabled beavers to start building lodges, which would have been warmer than burrowing in the earth. Both theories are considered highly plausible.

In terms of beaver research and environmental restoration in Europe, countries leading the way include Great Britain, the Netherlands, Bavaria, and Norway. Individuals at the forefront include Gerhard Schwab (Bavaria); Frank Rosell (Norway); Róisín Campbell-Palmer (UK); and Derek Gow (Scotland). There is a fun article about Derek Gow's work rewilding beavers in Great Britain in the *Guardian*—"'It's Going to Be Our Way Now': The Guerilla Rewilder Shaking Up British Farming," by Phoebe Weston,

September 4, 2020. Gow's book, *Bringing Back the Beaver* (Chelsea Green, 2020), tells the story of his efforts over twenty-five long years to restore Britain's waterways by bringing back beavers.

Chapter 9. *The Underwater People*

This chapter is based on a day I spent with Dr. Denise Burchsted and Andy Fallon hiking through the Yale-Myers Forest to locate some of the beaver-damming sites along Branch Brook that Dr. Burchsted had studied for her doctorate thesis at the University of Connecticut in 2011. In addition to reportage and notes taken in the field, I had several follow-up phone calls and Zoom meetings with Dr. Burchsted, who was incredibly generous with her time. I similarly benefited from follow-up calls and correspondence with Andy Fallon, who at the time was a Ph.D. graduate student in the Department of Earth Sciences at the University of Connecticut and a member of the geomorphology and Earth Surface Processes research lab.

It was remarkable to me to discover just how many connections came together at the Yale-Myers Forest in Union and through the beavers living there. The Yale Forestry School (now called the Yale School of Forestry and Environmental Studies) was founded in 1900. Aldo Leopold, the eventual father of ecology studies, entered the Yale Forestry School in 1905 at the age of eighteen. More than likely, there were no beavers in the Yale Forest when Leopold was in the newly formed forestry school, largely because beaver reintroduction efforts did not begin in Union, Connecticut, until 1914 (and the 7,840 acres of forest were not completely set aside and named the Yale-Myers Forest until the 1950s). But the beavers that Dr. Burchsted had studied in 2011 were more than likely later generations of beavers descended from the initial pair imported from Oregon. The beaver pond I describe at Edwin Teale's farm in nearby Hampton would most likely have also been populated by beavers that dispersed from this original 1914 release.

Aldo Leopold is perhaps most famous for the "land use ethic" he put forward in his 1949 classic, *A Sand County Almanac.* He wrote: "A thing is right when it tends to preserve the integrity, stability, and beauty of the biotic community. It is wrong when it tends otherwise."

Chapter 10. Beavers in the White Mountains

This chapter is based on a day I spent with Dr. Denise Burchsted and Dr. Scott Bailey hiking through the Hubbard Creek Watershed in the White Mountains of New Hampshire in 2020. And upon many follow-up conversations and emails in which they generously answered my many questions.

Chapter 11. The Beaverhood

For five years I documented the beavers who arrived in the woods just a few minutes' walk from my house. I kept a daily journal of their activities and my awe and wonder at the pond they created, then my sense of loss when they disappeared.

In many ways this book began with the completion of another. In 2015, I wrote a poem titled "Water Rising," about watching a beaver watch me at the beaver pond. That poem would be the first in a series of poems I would go on to write for an art collaboration that came to be called *Water Rising* and resulted in a book of poetry and watercolors published in 2016 by New Rivers Press. The collaboration began with the sculptor Garth Evans but grew to include the composer Shirish Korde, then others, and led to musical performances, a film, and a video installation that has been shown widely. The art collaboration also developed an environmental mission. To learn more, see http://www.water-rising.com. But once the poem, the book, the film, and the video installation were out in the world, I realized that my interest in beavers and in that particular beaver pond had only just begun.

Chapter 12. Stone Walls

In 1934 Connecticut became the first state to conduct an aerial survey. I used these initial aerial surveys as well as later surveys from 1951–1952, 1965, 1970, 1985–1986, and 1990 to reconstruct a history of the beaver sites near where I live in Woodstock, Connecticut. These images are available at the University of Connecticut Map and Geographic Information Center (MAGIC) at http://magic.lib.uconn.edu/.

The visual timeline of these beaver sites, in particular to identify their size and how much open water they contained at different times, was further researched and reconstructed using Google Earth. For help in locating the GIS images of the beaver sites in Woodstock, I am grateful to Ruolin "Eudora" Miao, who was a Master of Forestry student at The Forest School at Yale School of the Environment at the time.

To research this chapter, in addition to the works listed in the Sources, I made use of the Archives at Connecticut State Library and at the Killingly Historical Society. Of particular value were State Gazeteers, and State Agricultural Census Records from 1850. I learned a great deal from the following local Histories: Clarence Bowen's *The History of Woodstock*, vols. 1–10, 1926. Much of Bowen's history of Woodstock was plagiarized from the work of Ellen D. Larned, who was commissioned by Bowen's father to write the *History of Windham County 1760–1880*, vols. 1 and 2 (first edition published by the author, 1880); Susan J. Griggs's *Early Homesteads of Pomfret and Hampton*, Abington, CT; Cheryl R. Wakely's *From the Roxbury Fells to the Eastward Vale: A Journey Through Woodstock 1686–2011*, Woodstock, CT: Woodstock Historical Society (with Donning Company Publishers), 2011; *Windham County Business Directory*, printed at the Windham County Transcript Office, West Killingly, 1861.

As Jill Lepore points out in her powerful book *The Name of War: King Philip's War and the Origins of American Identity*, when the Algonquian and English colonists of seventeenth-century New England went to war in 1675, they devastated one another.

I am grateful to Dr. Robert M. Thorson, the author of *Stone by Stone*, a remarkably authoritative account of stone walls in New England. Dr. Thorson generously traveled to Woodstock from the University of Connecticut, where he is a professor, and spent a morning hiking the perimeter of the beaver pond with me to measure and document the stone walls that ring it. It was Dr. Thorson's observations about the design of the stonework to the right of the brook that helped me identify that the beaver pond had been harnessed at some point for water power with a mill of some type, or as the water storage for a mill farther downstream. The number of miles of stone walls in New England was drawn from *U.S Department of Agriculture Report*, "Statistics of Fences in the United States," 1871.

Chapter 13. Thinking Like a Watershed

Before the pandemic disrupted travel and put a hold on many scientific studies, I planned to travel to Voyageurs National Park in Minnesota in order to include the new research being done by Tom Gable on the interaction between wolves and beavers. Since 2015, Gable has overseen the Voyageurs Wolf Project. Among the many discoveries about wolves revealed by this ongoing study, one of the most significant is the finding that the summer diet of wolves includes a lot of beavers. This information impacts how scientists now think about trophic cascade in places like Yellowstone National Park and at Voyageurs, and it underscores the extent to which an apex predator like the wolf is intricately connected to an animal as seemingly low down on the food chain as *castor canadensis*, the North American beaver. It also reveals how the health of both animals is intricately tied to the health of the wetlands and vice versa. The official website of the Voyageurs Wolf Project is supported by the University of Minnesota and is ongoing. To learn more, see https://www.voyageurswolfproject.org/.

Chapter 14. Teale's Beavers

When beavers create problems for humans, they tend to make the news. Researchers at the University of Alaska in Fairbanks have been monitoring the impact of beavers in a broad swath of northwestern Alaska. The warming climate has enabled beavers to move north, and they now inhabit three watersheds infiltrating an area larger than Connecticut. Making use of data collected by Landsat satellites in summer months from 1999 through 2014, the researchers looked for new areas of wetness that covered at least 1.24 acres. They found fifty-six new beaver pond complexes; the beavers have expanded their range in Alaska at a rate of about six kilometers per year. This is bad news for greenhouse gas emissions. As beavers move in, creating ponds, the permafrost melts, releasing methane gas. To learn more, start by reading the excellent article by Sid Perkins, "Beavers Are Engineering a New Alaskan Tundra," *Science News*, November 28, 2018.

Another place where beavers are creating large-scale problems is in the unlikely terrain of Tierra del Fuego, a windswept archipelago on the tip of South America. In 1946, Argentina attempted a bizarre wildlife experiment that was designed to both "enrich" the resident wildlife and produce new income sources by fostering a fur trade—they released North American beavers. To be fair, in 1946, beaver pelts were bringing good money in the global fur market. But flash-forward a few decades, and a few hardy beavers had managed to swim across the icy strait and establish them-selves on the Patagonian mainland. By 2009, their population had risen to almost two hundred thousand, and the beavers were busily transforming the landscape—chewing down everything they could get their teeth into, leaving the land essentially clear-cut. An ecologist at the Universidad de Magallanes in Chile, who studied the problem, estimated that beavers had reshaped up to 16 percent of Tierra del Fuego's total land area. In 2016, Chile and Argentina announced plans to cull one hundred thousand bea-vers, which in their countries are identified as an invasive species. To learn more, start with Ben Goldfarb's excellent piece for the *Washington Post*, "Why Two Countries Want to Kill 100,000 Beavers," August 9, 2018.

In Martinez, California, beaver advocacy has evolved to the extent that each summer Martinez hosts an annual beaver festival. Heidi Perryman, the founder and leader of the Martinez beaver group "Worth a Dam," is known for her witty comment: "Beavers are the trickle down economy that works." To learn more, see https://www.martinezbeavers.org/.

Chapter 15. Kintsugi

From 1983 to 1985 I lived in Japan and apprenticed to a master potter there in the village of Miyama, in southern Kyushu. That experience became the basis of my first book, *The Road Through Miyama* (Random House, 1989). While I no longer actively make pots, that experience forever shaped how I see the world. When I looked at the beaver pond that October day, it was thus natural for me to think of the art of tea and Japanese ceramics and the ancient art of joinery, *kintsugi*.

Climate change is the defining environmental concern of the twenty-first century, and climate is entangled with every environmental concern—clean water and air, energy use, food security, protection of land and oceans, biodiversity, desertification. To read more about greenhouse gas emissions and climate change, see the exceptional work being done at the *Washington Post* by reporters like Chris Mooney, who received a Pulitzer Prize for his writings about global greenhouse emissions in 2020.

In his compelling book *Inheritors of the Earth: How Nature Is Thriving in the Age of Extinction*, published in 2017, Dr. Chris Thomas, a professor of biology at the University of Leeds. argues that we need to fundamentally change the way we consider nature if we are to survive our new era of climate instability. He argues that the only constant of nature is biologic change. And humans have so influenced the biologic and physical processes of the earth for such a long period of time that we can no longer afford to think of nature as an old master we need to conserve or restore to its previously undamaged state. Only an embrace of this new natural order—the Anthropocene—will enable us to understand how to best help the natural world around us, and . . . survive.

In other words, the enduring idea of nature being in some perfect finished state before humans pitched up is a fallacy because humans—as part of nature—are part of the continuum of the earth's larger picture of biologic change. (This is, I admit, a bit hard to accept: How can our human propensity for greedily trampling the world around us be a helpful biologic process in evolutionary terms?) Dr. Thomas points out that over the last 2 million years, as the earth's climate shifted between glacial and warmer climes, an ongoing pattern of rare species becoming common and common species becoming rare has been on repeat. What is different now, of course, is that human-influenced change has accelerated that process. We face a new natural world in which any number of species of plants and animals are living in locations that they did not previously inhabit. Beavers moving into Alaska are just one example of this.

The main takeaway from Dr. Thomas's provocative book is that we waste a lot of precious time and resources when we put our efforts into trying to return nature to its previous state. We would be better off thinking of the Anthropocene as a possible new start for life on earth. Far from promoting climate change denial or a laissez faire approach to the environment, Dr. Thomas argues for a vigilant embrace of dynamism. Yes, you might say he wants us to try to think a bit more like a beaver: Transformation can be good.

Afterword to the Trade Edition

Beaverland sets out to show how beavers are central to the health of the river network—that vast circulatory system that pulses water throughout the continent. By building their networks of dams, beavers create a rhythm of ponds, wetlands, and beaver meadows that not only result in structures we can see but set in motion ecological, biological, hydrological, and geomorphic processes that profoundly impact the ecology and function and thus health of the river system. For eons, the 400 million beavers that have lived throughout North America have helped manage our waters.

This new paperback edition comes out at a time when there is much to celebrate in Beaverland. Below I describe some of the ways the movement to bring beavers back to North America has grown in the past sixteen months since the book first went to press. "Beaver believers" are moving from the fringe into the mainstream. Government agencies, federal and state employees, tribal governments, and state legislators are joining nonprofits, scientists, individuals, ranchers, farmers, and other landowners in new partnerships with the shared goal of harnessing what beavers do to help restore river systems and create watershed resiliency.

Oregon passed legislation that removes the "predatory" status of beavers, meaning they can no longer be killed without a permit by landowners and the state must document numbers of beavers killed. This bill awaits signature by the governor.

California passed a statewide initiative to support projects that harness beavers' natural abilities to help protect biodiversity, restore habitat, build fire-resilient landscapes, and restore watershed resiliency. The state has also implemented a new beaver management policy prioritizing nonlethal deterrents.

In Congress, Washington State representative Suzan Delbene put forward the Developing Alternative Mitigation Systems (DAMS) for Beavers Act. Supported by over eighty organizatons and tribes, the DAMS Act would establish a five-year pilot grant program administered by the U.S. Fish and Wildlife Service. Each year $1 million would be allocated for nonlethal beaver coexistence projects across the United States. Tribes, states, federal agencies, and local governments, landowners, and nonprofits would all be eligible for this grant funding.

In the eastern United States, the nonprofit Beaver Institute has received grant funding and grown in size and scope. The institute's core program, BeaverCorp, offers beaver coexistence training and the installation of flo devices, as well as strategies for protecting trees from beaver damage. Its new initiatives include training individuals in tribal, state, and federal agencies, as well as individuals working in education and advocacy. The institute aims to provide a trained BeaverCorp volunteer within two hours of any beaver-human conflict anywhere in the contiguous United States.

The organization has also launched national working groups in the areas of policy and legal strategies, education, funding, beaver management, communication, and science and research. A pilot Beaver Habitat Lease Program is underway to create financial incentives for farmers willing to support beaver wetlands on their lands.

With equal ambition, a team at Google Earth is working with scientists to upload images of beaver damming complexes in order to train Google Earth to identify them. Using artificial intelligence to locate, map, and count the beaver damming complexes of North America would greatly aid current research projects looking at fire and flood resiliency, as well as the biologic, ecologic, hydrologic, and geomorphic impacts of beaver dams and canals.

Slowly but surely, the value of beavers as part of the landscape is becoming more widely known. For years most farmers and ranchers have fought beavers on their lands. Recently a farmer who once proudly reported killing ninety beavers in a single summer called up an environmental consultant after reading an article about the water gains of beaver wetlands on grazing lands. He had a blunt question: "How many beavers did you say you could get me?"

Back here in Connecticut, early in 2023, I watched beavers near my house rebuilding a broken dam and a damaged lodge. Their new dam pulled thousands of gallons of water up from below the surface, restoring a hidden section of the stream system in an area that previously had been so dry you could walk through it and keep your sneakers clean. On that winter day, when I walked out and saw the trees down and the water swelling between the drumlins, I felt a marvelous sense of déjà vu. I recalled my first encounter with beavers all those years ago, when the sight of that gleaming water through the trees first stopped me in my tracks, then led me to write *Beaverland*.

With three wildlife cameras I continued to capture images of the new beavers over the coming months, documenting their growing pond, then the building of a second dam. At last measurement, the upper pond covered 4.7 acres and held as much as two million gallons of water. A beaver pond can hold three times as much water underneath the basin than we can see, a vast body of both observable and hidden water. More significant still, these young beavers had reconnected the upper section of the stream to its lower section by the building of just two dams in sixteen weeks. They had not stopped visible stream flow but had actually enabled subsurface water to collect and rise to the surface, drawing on the ways rivers flow beneath the ground, at times spreading out like a meadow, at other times following beneath the stream's channel, the river's dark shadow.

Half of the wetlands of the contiguous United States have been destroyed since the onset of colonization. Even river scientists with sophisticated ground-penetrating radar can't detect the full extent of the river systems' original tributaries because so many have been filled in, paved over, or dried up. They do know, however, that the river network of North America once looked more like a multi-threaded system of branching arteries than today's largely single-channel river systems.

Until recently, the stream my beavers have been working in would have been protected by the Federal Clean Water Act, so that even if Connecticut law failed to protect it, the Clean Water Act would have. This section of the river system could not have been filled in, or built upon, or drained for agriculture. It would have been allowed to remain in rhythm with the stream network, its wetland corridors arising and subsiding over time.

But in May 2023, the United States Supreme Court adopted a new and narrow standard for deciding which wetlands and waterways of the nation were entitled to protection under the 1972 Clean Water Act. A five-to-four majority overruled science (and Congress) in a decision that has left 70 percent of the river network now without federal protection from development, pollution, and destruction. As we watch the impacts of accelerating climate change, knowing that floods, fire, drought, rising seas, and erasing coastlines are all part of our problems with water, the decision seems nothing short of delusional.

To only protect the visible waters of a river system is as foolish as thinking we will stay healthy if we only lather on skin cream and brush our hair. Wetlands are called the "kidneys" of the river because they cleanse its waters. Deep below, in the hyporheic zone where soil and water mix, complex geochemical processes begin and a world of microbial life is in motion.

We say water is life, but our story with water is more directly personal. Water is not just life, water *is* us. I myself am composed of 97 percent water. If I don't replenish myself, I will die within a matter of days. The human body has 60,000 miles of arteries, veins, and capillaries. If we unfolded each tuck of the origami of our lungs they would cover a soccer field. We don't question this vast circulatory system that keeps us alive even though we can't see it. Everything would change if we could accept the fact that a vital part of the river network is circulating with waters we also cannot see.

From the birth of the universe, long before our galaxy, our solar system, even our beloved planet earth formed, there was water. When humans emerged from the end of the last great ice age to create the first preindustrial cultures, religions, languages, art, then empires, they did so in large part because they learned to harness the earth's water.

We have now dammed up so many of the world's rivers, we have stored so many thousands of cubic kilometers of water in places where it did not used to be, that we have changed the length of a day on earth. The weight of this impounded water has literally altered the rotation of the planet, and as a result, each day is a few microseconds shorter.

Put bluntly, we have developed awe-inspiring technologies—we can literally reshape planet earth—but this power has come to us before we have learned how to live on our planet sustainably.

And yet the story of beavers here in North America and the growing movement to harness them to address our water problems brings me real hope. There are so many signs that the light bulb is turning on, that we are coming to grips with the ecological consequences of our long history of ecological abuse in the ways we have used our water.

We urgently need to reset our relationship with the natural world, which we can begin to do, in large part, by simply looking anew at the places where we live. I begin *Beaverland* with the Indigenous story of Great Beaver, and throughout I weave information about Great Beaver stories and Indigenous teachings about beavers that proliferate throughout the continent because our interconnectedness with beavers in North America has been acknowledged for thousands of years. The surface connection that the beavers set in motion here in this little stream near my home is just the observable beginning. The underlying connections that we cannot see, the increased flow of water through the land and the increased connection between water and land through the beaver damming complex and the start of canals, has initiated biologic, ecologic, hydrologic, and geomorphic processes that we are only beginning to understand and thus begin to quantify.

Since *Beaverland* has been out, I have been gratified by the immense interest it has received. It joins a number of books now on the shelves about nature-based solutions that can lead us toward a sustainable future. Readers often contact me, asking what they can do to help. Here is my answer: Find out about the waters where you live. Learn about them and do whatever you can to protect them, locally and nationally.

If you are lucky, there just might be some beavers already living nearby.

Sources

The gold ore of *Beaverland* is immersion journalism, which includes extensive field notes and interviews conducted from 2016 to 2020. These are described in the narrative notes for each chapter. The following is a list of the books, articles, and films I used to further research this book. To help readers who may wish to further explore particular areas of research, I have grouped the sources by category. Of course, these categories are subjective and overlap.

Native American and Indigenous Studies

Baron, Donna Keith. "They Were Here All Along: The Native American Presence in Lower-Central New England in the Eighteenth and Nineteenth Centuries." *William and Mary Quarterly*, Third Series, vol. 53, no. 3, 1996, pp. 561–586.

Brooks, Lisa. *The Common Pot: The Recovery of Native Space in New England.* Minneapolis: University of Minnesota Press, 2008.

———. *Our Beloved Kin: A New History of King Philip's War.* New Haven: Yale University Press, 2018.

Bruchac, Margaret M. *Savage Kin: Indigenous Informants and American Anthropologists.* Tucson: University of Arizona Press, 2018.

Ewers, John C. *The Blackfeet: Raiders on the Northwestern Plains.* Norman: University of Oklahoma Press, 1958.

Gookin, Daniel. *Historical Collection of the Indians of New England: Of Their Several Nations, Numbers, Customs, Manners, Religion and Government, Before the English Planted There.* Collection of Massachusetts Historical Society, 1972; Bibliobazaar, 2010.

Gould, Donna Rae. *A Wabbaquasett: An Ethnohistorical Analysis and Methodology for Locating a 17th Century Praying Village.* Master of Arts Thesis, University of Connecticut, Department of Anthropology, 2005.

Kimmerer, Robin Wall. *Braiding Sweetgrass: Indigenous Wisdom, Scientific Knowledge and the Teachings of Plants.* Minneapolis: Milkweed Editions, 2013.

Krech, Shepard III. *The Ecological Indian*. New York: W. W. Norton, 1999.

O'Brien, Jean M. *Firsting and Lasting: Writing Indians Out of Existence in New England*. Minneapolis: University of Minnesota Press, 2010.

Richter, Daniel K. *The Ordeal of the Longhouse: The Peoples of the Iroquois League in the Era of European Colonization*. Chapel Hill: University of North Carolina Press, 1991.

Stark, Heidi Kiiwetinepinesiik. "Respect, Responsibility and Renewal: The Foundations of Anishinaabe Treaty Making with the United States and Canada." *American Indian Culture and Research Journal*, vol. 34, no. 2, 2010, pp. 145–164.

Waller, Donald M., and Nicholas J. Reo. "First Stewards: Ecological Outcomes of Forest and Wildlife Stewardship by Indigenous Peoples of Wisconsin, USA." *Ecology and Society*, vol. 23, no. 1, 2018, p. 45.

Young, William R., ed. *An Introduction to the Archeology and History of the Connecticut Valley Indian*, vol. 1, no. 1, 1969.

Native American and Indigenous Storytelling, Religion, and Beaver Stories

Beck, Jane C. "The Giant Beaver: A Prehistoric Memory?" *Ethnohistory*, vol. 19, no. 2, Spring 1972, pp. 109–122.

Bruchac, Margaret M. "Earthshapers & Placemakers: Reflections on Algonkian Indian Stories and the Landscape." *Indigenous Archaeologies: Decolonizing Politics and Practice*, edited by H. Martin Wobst and Claire Smith. London: Routledge Press, 2005.

Jones, William. *Ojibwa Texts*. Publications of the American Ethnological Society. 1917, pp. ix–23.

———. *Ojibwa Texts*, vol. 7, part 2. Publications of the American Ethnological Society. 1919, pp. 250–259, 530–561.

Krickeberg, Walter et al. *Pre-Columbian American Religions*. New York: Holt, Rinehart and Winston, 1968.

Lapier, Rosalyn R. *Invisible Reality: Storytellers, Storytakers, and the Supernatual World of the Blackfeet*. Lincoln, NE: Board of Regents of the University of Nebraska, 2017.

Leland, Charles G. *The Algonquin Legends of New England: Myth and Folk Lore of the Micmac, Passamaquoddy, and Penobscot Tribes*. Boston: Houghton Mifflin, 1884.

Martin, Calvin. *Keepers of the Game: Indian-Animal Relationships and the Fur Trade*. Berkeley and Los Angeles: University of California Press, 1978.

Mayer, Adrienne. *Fossil Legends of the First Americans*. Princeton: Princeton University Press, 2007.

Morgan, R. Grace. *Beaver, Bison, Horse: The Traditional Knowledge and Ecology of the Northern Great Plains*. Regina, Sask.: University of Regina Press, 2020.

Morgan, R. Grace. "Beaver Ecology/Beaver Mythology" Ph.D. dissertation, University of Alberta, 1991.

Ong, Walter J. *Orality and Literacy*. New York: Routledge, 1982.

Savageau, Cheryl. "Stories, Language, and the Land." *The Land Question*, 2020, pp. 1–39.

Simpson, Leanne. *Dancing on Our Turtle's Back: Stories of Nishnaabeg Re-Creation, Resurgence and a New Experience.* Winnipeg: ARP Books, 2011.

Simpson, Leanne. *A Short History of the Blockade: Giant Beavers, Diplomacy, and Regeneration in Nishnaabemwin.* Alberta: University of Alberta Press, 2021.

Speck, Frank Gouldsmith. "Penobscot Shamanism." *Memoirs of the American Anthropological Association*, vol. 6, 1919, pp. 237–288.

———. "Penobscot Tales and Religious Beliefs." *The Journal of American Folklore*, vol. 48, no. 187, Jan.–Mar., 1935, pp. 1–107.

———. "Totems Among the Northeastern Algonkians." *American Anthropologist*, vol. 19, no. 1, pp. 16+.

Tanner, Adrian. *Bringing Home Animals: Religious Ideology and Mode of Production of the Mistassini Cree Hunters.* New York: St. Martin's Press, 1979.

Treuer, Anton, ed. *Living Our Language: Ojibwe Tales & Oral Histories.* St. Paul: Minnesota Historical Society Press, 2001.

Wissler, Clark. "Ceremonial Bundles of the Blackfoot Indians." *Anthropological Papers of the American Museum of Natural History*, vol. 7, part 2, 1912.

Wissler, Clark, and D. C. Duvall. "Mythology of the Blackfoot Indians." *Anthropological Paper of the American Museum of Natural History*, vol. 2, part 1, 1909, pp. 5–105.

American History

Ayres, Harral. *The Great Trial of New England.* Boston: Meader Publishing, 1940.

Cronon, William. *Changes in the Land: Indians, Colonists, and the Ecology of New England.* New York: Hill and Wang, 1983.

Grandjean, Katherine A. "New World Tempests: Environment, Scarcity, and the Coming of the Pequot War." *William and Mary Quarterly*, Third Series, vol. 68, no. 1, 2011, pp. 75–100.

Hearne, Samuel. *A Journey to the Northern Ocean: A Journey from Prince of Wales's Fort in Hudson's Bay to the Northern Ocean in the Years 1769, 1770, 1771, 1772.* Toronto: Macmillan Company of Canada, 1958.

Kerson, Arnold L. "The Republic of Beavers: An American Utopia." *Utopian Studies*, vol. 11, no. 2, 2000, pp.14–32.

Lepore, Jill. *The Name of War: King Philip's War and the Origins of American Identity.* New York: Vintage, 1999.

Lewis, Meriwether, and William Clark. *The Lewis and Clark Journals: An American Epic of Discovery.* Lincoln, NE: Board of Regents of the University of Nebraska, 2003.

Main, Jackson Turner. *Society and Economy in Colonial Connecticut.* Princeton: Princeton University Press, 1938.

Montanus, Arnoldus. *De Niewe en Onbekende Weereld* [America being the latest and most accurate description of the New World]. Translated by John Ogilby. London, 1671.

Morton, Thomas. *New English Canaan*. Amsterdam: Theatrum Orbis Terrarum; New York: Da Capo Press, 1969.

Newell, Margaret Ellen. *Brethren by Nature: New England Indians, Colonists, and the Origins of American Slavery*. Ithaca: Cornell University Press, 2015.

Reséndez, Andrés. *The Other Slavery: The Uncovered Story of Indian Enslavement in America*. New York: Mariner Books, 2016.

Russell, Howard S. *A Long Deep Furrow: Three Centuries of Farming in New England*. Hanover: University Press of New England, 1976.

Stark, Peter. *Astoria: Astor and Jefferson's Lost Pacific Empire: A Tale of Ambition and Survival on the Early American Frontier*. New York: HarperCollins, 2015.

Taylor, Alan. *American Colonies: The Settling of North America*. New York: Penguin Books, 2002.

Thorson, Robert M. *Stone by Stone: The Magnificent History in New England's Stone Walls*. New York: Bloomsbury, 2002.

Van Der Donck, Adriaen. *A Description of New Netherland*. Originally published in 1655; Lincoln, NE: University of Nebraska Press, 2008.

Warren, Wendy. *New England Bound: Slavery and Colonization in Early America*. New York: Norton, 2016.

Fur Trade (North America)

Chittenden, Hiram Martin. *The American Fur Trade of the Far West*. New York: Francis P. Harper, 1902.

Cleland, Robert Glass. *This Reckless Breed of Men: The Trappers and Fur Traders of the Southwest*. New York: Alfred A. Knopf, 1950.

Connecticut Trapper Education Manual: A Guide for Trappers in the United States. Connecticut Department of Energy & Environmental Protection, Bureau of Natural Resources, Wildlife Division, 2005.

Coyner, David. *The Lost Trappers*. Originally published in 1847; Carlisle, MA: Applewood Books, 2010.

Dolin, Eric Jay. *Fur, Fortune, and Empire: The Epic History of the Fur Trade in America*. New York: W. W. Norton, 2010.

Hanson, James A. *When Skins Were Money: A History of the Fur Trade*. Chadron, NE: Museum of the Fur Trade, 2005.

Hayes, Derek. *First Crossing: Alexander Mackenzie, His Expedition Across North America and the Opening of the Continent*. Seattle: Sasquatch Books, 2001.

Holland Braund, Kathryn. *Deerskins & Duffels: Creek Indian Trade with Anglo-America, 1685–1815*. Lincoln, NE: University of Nebraska Press, 1993.

Innis, Harold A. *The Fur Trade in Canada*. Originally published in 1930; New Haven: Yale University Press, 1962.

Kay, Jeanne. "Native Americans in the Fur Trade and Wildlife Depletion." *Environmental Review*, vol. 9, no. 2, Summer 1986, pp. 118–130.

Kurlansky, Mark. *The Basque History of the World*. New York: Walker, 1999.

Maloney, Francis Xavier. *The Fur Trade in New England*. Cambridge, MA: Harvard University Press, 1931.

Mason, Otis T. "Traps of the American Indians—A Study in Psychology and Invention." In *Annual Report of the Board of Regents of the Smithsonian Institution*. Washington: Government Printing Office, 1902, pp. 461–474.

Newman, Peter. *Company of Adventurers: How the Hudson Bay Empire Determined the Destiny of a Continent*. Toronto: Penguin Canada, 2004.

Outwater, Alice. "The Fur Trade." In *Water: A Natural History*. New York: Basic Books, 1997.

Parr, Tom, and Blaise Andreski. *The Trap Collector's Guide*. Galloway, OH: Tom Parr, 2000.

Perreault, Jean Baptist. *Relation des traverses et des avantures d'un marchant voyageur dans les terrytoires sauvages de l'Amerique* [(Adventures of a Merchant Voyageur in the Savage Territories of North America (Leaving Montreal on the 28th Day of May, 1783 to 1820)]. Montreal: L. P. Cormier, 1978; H. R. Schoolcraft papers, Library of Congress, Washington, DC.

Schmidt, Benjamin. "Mapping an Empire: Cartographic and Colonial Rivalry in Seventeenth-Century Dutch and English North America," *William and Mary Quarterly*, Third Series, vol. 54. no. 3, 1997, pp. 549–578.

Silver, Helennette, *A History of New Hampshire Game and Furbearers*. Survey Report no. 6, Concord, NH: Fish and Game Department, May 1957.

Terrell, John Upton. *Furs by Astor*. Scranton, PA: Haddon, 1963.

Fur Trade (Europe)

Coles, Bryony. *Beavers in Britain's Past*. Oxford: Oxbow Books and WARP, 2006.

Veale, Elspeth M. *The English Fur Trade in the Later Middle Ages*. Oxford: The Clarendon Press, 1966.

Beavers: Ancient History and Medieval Europe

Barber, Richard. *Bestiary: Being an English Version of the Bodleian Library, Oxford M.S. Bodley 764 with All the Original Miniatures Reproduced in Facsimile*. Woodbridge, UK: The Boydell Press, 1993.

George, Wilma, and Brunsdon Yapp. *The Naming of the Beasts: Natural History in the Medieval Bestiary*. London: Gerald Duckworth, 1991.

Kitchell, Kenneth F. Jr. "A Defense of the 'Monstrous' Animals of Pliny, Aelian, and Others." *Preternature: Critical and Historical Studies on the Preternatural*, vol. 4, no. 2, 2015, pp. 125–151.

Secundus, C. Plinius. *The History of the World Commonly Called the Natural History of C. Plinius Secundus, or Pliny*. Translated by Philemon Holland. New York: McGraw-Hill, 1962.

Šedinová, Hana. "The 'Lamia' and Aristotle's Beaver: The Consequences of Mistranscription." *Journal of the Warburg and Courtauld Institutes*, vol. 79, 2016, pp. 295–306.

White, T. H., ed. *The Book of Beasts: Being a Translation from a Latin Bestiary of the Twelfth Century*. New York: G. P. Putnam's Sons, 1954.

Beavers: Natural History

Campbell-Palmer, Róisín et al. *The Eurasian Beaver Handbook: Ecology and Management of* Castor fiber. Exeter, UK: Pelagic Publishing, 2016.

Feldhamer, George et al. *Wild Mammals of North America.* Baltimore: Johns Hopkins University Press, 2003.

Hood, Glynnis A. *Semi-aquatic Mammals: Ecology and Biology.* Baltimore: Johns Hopkins University Press, 2020.

Johnston, Carol A. *Beavers: Boreal Ecosystem Engineers.* Cham, Switzerland: Springer, 2007.

Müller-Schwarze, Dietland, and Lixing Sun. *The Beaver: Natural History of a Wetland Engineer.* Ithaca, NY: Cornell University Press, 2003.

Rosell, Frank, and Róisín Campbell-Palmer. *Beavers: Ecology, Behavior, Conservation, and Management.* Oxford: Oxford University Press, 2022.

Seton, Ernest Thompson. *Lives of Game Animals,* vol. 4, part 2. Boston: Charles T. Branford, 1953.

Beavers: Rivers, Wetlands, and Environmental Restoration

Brown, Sharon, and Suzanne Fouty. "Beaver Wetlands." *Lakeline,* Spring 2011, pp. 34–38.

Burchsted, Denise et al. "The River Discontinuum: Applying Beaver Modifications to Baseline Conditions for Restoration of Forested Headwaters." *Bioscience,* vol. 60, no. 11, 2010, pp. 908–922.

Fairfax, Emily. "Smokey the Beaver: Beaver-Dammed Riparian Corridors Stay Green During Wildfire Throughout the Western United States." *Ecological Applications,* vol. 30, no. 8, 2020.

Fouty, Suzanne C. "Euro-American Beaver Trapping and Its Long Term Impact on Drainage Network Form and Function, Water Abundance, Deliver, System Stability." Chapter 7 in *Riparian Research and Management: Past, Present, and Future,* vol. 1. Washington, DC: USDA Forest Service, RMRS-GTR-377, 2018.

Gable, Thomas D. et al. "Where and How Wolves Kill Beavers, and Confronting Biases in Scat-Based Diet Studies." *All NMU Master's Theses,* vol. 11, no. 12, 2016.

Gow, Derek. *Bringing Back the Beaver.* White River Junction, VT: Chelsea Green, 2020.

Halley, Duncan et al. "Population and Distribution of Beavers *Castor fiber* and *Castor canadensis* in Eurasia." *Mammal Review,* vol. 51, no. 1, 2021.

Heter, Elmo W. "Transplanting Beavers by Airplane and Parachute." *Journal of Wildlife Management,* vol. 14, no. 2, 1950.

Hood, Glynnis A., and Suzanne E. Bayley. "Beaver (*Castor canadensis*) Mitigate the Effects of Climate on the Area of Open Water in Boreal Wetlands in Western Canada." *Biological Conservation,* vol. 141, no. 2, 2008, pp. 556–567.

Johnson-Bice, Sean M. et al. "A Review of Beaver-Salmonid Relationships and History of Management Actions in the Western Great Lakes (USA) Region." *North American Journal of Fisheries Management*, vol. 38, no. 6, 2018, pp. 1203–1225.

Johnston, Carol A. "Fate of 150 Year Old Beaver Ponds in the Laurentian Great Lakes Region." *Wetlands*, vol. 35, 2015.

Liao, Qian et al. "Project Hydrological Impact of Beaver Habitat Restoration in the Milwaukee River Watershed." MMSD Contract P-2890, November 2020.

Montgomery, David R. *King of the Fish: The Thousand-Year Run of Salmon.* Boulder: Westview Press, 2003.

Naiman, Robert. "Alteration of North American Streams by Beaver." *Bioscience*, vol. 38, no. 11, 1988.

———. "Beaver Influences on the Long-Term Biochemical Characteristics of Boreal Forest Drainage Networks." *Ecology*, vol. 75, no. 4, 1994.

Naiman, Robert J., and Jerry M. Melillo. "Nitrogen Budget of a Subarctic Stream Altered by Beaver (*Castor canadensis*)." *Oecologia*, vol. 62, no. 2, 1984, pp. 150–155.

Outwater, Alice. *Water: A Natural History.* New York: Basic Books, 1996.

Perryman, Heidi. "Beavers Are Nature's Firefighters. So Why Is California Killing Them?" *San Francisco Chronicle*, June 26, 2021.

Pollock, Michael M., Timothy J. Beechie, and Chris E. Jordan. "Geomorphic Changes Upstream of Beaver Dams in Bridge Creek, an Incised Stream Channel in the Interior Columbia River Basin, Eastern Oregon." *Earth Surfaces Processes and Landforms*, vol. 32, no. 8, 2007, pp. 1174–1185.

Pollock, Michael M., Gregory Lewallen et al. *The Beaver Restoration Guidebook: Working with Beaver to Restore Streams, Wetlands and Floodplains*, version 1.0. Portland, OR: U.S. Fish and Wildlife Service, 2015.

Pollock, Michael M., Robert J. Naiman, and Thomas A. Hanley. "Plant Species Richness in Riparian Wetlands—A Test of Biodiversity Theory." *Ecology*, vol. 79, no. 1, 1998.

Puttock, Alan at al. "Eurasian Beaver Activity Increases Water Storage, Attenuates Flow and Mitigates Diffuse Pollution from Intensively-Managed Grasslands." *Science of the Total Environment*, vol. 576, 2017, pp. 430–443.

Ruedemann, Rudolf. "Beaver Dams as Geologic Agents." *Science*, New Series, vol. 88, no. 2292, December 2, 1938, pp. 523–525.

Vannote, R. L. et al. "The River Continuum Concept." *Aquatic Science*, vol. 37, 1980, pp. 130–137.

Walter, Robert C. et al. "Natural Streams and the Legacy of Water-Powered Mills." *Science*, vol. 319, 2008.

Wohl, Ellen. *Disconnected Rivers: Linking Rivers to Landscapes.* New Haven: Yale University Press, 2004.

———. *Saving the Dammed: Why We Need Beaver-Modified Ecosystems.* New York: Oxford University Press, 2019.

Beavers: Animal Behavior and Cognition

"The Beaver Is Not a Great Diver." Universitetet i Sørøst-Norge, March 17, 2017.

Burroughs, John. "Real and Sham Natural History." *Atlantic*, March 1903.

Cabré, Laura Bartra et al. "Beaver (*Castor fiber*) Activity and Spatial Movement in Response to Light and Weather Conditions." *Mammalian Biology*, no. 100, 2020, pp. 261–271.

Campbell, Ruairidh D. et al. "Proximate Weather Patterns and Spring Green-Up Phenology Effect Euroasian Beaver (*Castor fiber*) Body Mass and Reproductive Success: The Implications of Climate Change and Topology." *Global Change Biology*, vol. 19, no. 4, 2013.

Dennett, Daniel C. *Kinds of Minds: Towards an Understanding of Consciousness.* New York: Basic Books, 1996.

Godfrey-Smith, Peter. *Metazoa: Animal Life and the Birth of the Mind.* New York: Farrar Straus & Giroux, 2020.

Heffernan, Ellie. "UNC Researchers Receive Grant to Study Potential Benefits of Beaver Dams." UNC Institute for the Environment. November 1, 2020.

Herzog, Hal. *Some We Love, Some We Hate, Some We Eat: Why It's So Hard to Think Straight About Animals.* New York: Harper Perennial, 2021.

Nolet, Bart A., and Frank Rosell. "Comeback of the Beaver *Castor fiber*: An Overview of Old and New Conservation Problems." *Biological Conservation*, vol. 83, no. 2, 1998, pp. 165–173.

Roosevelt, Theodore. "Nature Fakers." *Everybody's Magazine*, September 17, 1907.

Rybczynski, Natalia, "Castorid Phylogenetics: Implications for the Evolution of Swimming and Tree-Exploitation in Beavers." *Journal of Mammalian Evolution*, vol. 14, no. 1, 2007, pp. 1–35.

Wohlleben, Peter. *The Inner Life of Animals: Love, Grief, and Compassion: Surprising Observations of a Hidden World.* Translated by Jane Billinghurst. Vancouver and Berkeley: Greystone Books, 2017.

Natural History of the Forest

Bailey, Scott W., and Gene E Likens. "The Discovery of Acid Rain at the Hubbard Brook Experimental Station Forest: A Story of Collaboration and Long-Term Research." In *USDA Forest Services Experimental Forests and Ranges.* Edited by D. C. Hayes et al. New York: Springer, 2014.

Haskell, David George. *The Forest Unseen, A Year's Watch in Nature.* New York: Viking, 2012.

Sheldrake, Merlin. *Entangled Life: How Fungi Make Our Worlds, Change Our Minds, & Shape Our Futures.* New York: Random House, 2021.

Simard, Suzanne. *Finding the Mother Tree: Discovering the Wisdom of the Forest.* New York: Knopf, 2021.

Wohlleben, Peter. *The Hidden Life of Trees: What They Feel, How They Communicate—Discoveries from a Secret World.* Translated by Jane Billinghurst. Vancouver and Berkeley: Greystone Books, 2016.

Environmental Writings

Berry, Wendell. *The Unsettling of America: Culture and Agriculture*. San Francisco: Sierra Books, 1977.

Cronon, William. *Uncommon Ground: Rethinking the Human Place in Nature*. New York: W. W. Norton, 1996.

Flores, Dan. *Coyote America: A Natural and Supernatural History*. New York: Basic Books, 2017.

Kolbert, Elizabeth. *Under a White Sky: The Nature of the Future*. New York: Penguin Random House, 2021.

Leopold, Aldo. *A Sand County Almanac and Sketches Here and There*. New York: Oxford University Press, 1949.

Marsh, George Perkins. *Man and Nature*. Edited by David Lowenthal. Originally published in 1864; Seattle: University of Washington Press, 2003.

McKibben, Bill. *Hope, Human, and Wild: True Stories of Living Lightly on the Earth*. Boston: Little, Brown, 1995.

McPhee, John. *The Control of Nature*. New York: Farrar, Straus & Giroux, 1989.

Philip, Leila. "North American Wildlife Depends on Gun Sales for Survival." *Boston Globe*, August 1, 2018.

Price, Jennifer. *Flight Maps, Adventures with Nature in Modern America*. New York: Basic Books, 1999.

Quammen, David. *The Tangled Tree: A Radical New History of Life*. New York: Simon and Schuster, 2018.

Sterba, Jim. *Nature Wars: The Incredible Story of How Wildlife Comebacks Turned Backyards into Battlegrounds*. New York: Broadway Books, 2012.

Thomas, Chris D. *Inheritors of the Earth: How Nature Is Thriving in an Age of Extinction*. New York: Public Affairs, 2017.

Thoreau, Henry David. *Thoreau's Journals*. March 23, 1853.

Wilson, Edward O. *Biophilia: The Human Bond with Other Species*. Cambridge, MA: Harvard University Press, 2009.

Wulf, Andrea. *The Invention of Nature: Alexander Humboldt's New World*. New York: Alfred A. Knopf, 2017.

Biography and Miscellaneous

Becker, Howard S. *Outsiders: Studies in Sociology of Deviance*. New York: Simon & Schuster, 1963.

Bly, Robert. *Iron John: A Book About Men*. New York: Addison Wesley, 1990.

Dickson, Lovat. *Wilderness: The Strange Story of Grey Owl*. Toronto: Macmillan of Canada, 1973.

Hochschild, Arlie Russell. *Strangers in Their Own Land: Anger and Mourning on the American Right*. New York: Perseus, 2016.

Moses, Daniel Noah. *The Promise of Progress: The Life and Work of Lewis Henry Morgan*. Columbia and London: University of Missouri Press, 2009.

Petersen, David. *A Hunter's Heart: Honest Essays on Blood Sport*. New York: Henry Holt, 2016.

Smith, Donald B. *From the Land of Shadows: The Making of Grey Owl*. Saskatoon, Sask.; Western Producer Prairie Books, 1990.

Swan, James A. *In Defense of Hunting*. New York: HarperOne, 1995.

Films

The Beaver Believers. Sarah Koenigsberg. (https://www.thebeaverbelievers.com/)

The Beaver People. Archibald Belaney (Grey Owl)'s first film can be viewed on the National Film Board of Canada's website (https://www.nfb.ca/film/beaver_people/)

Beavers of the North County. Jacques Cousteau. (https://www.youtube.com/watch?v=EvYJHYObTGs)

How Beavers Bring Biodiversity. High Desert Museum, Oregon. Interactive website. (http://highdesertmuseum.org/beaver-interactive/)

Meet the Beavers. Owen and Sharon Brown. (https://www.beaversww.org/about-us/)

My Forty Years with Beavers. Dorothy Richards. (https://www.beaversww.org/about-us/)

Parachuting Beavers. Idaho Department of Fish and Game, footage of the Beaver Drop, 1948. (https://www.youtube.com/watch?v=rpWKd9uT2Ro)

Water's Way: Thinking Like a Watershed. Chesapeake Bay Journal. 2021. Film by Dave Harp, Tim Horton, and Sandy Cannon-Brown. (https://www.bayjournal.com/multimedia/waters-way-thinking-like-a-watershed/video_abd786f4-2377-11ec-9f8a-53da57c1cc7d.html)

Worth a Dam (The Beavers of Martinez). Heidi Perryman. 2020. (https://www.youtube.com/watch?v=-XjgfOFiznA)

A Brief, Canonical Timeline of American Nature Writing About Beavers

1868 Morgan, Lewis H. *The American Beaver and His Works*. Philadelphia: J. B. Lippincott.

1892 Martin, Horace Tassie. *Castorologia, or the History and Traditions of the Canadian Beaver*. Montreal: William Drysdale.

1913 Mills, Enos. *In Beaver World*. New York: Harper.

1915 Dugmore, A. Radclyffe. *Romance of the Beaver*. Philadelphia: J. B. Lippincott.

1935 Belaney, Archibald Stansfeld. *Pilgrims of the Wild*. Toronto: Macmillan of Canada.

1959 Collier, Eric. *Three Against the Wilderness*. New York: E. P. Dutton.

1964 Rue, Leonard Lee III. *The World of the Beaver*. Philadelphia: J. B. Lippincott.

1968 Willson, Lars. *My Beaver Colony*. New York: Doubleday.

1983 Richards, Dorothy. *Beaversprite*. New York: Heart of Lakes Publishing.

1989 Ryden, Hope, and William Morrow. *Lily Pond: Four Years with a Family of Beavers.* New York: Harper Perennial.

2003 Tournay, Audrey. *Beaver Tales: Audrey Tournay and the Aspen Valley Beavers.* Boston: Mills Press.

2011 Hood, Glynnis A. *The Beaver Manifesto.* Victoria, BC: Rocky Mountain Books.

2015 Backhouse, Frances. *Once They Were Hats: In Search of the Mighty Beaver.* Toronto: ECW Press.

2018 Goldfarb, Ben. *Eager: The Surprising, Secret Life of Beavers and Why They Matter.* White River Junction, VT: Chelsea Green.

Photo Credits

Acknowledgments

In many ways this book began long before I first saw beavers building their pond in my adopted home of Woodstock, Connecticut. It began on the Hudson River when I was much younger. I was in a small boat just before dawn, helping a man named Everett Nack, who was among the last of the Hudson River shad fishermen (and an environmental vigilante), pull his heavy nets up from the river, which at that moment was smooth as glass. Only now when I have finished this book do I understand the complex strands of American history and culture that a commercial fisherman and fur trapper like Everett Nack represents. But the way he looked in that moment—as if bursting with wild gladness for the river and for the huge primeval-looking fish he was about to pull up from below, and for everything around us as dawn began to break—was something I would remember years later in northeastern Connecticut when I met fur trappers on my quest to find out what had happened to my beavers. No doubt, my having known Everett Nack had in part helped me cross over some of the seismic divides in our country that were revealed in 2016. I have to first thank my mother for supporting my sense of adventure and selflessly driving me to the river at five in the morning. And I have to thank both of my parents for teaching me, early on, to love and care for the natural world, both plant and animal.

Many individuals and institutions helped me in the course of writing *Beaverland*, and I'd like to acknowledge as many as I can here.

Generous funding for this book came from the Society for Environmental Journalists, which awarded me a storytelling grant for work on this book. Similarly, a grant from Furthermore: A Program of the Kaplan Fund enabled me to pursue an exciting new path of research at a critical time. The College of the Holy Cross, where I teach, generously supported my work on this book in various ways, including the award of a research leave and supporting grants for travel. I received a Baron Artist Fellowship from the American Antiquarian Society in Worcester to work for many weeks in the incredible national research library there.

This book would never have happened without the ongoing support of my literary agent, Miriam Altshuler. She believed in what this book could be from the start and has been there for me at every step: reading drafts, shepherding the book proposal, and connecting me to a wonderful publisher. To both Miriam and her assistant at the time, Reiko Davis, I cannot thank you enough.

I feel fortunate beyond measure to have worked with the people at Twelve Books. From the beginning, this has felt like a team effort. Rachel Kambury, the book's first editor, seemed to know where I was going even before I did. Her comments pushed me and the book in critical ways. Then Sean Desmond's keen eye and ear for story and pace showed me ways to bring it all together. Zohal Karimy, his editorial assistant, kept so many details going with grace and good cheer. Bob Castillo, the book's production editor, worked tirelessly to make *Beaverland* the book it is. Thank you to everyone who helped in that process, from copyediting to design, especially the people in the art department who came up with the book's fantastic cover. Estefania Acquaviva and Megan Perritt-Jacobson, who run a truly phenomenal publicity and marketing group, paved the way for the book to enter the world. To everyone at Twelve who has been a part of team *Beaverland,* thank you.

For reading and offering insight on early chapters, I'd like to thank Angela Miller, Jennifer Price, and Natalia Rachel Singer. I am grateful for interest and support from Joan Davidson, Adam Weinberg, Shareen Hertel, Todd Lewis, Sean Prentiss, Robin Hemley, and Gish Jen.

Some of the material covered in *Beaverland* began with opinion pieces that I wrote for the *Boston Globe.* I am grateful to Editorial Page editors Ellen Clegg and Marjorie Pritchard for giving me that opportunity.

Ellen Clegg and Tim Weiner were generous beyond measure, reading drafts of the book with insight and offering invaluable feedback. Jeanne Jordan read the book with a filmmaker's eye for story and helped me see some things with fresh eyes.

I am indebted to two important linguists. Ives Goddard, considered a leading expert on the Algonquian languages and the larger Algic family, generously responded to my questions about certain Algonquian words. Steven Bird, who is based in Darwin, Australia, and studies Indigenous languages, generously read sections of the book, offering advice and insight.

Archeologists Kristine Heitert and Nick Bellantoni helped me research Woodstock colonial history. Native scholar Thomas Doughton helped me untangle complex aspects of Nipmuc history and their ongoing local presence. Robert Thorson, a renowned geologist, shared his vast knowledge of New England stone walls. Native scholar Rae Gould generously answered my questions about seventeenth-century "praying villages." Classics scholars Ellen Perry and Thomas Martin helped me track down obscure classical references. Historian Sahar Bazazz helped me with similarly obscure questions about the ancient Middle East. Louise Cort, renowned for her work in the history of Japanese ceramic art, read the final chapter and responded to my questions. My heartfelt thanks to them all.

Finally, I owe a debt of gratitude to Linda Coombs, a museum educator, historian, and author from the Wampanoag Tribe of Gay Head/Aquinnah in Massachusetts, who read the book and strengthened it with her feedback.

For images, thanks to Vicky Osborne at the Idaho Fish and Game Department. Thanks to Ruolin Eudora Miao and Andy Fallon for help generating GIS images of beaver ponds. Thanks to Jordan Kennedy for sharing her amazing images of beaver damming complexes. Thanks to Sharon Brown for help locating photographs of Dorothy Richards. Thanks to Sherri Sobanski for the great picture of Herb. Thanks to Jan Desmaris, for help in preparing many images. Thanks to John Earle, for his generosity and good humor the day we took my author photograph. Thanks to Heidi Perryman and Libby Corliss for the wonderful beaver silhouette used in the interior.

I would be remiss not to mention my three wonderful student interns who, at different times, helped with many of those mundane tasks that must get done and helped with fact-checking: Olivia Sahovey, Grace Keith, and Sloane Larsen.

Librarians and archivists have to be among the most helpful and generous people in existence. At Holy Cross, special thanks to Philippe

Telemarque, who kept me supplied with books via interlibrary loan; and Barbara Merolli, who helped me with many arcane research questions. Thanks to all the librarians at the many libraries where I conducted research or made use of existing collections. Thanks also to the generous souls who conduct volunteer outreach for small salaries to keep local historical societies going. Your work is more valuable than you might know.

Thank you to all those who allowed me to interview them for this book and gave generously of their time and expertise. Their names are listed in the notes for each chapter.

I am deeply indebted to Herb Sobanski, who welcomed me to the secretive world of contemporary fur trapping when others were wary. Sadly, Herb did not live to see the final book. I am tremendously grateful to his widow, Sherri, for her ongoing support.

Another person who deserves special thanks is the fur trader who appears in chapter five. He generously spent more hours with me than I can count, answering any number of questions, often guiding me toward the important issues and introducing me to others.

In Michigan, Pasqua Warstler, then working at the Bonifas Arts Center in Escanaba; Jon Magnussen, director of the Cedar Tree Institute; and Tina Harris, of the Peter White Public Library, helped with many aspects during my visit to Marquette. I am also grateful to Carl Lindquist and Jeff Koch, of the Superior Watershed Partnership and Land Conservancy, for helping me in my hunt to find Morgan's beaver dams.

In Maryland, I want to thank MaryBeth O'Bryan for helping arrange my Ecotone site visits and interviews with Scott McGill and Glenn Gibson. I also want to thank the many "beaver believers" I have met at BeaverCon conferences, who generously shared what they knew of beavers with me in any number of formats. Their generosity and dedication to educating the world about the valuable roles beavers can play in the ongoing climate crisis are an inspiration.

Here in southern New England I especially want to thank Mike Callahan, of the Beaver Institute, for generously allowing me to follow him in and out of so many beaver sites. Also Sarah Heminway, the director of the Connecticut Audubon Society's Northeast Region, for her time and for access to the Teale Nature Center.

To all those who work on behalf of the natural world, whether through research, conservation, or climate activism, a resounding thank-you. Your efforts give me hope.

Finally, I must mention my deep gratitude for the two canine companions who appear in this book. My wonderful field Golden, Coda, first led me to the beavers. Her sense of humor will be with me always. Then Obie, my handsome English Shepherd pup, was there when I discovered the new beaver colony and shared in that joy, as well as the daily work of writing this book. You taught me more than you can know.

Books take time and writers need space to put aside the tasks and obligations of daily life and get to work. Thanks to Ted and Cindy Gaty, who generously lent me their house on the Oregon coast for several blissful weeks of isolated time to write. Most of the book was written during the pandemic, which shut down travel and writing residencies. Thanks to the foresight of my mother and her siblings, I was able to retreat at times to a small cottage on Willoughby Lake in Vermont that my extended family now owns.

Working at home during the pandemic challenged us all. I found it increasingly difficult to juggle the demands of full-time teaching and work on the book from my cramped home office. One morning my husband came out with a sketch of a small barn and put it quietly on the table. It showed the shed we'd been saving up to build for some time, but with the addition of a writing studio. We hired a carpenter, and within a few months, I had a beautiful place to write that overlooked the woods. I would work there day after day until the book was done. My clever sheepdog, Obie, who has an excellent sense of order and time, kept me company. If I was not heading out to the writing shed, coffee in hand, by eight thirty, he'd find me and bark until I got going.

For their interest, encouragement, and general support, I want to thank many friends and extended family members. To research and write a book like this demands a certain willingness to venture into the unknown, whether they be real places or an exploration of places in the mind and heart. I would never have been able to maintain the kind of research and sustained thinking this book required without the enduring patience, support, and love of my immediate family.

My husband, Garth Evans, who has his own busy career as a sculptor and a full art practice, never hesitated to pick up the slack on any number of shared aspects of keeping a house when my deadlines were near. On top of that, he read everything I put before him with more insight than I can describe. Rhys, our son, was just out of college and recently trained as an EMT when the pandemic hit. Throughout Covid, he threw himself without hesitation into work as a first responder, and he soon began a rigorous course of training to become a paramedic. Despite this incredibly hard schedule, he has always been ready to help, or be at hand with his sense of humor and beautiful smile. Garth and Rhys, you are my true north, and I dedicate this book to you.

Index

About the Author

Leila Philip is the author of award-winning books of nonfiction that have received national glowing reviews. A Guggenheim Fellow, she has also been awarded fellowships from the National Endowment for the Arts and the National Endowment for the Humanities. Philip was a popular contributing columnist at the *Boston Globe* and teaches in the Environmental Studies Program at the College of the Holy Cross in Massachusetts, where she is a professor in the English Department and holds the Brooks Chair in the Humanities.